SOME FAMOUS (AND NOT SO FAMOUS) PRAISE FOR
NOT ANOTHER SELF-HELP BOOK

"We learn best from real people who have lived some real life and done some real work . . . Let's look to the ones who've come through the flames, even if they still smell a little singed. That is trustworthy leadership. And that is Lindsey."

—Jen Hatmaker, *New York Times* best-selling author, speaker, host of *For the Love* podcast, and personal friend and mentor

"This book! If you know Lindsey, you know there are stories upon stories that make up this amazingly energetic, passionate, and brave person in front of you—and this book is a laugh-out-loud, vulnerable, ride through her rollercoaster of a journey. From her relationship with her faith to coming out, she shares in so many ways how challenges teach us so much, that teachers are everywhere around us, and to have so much humanity for ourselves and all of our flaws. Every page made me feel like being kinder to myself and reminded me that there is so much room for us to discover our true selves and to treat them with love and forgiveness!"

—Jennifer Brown, keynoter and *Wall Street Journal* best-selling author of *How to be an Inclusive Leader* and host of the podcast *The Will to Change*

"I ain't reading her damn book until she starts putting her trash bins away *shortly* after trash day so I don't have to keep looking at them."

—Buford W. Tannahill, SR., my crotchety old neighbor

"Our daughter Lulu is one of a kind, and so is this book."

—Mark and Vicki Leaverton, parental units

"Mama, what's for dinner?"   **—Annabelle and Liv, my twins**

Not Another

SELF-HELP BOOK

Finding Gifts in the Midst of Life's Sh*t

Lindsey Kane Leaverton

RIVER GROVE
BOOKS

2023908384

Published by River Grove Books
Austin, TX
www.rivergrovebooks.com

Distributed by River Grove Books

Design and composition by Greenleaf Book Group and Sheila Parr
Cover design by Greenleaf Book Group and Sheila Parr
Cover photo by Steven Miura
Author photo by Sally Lok

Publisher's Cataloging-in-Publication data is available.

Print ISBN: 978-1-63299-742-5

eBook ISBN: 978-1-63299-747-0

First Edition

CONTENTS

FOREWORD

Somewhere around 2002, Lindsey asked me to be her "spiritual mentor." Good reader, let me recount the folly:

I was 26 years old and didn't know jack about shit.

I had done zero internal work and was still playing my prescribed role inside both the patriarchy and the religious industrial complex.

My primary tools were Christian jargon, unexamined theology, and good behavior.

I'd married at 19 and had three kids by the time Lindsey requested my mentorship. I couldn't even drink at my own wedding, not that there was alcohol in the Baptist fellowship hall.

My favorite spiritual practice was certainty.

When I think about what sort of religious nonsense I must've handed poor Lindsey, I want to bury myself in the backyard. What a sham. What thin, uninteresting drivel I parroted. I actually have endless compassion for both of us: We were trying so very hard to shape-shift into the template we'd been assigned, incredibly well-intentioned inside our prisons. Our options were limited, so we attempted to master the model.

The beauty of this very moment for me, sitting here writing the foreword for Lindsey's book, is that we are now two self-actualized grownups who have lost more than we ever thought, learned more than we ever imagined, and have grown more than we ever dreamed. Those old containers are in our rearview mirror. Turns out, we never mastered that model because we couldn't stay small enough to comply.

A couple of caveats. First, do not hear me say we have it figured out and all we do is slay. That is part of the fake construct we left behind. There is no such thing as nonstop slaying except for Beyonce and Michelle Obama. As recently as two weeks ago, I got an inch away from one of my teenagers' faces and said through gritted teeth: "You ABSOLUTELY have to get your shit together." So in some ways it is still a race to the bottom. As I say often: I can't care about everything.

Second, as much as I wish growth occurred through happiness, sparkles, and endless joy, it actually materialized through suffering, failure, trauma, and loss. This point matters, because Lindsey is about to walk you through a bunch of big ideas, and the guides we choose through this terrain will either lead us well or lead us astray. The best leaders have scars. Someone unscathed by life's shadow side cannot illuminate the path for anyone else. They can say impressive words or regurgitate talking points, but it rings hollow.

We learn best from real people who have lived some real life and done some real work. This is why we don't ask 26-year-old former teen brides to be our mentors. Let's look to the ones who've come through the flames, even if they still smell a little singed. That is trustworthy leadership.

And that is Lindsey.

We've been friends now for over twenty years. I know all the curves and twists in her story and she knows mine. You couldn't have told either of us back in 2002 where we'd be sitting today. Lindsey married to a woman?? Jen divorced and saying swears online?? Oh, life! You maniac!

And yet I can tell you with full confidence: Lindsey has earned her wisdom. It takes a lot to live truthfully when your inherited ecosystem doesn't have enough oxygen. You have to find new spaces where you can breathe, and that is a hero's journey, a difficult one with losses and unprecedented change. You are probably there too because that is how life works. Life just keeps on life-ing, and we get to choose what to make of it.

Good news: you aren't alone. As Moira from *Schitt's Creek* says (which Lindsey will pepper you with ad nauseum in the following pages): "Why should I be the only one encumbered with this emotional cargo?" You aren't, dear one. Come find your reflection in these stories. We are all in this together. We have loads to learn from each other, and oh it is a relief to not feel alone.

Finally, suuuuuuuper sorry for whatever "instruction" I yammered about in 2002, Lindsey. It probably made you gay, and that is why women shouldn't be allowed to teach in church with their heads uncovered. My apologies. Glad to see you recovered nicely. I love you, sister. You're one of the good ones.

—Jen Hatmaker

A NOTE FROM THE AUTHOR

If any of the following phrases resonate with you like they do with me, then you have undoubtedly chosen the right book to read. If not, you may want to put this book down and opt for an alternate activity. (I hear pickleball is HUGE these days.) Here are the phrases. Ready?

Feeling stuck and hopeless and having zero idea where to take your next step

Struggling with a personal crisis, such as a health issue, the loss of someone you love, a major life change or transition, and having trouble seeing any way out

Doubtful of the alleged light-at-the-end-of-the-tunnel promise since the only light you've ever seen is from a train coming at you

Overwhelmed in the way that makes your very bones ache

Too stressed to be blessed, while judging dumb phrases like "Too blessed to be stressed"

Unsure of how to move forward and wondering if it's *even* possible

Hopeless, burned out, fed up, and trying not to lose your shit on the daily

If any of those phrases landed with you, I'm beyond thrilled you picked up this book. Now, we can get to work. But don't worry—it won't feel like work. We're beginning an awareness process of discovery, letting the pages of this book serve as our guide and walking with each other as we find hope and meaning—and dare I say *gifts*—in the midst of life's shit, pain, and unbearable discomfort. If you're open to it and approach this with a willing heart, the words you're about to read will bury themselves so deeply within you that you'll leave these pages feeling inspired, motivated, and believing there's maybe, just maybe, another way to look at life: it's happening FOR you, not TO you.

First, a few words of clarification about this book.

I can't heal you. This book can't heal you. No one else can heal you *BUT YOU*. My hope is that this book will serve as a resourceful tool you can bring with you on your journey. I hope each word resonates so intensely with you and in you that a deep seed is planted as you read the pages of this book, and that your unique experiences will water that seed in some way, no matter how significant or seemingly insignificant.

I feel it is my calling to help you with an awareness process, working alongside you to challenge the way you think about life and how you respond to it.

Our lives will be deeply impacted if we learn this truth: you and I both have a treasure chest of gifts within each of us (regardless of what life throws our way), but because of various factors, we can't access these gifts. The greatest hurdle to overcome in discovering these gifts is determined by the way we see and experience ourselves and the world.

You and I have unique perspectives and perceptions based on our experiences up to this point. We interact with the world in our own unique ways. Your journey may be similar to mine, but our steps are wholly unique. Our steps are well-worn tracks that have led us here. We tend to see what we want to see and hear what we want to hear.

I want these pages to be filled with words you may not want to hear but may *need* to hear. Namely, NOT everything happens for a reason. Awareness is the first stage in this journey, and I hope you'll join me step by step, together. It won't be easy, and some parts may be excruciating—but if you can, stick with it. Stay with me. We have to own our individual journey. No one is coming to rescue you or make you whole. This isn't a Disney movie, and there won't be birds singing and rainbows shooting out of clouds. It's time we *do* things differently by *seeing* differently. Let's do our own damn thing but with new ears, eyes, and open-mindedness.

There's no one-size-fits-all approach to life because each person is profoundly unique. Some of what you read in the following pages will resonate deeply with you and yet fall on deaf ears to others. Every reader will take something completely different from our upcoming experience together. Take what you like and leave the rest. Don't let this just be another book you read or listen to yet remain unchanged by. Commit to the process and be brave.

Before we move on to Chapter 1 and officially get started, it's important I take a moment to speak *specifically* to those of you reading this book at a moment when you are currently, in real-time, in the here-and-now wallowing in the depths of pain, grief, loss, fear, or a myriad of other traumas and challenges. I find myself struggling with intense anxiety when I think about a potential reader who may be in the *midst* of trauma while reading about the *gift* of trauma. The last thing I wanted to hear about when I was in the throes of my various traumas and tragedies was how many gifts were hidden deep within each of these situations and circumstances.

I write all this to say: one of these chapters may be too triggering for you, depending on where you are emotionally at the exact moment you read these pages. Before you begin a chapter, ask yourself if this is something you are open to hearing. If you find yourself in the middle of a chapter that you aren't ready to read, move on to the next. If you're in the middle of a painful divorce and it's fresh with a still-bleeding wound, then the chapter about the gift of heartbreak might be far too painful for you. And that's okay! All I ask is that you be aware in those moments. If you read something and get triggered, or it hits you a certain way that makes you feel sideways or off balance, get curious about your reaction. Journal about it, and be fully present with whatever comes up for you.

I've spent the majority of my adult life trying desperately to find healing *outside* of myself. For the better part of two decades, I was convinced that maybe the next diet, prescription pill, episode of *Real Housewives*, vitamin blend, book, journal prompt, kickboxing class, chiropractic adjustment, healthy smoothie, counseling session, more comfortable mattress, exercise regimen, and about a thousand other things would be the magic. I'm not discounting any of those things, and I'm not discounting whatever you've tried or are currently trying.

What I *am* hoping to convey is that the answer isn't over there or outside of you at all. Whatever you came to this book looking for, you came to the book *with*. Let's start there—a "let it begin with me" mindset. Then, once we've built that foundation of awareness and begun looking internally, we can fine-tune and dive deeper into the list of self-care activities we need to prioritize based on what works best for each of us.

Double down on self-love and self-care as you make your way through this book. As you become aware of frustration, confusion, or discomfort rising up in you as you read, remember this: you are about to learn something new. Newness can feel uncomfortable, but as you'll soon read, there's beauty in turning the concept of discomfort—and our obsession with being comfortable—on its head, too.

There are gifts in all of it.

Too often, I read a book and go from chapter to chapter without letting anything truly sink in. By the time I read chapter 2, I've already forgotten everything from chapter 1. To ensure this doesn't happen to you as you move through the book, I've curated an experiential journey for you. Between each chapter you will find a QR code that will take you directly to one of my original songs, as well as a coloring book page designed by *moi*. Before moving on to the next chapter, sit with what you've just read. Journal. Doodle. Listen to music. Let the words percolate within you. For extra points, if you really want to give into the whole experiential journey aspect, check out the Spotify playlist I created specifically for this book.

https://spotify.link/odNbP5OiNDb

I'M FINALLY WRITING THIS DAMN BOOK

> "You have to write the book that wants to be written. And if the book will be too difficult for grown-ups, then you write it for children."
> —Madeleine L'Engle

My soul has craved this literary outlet for as long as I can remember. I've been writing this book over and over again in my head, heart, soul, and spirit for the greater part of a decade. But each time I think about pulling the trigger and typing those first few intimidating words, I get sidetracked. Or I let fear in.

I have found every excuse in the book to not write the book. Those excuses stop today. I'm not sure what happened to make me finally suck it up and start typing today, but I plan on being mindful of and acting upon this prodding. I've officially run out of excuses, and fear holds no power over me anymore—at least in this area. Now, I am feeling a deep sense of urgency and longing to do the damn thing. It's time.

Too often throughout my life, I've chosen not to do something because of fear or insecurity. I've silenced that still, small voice inside of me one too many times because the perceived judgment of others rang too loudly. Gone are the days of allowing the naysayers and dream-dashers to block my path. I'm done with giving my power away. I'm done with allowing others to dictate what I do with my life, how I live my life, and where I choose to spend my time and energy.

In the subsequent pages, you can expect to read about the following:

- Pain . . . deep, intense, excruciating pain
- Hope, perseverance, resilience, grit
- Suffering, conflict, heartache, heartbreak
- Getting married at a drive-in theater during Covid and ending up on *The Today Show* and in the *New York Times*, *People* magazine, *BuzzFeed*, *Huff Post*, and countless other publications
- Going through a divorce and co-parenting with my ex
- Open adoption of twins and becoming a stepparent
- Receiving a real diamond engagement ring from a complete stranger at an airport
- Touring the country as a full-time professional recording artist
- Witnessing two deaths first-hand and erroneously thinking I was responsible
- Growing up gay (and very much in the closet) in a conservative Christian home
- Countless failed attempts at praying the gay away
- Why you'll *never* hear me say, "Everything happens for a reason"

If anything on that list made you uncomfortable, good! Keep reading . . . Lean into the discomfort because we go on a Pilgrim's

Progress of sorts in the following pages. A journey into a world where you and I can realistically learn to discern the presence of an unexpected gift in everything that happens in our lives. Yes, *everything*.

It's not an easy journey or a path for the faint of heart. But it's a worthy path because it's a path of struggle. If life is about the journey and not the destination, then it's also *about* the struggle, and not just what comes as a result of the struggle. The magic is in those moments when you feel you can't get off the struggle-bus. In the rooms of Al-Anon, I once heard an old man wisely say, "It's the struggle itself that defines us." That's when we grow and see what we're really made of . . . what we're really capable of.

Here's the truth—my truth—and what I am shamelessly confident in: this book cannot wait. This book is begging to be written.

> **Disclaimer**: What you read in the following pages may or may not be too difficult for you, my grown-up friends and peers. I *do* know it is not a children's book. I have way too foul a mouth to write a children's book (Sorry, Madeleine . . . and Mom). I can say this though: it *will* challenge you. This book has the potential to spur you on to reframe your thinking, deepen your awareness, and embrace new perspectives and perceptions.

This book is filled with true stories that touch on a variety of topics, including but not limited to the topics already listed. Ideally, this book will also touch a piece of your soul and foster fresh perspectives.

Benji Franklin once said, "Either write things worth reading or do things worth the writing."[1] When I read that, I felt it deeply. I finally let myself off the hook for not writing over the past few decades. I've been doing a lot of living, and I've been doing a lot of *somethings* worth writing about.

INTRO MUSINGS

If my mentor Jon has said this once, he's said it a thousand times:

"We ALL have gifts, but because of many factors, we can't access them."

Today, I know that the same is true about every single thing that happens to me in my life. Scratch that. Every single thing that happens FOR me in my life.

My hope for this book is to bring awareness. It is my sincere and deep desire that the pages of this book help you build an awareness process. And let me tell you, it's definitely a process. Every situation, no matter how dire, has treasures locked up deep inside. Even in the worst of times, in the midst of the most horrific situations, there are treasures to be found.

But it's never been about the treasure. This is not one of those "the ends justify the means" books. Far from it. This book is about gifts hidden deep within the recesses of shitty moments. It's about the journey and the intense transformative process that takes place within us and around us whenever we go through the shitstorm.

We are all connected. You know this. I know this. Even if you don't know it fully, you know it somewhere deep down intuitively. We've got this, so let's do the dang thang!

I wonder when your moment will be.

I wonder where you'll be sitting or standing or what you'll be doing when it clicks and you have that moment of realization, the same moment of realization I had over a year ago. During the beginning stages of my journey into changing the way I thought about pretty much everything in life, I got a sense that my pain was and is a gift. I had an acute awareness that all the pain I'd experienced in my life was actually love. Love Intelligence pursuing me and calling me in.

As I sit here today, writing these words on my tiny laptop surrounded by three of the laziest dogs on the planet, accompanied by a lovely glass of tempranillo, shrouded in the biggest blanket, with the kids' leftover crap and stains of who-knows-what all over the place, I can type this next sentence with utmost confidence and clarity:

My pain was and is my greatest teacher.

PART ONE

"Every great work of art contains a message. And the message of this painting is 'Get out of my way unless you want an arrow in your ass.'"

—Leslie Knope, *Parks and Recreation*[1]

HERE FOR THE SNACKS

Chapter 1

THE GIFT
OF FEAR

"The world is falling apart around us, and I'm dying inside."
—Moira Rose, *Schitt's Creek* (S1, E1)

"The cry we hear from deep in our hearts comes from the
wounded child within. Healing this inner child's pain
is the key to transforming anger, sadness, and fear."
—Thich Nhat Hanh

Fear is pretty much the basis for everything in our lives, and it has a good, bad, and ugly side. Fear can be our best teacher *and* our worst nightmare. Fear is a funny thing. I remember watching *Jaws* for the first time when I was a little girl. It was so real to me, and I was so terrified that I wouldn't swim in my grandad's pool for a month because I thought a shark secretly inhabited the deep end. I was convinced this shark would come for me when he got hungry.

You're not going to believe this next story when you hear it, but as my six-foot-six, former-Olympian, female, high school Bible class teacher used to say, "If I'm lyin', I'm dyin'." During my time at summer camp around age eight, I was able to celebrate my actual birthday.

Everyone at camp knew I had an obsession with daddy longlegs. Looking back, maybe it was because I was a daddy's girl? I honestly have no clue. But I was obsessed. I was fascinated to hear that they are the most poisonous spiders in the world but have too small of a mouth to bite. I still don't even know if this is a real thing and I'm too lazy to put in the time to research it, but suffice to say, these spiders were my favorite. And I hated spiders. I saw the movie *Arachnophobia* at a slumber party, and that was it for me. I hated all spiders except for the dads with the long legs.

To celebrate my birthday, there was a group of kids and even some counselors who thought it'd be hilarious to gather several daddy longlegs' nests that were strewn about the campgrounds and store them in a huge black trash bag. Later that evening, I remember singing "Happy Birthday" to myself, along with the campers and counselors. About halfway through the song, these well-meaning pranksters came up behind me, proceeded to open the trash bag, and emptied the nests on my head. Just take a second to soak that in.

As fast as my chubby little legs could take me, I sprinted to the nearby lake and jumped in the water as if I were rescuing my favorite stuffed animal from drowning. What felt like *millions* of daddy longlegs were all over me. The lake jump helped some, but the damage had been done. I can still feel them crawling all over me if I think hard enough or eat expired beef jerky. But hey, it could've been worse, right? It can ALWAYS be worse!

From that day on, I couldn't look at a daddy longlegs spider without having a full-blown panic attack. I would freeze at the mere sight of one. Until much later in life, I was plagued by fear of this Satan-spawned spider. In high school I saw one in our backyard and instantly fell to the ground, holding my knees to my chest and crying hysterically. I've done some work around this intense phobia, but I'll still make every effort to avoid this insect at all costs. If I see one, I'm not going to let it outside safely like I do other insects. Nope. That bitch is getting crushed under my sneakers.

I'm sure we've all experienced our own version of silly fears, serious fears, debilitating fears, and what (at the time) may have felt like life-ending fears. Someone smarter than me once encouraged me to think about fear in this way:

F-E-A-R = False Evidence Appearing Real

And yes, sometimes that's the case. However, there are other times when the evidence is quite real.

During my touring days post-college, I was on a flight to Nashville to sing. The weather was so bad that it felt as if the plane had joined a game of whack-a-mole in the sky. We were bouncing all over the place, and the women next to me started saying the Lord's Prayer. That's NEVER good when you're in midair. After about twenty minutes of this turbulence, the severity of which I'd never experienced before, I started praying for my family and friends. I came to a weird but peaceful place of acceptance with what was happening. If we didn't make it, I begged God to give extra comfort to the tens of people who would mourn my death. (The "tens" I just used wasn't a typo. I had pretty low self-esteem back then.) That was a *real* fear because the evidence indicated this plane might become one of those disappearing planes you hear about on *60 Minutes*.

After hearing twenty Hail Marys behind me and at least thirty Lord's Prayers next to me, the plane stopped acting like a newborn puppy fighting with itself in the mirror. We landed; no one died; it was fine. But I'll never forget that flight.

Another very real fear I had plagued me from the time I could comprehend what was going on around me. I knew I was different growing up. I couldn't pinpoint what exactly it was, but I knew I was different from my friends. I even felt out of place in my own family, through zero fault of theirs. It wasn't until years later that I realized why I'd always felt so odd: I was a little gay girl growing up in a conservative evangelical Christian culture. Oh, sorry, I *AM* gay. Not past tense. It's not a thing that just comes and goes like bloating or gas, despite what proponents of "ex-gay therapy" think.

I was filled with this fear of being different and being found out. What if someone caught on? What if I stayed quiet when my friends made fun of our gay volleyball coach instead of speaking up in defense of her? Would they instantly assume that I, too, was a homosexual destined for the pit of hell? I felt I *had* to join in the "fun" to throw everyone off my lesbian scent. As I got older, I perfected the art of closet living. I was athletic but could also code-switch to girly-girl when needed. If I even remotely suspected that someone was on to me, I would instantly be filled with the fight, flight, or freeze response that our bodies naturally produce when faced with fear.

Now, after decades of work, I'm finally learning how to reframe my thinking when it comes to fear. In addition to False-Evidence-Appearing-Real, I've also heard this explanation for fear: Fuck Everything And Run. I like that one, too, even though I'd rather eat a truck tire whole than go running.

SAY HELLO TO MY LITTLE FRIEND FEAR

My dance with fear has evolved from complete ignorance by way of utilizing the stick-my-head-in-the-sand approach, to the art of befriend-ing fear. WTF, Lindsey? I know, stay with me. Let me tell you about my hilarious best friend, Julia. She shared a story with me recently that genuinely made me tee-tee (another one of those "you know you're a mom when" terms) a bit in my sweatpants. She'd been bitten by a brown recluse spider when she was six. She has a physical scar (and a trove of unseen emotional scars) to prove it. She is TERRIFIED of spiders, even more so than I am.

Many, many years later, adult Julia attended a fiesta in a tiny vil-lage in Mexico—ya know, like you do. After the fiesta festivities ended, Julia made her way on foot back to the farm where she was staying. It was completely dark, and the only light source came from her head-lamp. Halfway to the farm, she saw what could only be described as twinkly (or is it twinkling?) lights. Lots and lots of lights. She initially thought nothing of it, until she kept seeing more and more of these "lights." Oh, and they were moving, not just twinkling.

WELL, dear reader, turns out that the twinkly lights were actu-ally the creepy eyes of *only-God-knows-how-many* spiders. She froze, thinking this might be the end of her life here on earth. She'd had a good run, she thought. Had an adorable kid (I'm the godmother). Married a wonderful man. Started a successful business. Maybe this was her time to go. Maybe she was supposed to sing her swan song in Mexico.

As her headlamp lit the (only) path of disaster, Julia was paralyzed with fear and couldn't move, blinded as she was by the refracting eyes of the spider army. She was terrified but knew she had to get home. What stood between her and the farm was a hill *filled* with spiders. She knew if she moved, the spider army would've been activated. But she wondered: If she stayed still, would she just fall asleep standing up while waiting on this hill until morning? Would the spider army devour her or just keep staring at her with those beady, judgmental eyes?

After what seemed like hours of internal deliberation, she had a eureka moment. Julia opted for *friendship*, a treaty of sorts. Here's the part that caused me minor urination. She told me she "had a moment with God" and started talking to the spiders. Her negotiation skills went a little something like this:

"Dear Spider Army. My name is Julia. I have a husband and child. I come in peace. If you leave me unmolested and allow me to pass safely and without attack, we will call a truce. I hereby promise that now and in the future, I will not seek to end your life or the lives of your spider relatives if and when you come into my household—as long as you are under a certain size. We won't be friends, but we will be cool."

Julia soldiered on through the droves of spiders and made it home to the farm that night in one piece, unscathed, and without being attacked. She believes it was that moment when she was cured of arachnophobia. Now, when spiders are in her house, she leaves them be and lets them "do what they need to do."

Julia didn't stop in the face of fear. She paused, got curious about her options, and moved forward. Likewise, when I have started to get curious about my fears, I have felt my mindset start to shift. To better understand fear, I know I need to not *fight* it but to *invite* fear to the table. This evolution can enable us to take back control of that fear-based part of our lives.

There's a logical and scientific explanation for why you and I tend to repeat the same unwanted fear-based patterns, regardless of the great extents we go to in order to improve ourselves and heal. It's written that, "Your brain is a three pound universe that processes 70,000 thoughts each day using 100 billion neurons that connect at more than 500 trillion points through synapses that travel 300 miles/hour. The signals that travel through these interconnected neurons form the basis of memories, thoughts, and feelings."[1] And who knows how many of those 70,000 thoughts are simply recycled from yesterday.

Think of all the countless aspects of life and our thinking that compete for our attention, causing us to *react* to what life throws at us when all we really needed to do was *respond* to it. Reacting is the instinctive, emotional, automatic response to a stimulus. Example: I see or smell mayo and immediately start gagging. Responding, on the other hand, is a more thoughtful, intentional, deliberate approach to stimuli. Example: Someone tricks me and puts mayo on my sandwich. Instead of immediately punching them in the throat, I pause and remember that hands are for loving, not for hitting. Julia gets an A+ in *responding* to the spider situation. I would've *reacted* and found a way to blowtorch all of them.

As you wade through the pages of this book, I share with you what has absolutely and significantly changed my life forever—so much so that I can't even see the world the same way I used to. Do I still struggle with unwanted patterns? Of course. Do I still struggle with fear and want to throw my hands up and yell, "Fuck everything and RUN!"? Hell yes. But now I am aware—and that's the difference. However, it doesn't stop there.

THE ~~DYNAMIC~~ DASTARDLY DUO: GUILT AND SHAME

There's one main culprit that is keeping you and me stuck in fear. I used to think the scapegoat was the hit list of patterns I'd developed throughout my life, starting from a young age. Patterns that used to serve me well yet no longer serve me in the life I'm trying to live today.

That culprit that keeps us trapped in fear is a dynamic duo I like to call shame and guilt. Spoiler alert: there is a reason you and I keep doing the stupid stuff we hate. There's a reason we keep swimming in the muck and mire that we swore we'd finally get out of someday. There's an explanation for why we can't seem to get off the hamster wheel that's also secretly trying to crush us into oblivion.

You may not see it now, but believe it or not, there is a magnetic field of guilt and shame surrounding you. This magnetic pull that lives in the very make-up of guilt and shame is what's keeping us stuck. It's not about the pattern. It's about the guilt and shame we *feel* about the pattern. Those two culprits are responsible for perpetuating those unwanted patterns in our lives.

The work we need to do is to shift those patterns through the magic of self-forgiveness. I say "magic" because that's truly what it is.

I started committing myself to this work more than two years ago, and I haven't been the same since. It didn't all change at once for me, but it's been changing slowly over time. A little bit each day. With every thought and moment.

With every step, I'm getting closer to living the life I've always dreamed of and didn't even know I so desperately needed.

Take my friend Patty, for example. Patty LOVES cheese. But she tries valiantly to swear off cheese and all things dairy because these food items tear her stomach to shreds. Every New Year's she vows anew to kick the habit, the addiction. But then *poof*, the commitment and willpower fly out the window. She's back on the couch with her hand in the grocery bag filled with shredded Mexican cheese.

Why can't she quit?

When Patty was a little girl, she was constantly bullied by her much older brother. It broke her more and more every time she suffered at his relentless hand.

When her brother would hurt her, Patty would run crying to her mother, who always had one answer for sad feelings: cheese. Patty's mom would find some cheese and tell her daughter, "Oh, Patty, eat the cheese. It will make you feel better." So, eat the cheese Patty did. But now Patty is forty-nine and has no idea why she keeps eating cheese when she knows it's counterproductive to her gastrointestinal (GI) goals.

You should also know that Patty is dedicated to self-development work, therapy, self-help books, and all kinds of other resources that women use to try to survive in this untenable world. She has success-fully dealt with the pain from her childhood bullying at the hands of her brother, finding sustainable freedom and forgiveness. She is healed. In fact, she and her brother have a fantastic relationship now. Everything seems to be good. Yet, Patty and cheese are closer than conjoined twins.

I enjoy using cheese to help drive home crucial points, so stay with me; we're almost there. For those of you who believe there are only five love languages, I challenge you. I firmly believe cheese (and sarcasm) should be added as the sixth (and seventh) love languages.

Patty isn't addicted to cheese because of the pain from her child-hood. She isn't even addicted to cheese because of the pattern that's sunk its deep claws into her soul. Patty can't stop eating cheese because of the guilt and shame she feels each time she eats cheese. The guilt and shame about the thing are the exact reasons the thing keeps happening.

Our guilt and shame about our patterns are the lifeblood of those patterns. The deeper work is in becoming aware and addressing the rampant nature of our own guilt and shame surrounding the patterns we hate, those parts of ourselves we wish we could kill off like your least favorite *Schitt's Creek* character. (Is that even a thing? I love ALL the characters on *Schitt's Creek*.)

Woven throughout this book is a thread dealing with this phenom-enon of guilt and shame, the power couple for perpetuating patterns. I'm going to share with you a very simple mantra, prayer, process, or whatever you want to call it. The purpose of this prayer is to kickstart your awareness of this dynamic duo, guilt and shame. Once we are aware of it, we can begin identifying where the pattern and subsequent guilt and shame originated.

FORGIVING YOURSELF IS THE SECRET SAUCE

Maybe you have a consistent pattern like me where I subconsciously or consciously choose to discount my own feelings because of fear. I then feel guilt and shame because of the way I've just discounted my feelings and essentially rejected them and myself. Turns out I've been placing the focus on the wrong thing this whole time. I've been obsessing over the unwanted pattern when I should have been hyper-focused on pursuing the patterns I DO want. Meanwhile, guilt and shame have been doing push-ups on the sidelines, just waiting for their big moment to shine. They're throwing fuel all over that fire you keep trying to put out.

The magic is in forgiving yourself of the guilt and shame you feel about the way you keep living your life despite wanting to live differently. Taking my previous example (pertaining to my pattern of discounting my own feelings and ignoring them at all costs), I'll share with you the way I tend to say this mantra of self-forgiveness in my heart.

After becoming aware of the pattern rearing its ugly head for the umpteenth time, I was ready to address the guilt and shame. With my mentor Jon's help, I've since conditioned myself and my spirit to simply say: "I'm aware of the guilt and shame I feel about my tendency to discount my own feelings and reject my emotions. I forgive myself for choosing to discount my own feelings because of fear. I forgive myself for choosing unconsciously to give in to the fear and ignore my feelings and emotions. I take responsibility for my life and my actions. Thank you for forgiveness."

Sometimes I say those words to myself, other times I say those words to God or my Spiritual Self. Maybe you are more of a spiritual guides type of person. Or maybe you have no faith in anything at all. Forgiveness doesn't care about any of that. We must take back the reins of what's going on in our lives and commit to doing the rigorous work of self-forgiveness.

You can't beat yourself up *and* forgive yourself at the same time.

In order to make room for forgiveness, you'll have to set down whatever weapon you're currently using to flog yourself for your indiscretions and addictions. When we do this work of forgiving ourselves—not only for our patterns but, more importantly, for the guilt and shame we feel about those patterns—something fascinating happens. Not all at once and not overnight. But piece by piece, like a puzzle, it all starts fitting together over time. When I genuinely forgive myself, something shifts. That magnetic field of guilt and shame that keeps causing my choices to be repeated slowly starts to change.

Love is about making decisions not based on fear. Love is about becoming more conscious of what already is so we can be open to what is to come. I believe that all answers are here if I know how to phrase the question without giving in to my biases and assumptions. One of my favorite sayings in Al-Anon is "Whatever you came here looking FOR, you came here WITH." Meaning, it's already inside you. The answers you so desperately seek day after day are already inside you, though they might be hidden and completely out of sight at this time. That's okay. It's all grace. It's all love.

If you'll allow for it, fear also wants to become one of your greatest teachers in addition to pain.

EXCERPT FROM *THE FOUR AGREEMENTS* BY DON MIGUEL RUIZ

"The experience of disappointment, for example, relates directly to your guilt and feelings of inadequacy. When your expectations are not met, you are merely receiving a correction. You are being told that you do not see the whole truth of the situation. You are being asked to expand your perceptions. Correction is not attack. It is not punishment. All experience happens for one purpose only; to expand your awareness. Resistance leads to suffering. Surrender leads to bliss. Resistance is the decision to act alone. Surrender is the decision to act with God . . . All the information you need in life is obtainable in the present moment through a simple method of inquiry. Of course, this method only works if you can ask for information from a neutral standpoint. Your preference will falsely influence and distort the answer you receive. To prevent distortion, earnestly state before asking: 'I place my preferences and prejudices aside and open myself to a free and truthful answer.'"[2]

After reading those words and adapting the steps to align with who I am and what I feel I need, I say the following statement to myself:

"I forgive myself for giving in to fear-based choices. I now understand and see that this addiction to fear-based decision-making is causing adverse, unintended consequences in my life, heart, spirit, and soul . . . wreaking havoc on my body. I forgive myself for this pattern and the toll it's taken on my body and those around me. I also forgive myself for any guilt or shame I may feel about my tendency to make fear-based choices that no longer serve me in the life I'm creating now."

This seemingly unremarkable patchwork of words helps to remove so much of the guilt and shame that surround me on all sides. This forgiveness prayer puts my fear-based choices in their place.

So, the next time you're driving out of the rental car parking lot, and you know you're fast approaching those horrifying road spikes that ALLEGEDLY only go one direction, think about what you're thinking about. Think about the fear and get curious about it. Why am I always, without fail, scared of driving over those spikes? I know they're not meant for me based on the direction I'm driving out of the rental car parking lot. I know these spikes aren't going to blow out all four tires. Yet, I start sweating and my heart starts racing when I approach the spikes and proceed to drive over them.

It's the same with cops. I could see a cop far off in the distance, and I am instantly convinced that I'll spend the night in jail. Have I done anything wrong or illegal? Nope. I was just driving to pick the kids up from school. But now, I won't be able to because I'll be in jail. The kids will be waiting, alone, scared, and cold because their felon of a mom couldn't pick them up because she got nabbed by the po-po. Anytime, to this day, I see a police car or motorcycle cop, fear convinces me that this is the end of the line. I'd better get ready for prison because I'll be there for a very long time due to whatever crime I don't remember committing.

This is what fear and anxiety look like. I'm sure you have some strange and even awkward fears and anxieties that you'd be too embarrassed to share with someone. Well, try it! It's liberating.

Before we dive into the next chapter, let's take a moment to digest this timely quote from Moira Rose in season four, episode five of *Schitt's Creek* after a rumor spread online that Moira had died. She appears to her stunned friends and proclaims, "FEAR NOT! She hath risen!"[3]

And so must we . . .

Break It Down for Me

- Fear is complex in nature. It can both help and hurt us. Approach with curiosity.

- The shame we feel about our unwanted patterns is exactly what perpetuates the patterns.

- You can't simultaneously beat yourself up and forgive yourself. Choose self-forgiveness.

- Don't play pranks on kids involving trash bags full of spiders. You can do better.

NORMALIZE NAPS

Chapter 2

THE GIFT OF ADDICTION

"This wine is awful. Give me another glass."
—Moira Rose, *Schitt's Creek* (S1, E6)

"I ate a brownie once, at a party in college. It was
intense. It was kind of indescribable actually. I felt like
I was floating. Turns out there wasn't any pot in the
brownie. It was just an insanely good brownie."
—Leslie Knope, *Parks & Recreation* (S2, E2)

Addiction, ugh. This is where I fear I might lose some of you because
we're all addicted to *something* and we typically don't like talking
about it, nor being challenged about it.

But that's not what this chapter is about. If I do have a challenge
for you, though, it's simply that you try to see addiction through a
new lens. There's a reason we get addicted to certain people, places,
and things. The addiction points to a much deeper meaning in our
lives and can be the canary in the coal mine. Here's my WHY with this
chapter specifically: I believe that the best way for me to help you find
your story (in this area and in general) is to share my story with you.

One of my all-time favorite books in the history of the universe is *The Spirituality of Imperfection* by Ernest Kurtz and Katherine Ketcham. Their combined work in the area of addiction is profound and played an integral role in reframing the way I see addiction. Here's what they have to say about this topic (don't worry, it only stings for a sec):

> Addiction represents the ultimate effort to control, the definitive demand for magic and the final failure of spirituality. Turning to the magic of chemicals signifies the desperate and doomed attempt to fill a spiritual void with a material reality—to make "magic" a substitute for miracle. Addiction has been described as the belief that whenever there is "something wrong with me," it can be "fixed" by something outside of me. That false start generates ever more drastic illusions. The search for "the quick fix," inevitably unfulfilled by drugs and unsated by material things, leaps next to spiritual realities and the search for "instant spirituality"—some sort of quick "spiritual fix." For a profound relationship exists between spirituality and addiction, as suggested by the ancient metaphor of thirst and the Jungian formulation spiritus contra spiritum. "Drunkenness can be a kind of shortcut to the higher life, the [attempt to] achieve a higher state without any emotional and intellectual effort," observed Dr. E.M. Jellinek, a pioneer in alcoholism theory and formulator of the modern disease-concept of alcoholism.[1]

Okay, so maybe it stung for longer than a few seconds. Is it 4:53 p.m., and am I about to pour myself a neat glass of local bourbon? Yep. Do I still very much resonate and agree with the previous paragraph? Yep. But how can both things exist? Because we're human. We were born with both darkness and light.

Jean Vanier puts it this way: "Somewhere in each of us we're a mixture of light and of darkness, of love and of hate, of trust and of fear."[2]

BEAUTY AND BROKENNESS: AN AWKWARD BALANCE

I write about this delicate balance later on in the book, but suffice it to say, we were born either already broken or born into a world where brokenness would eventually occur. If you are a human with a beating heart, you've experienced a brokenness so entrenched deep down in your soul that you'd do just about anything to get some relief from those overwhelming feelings it brings.

I don't know a lot about a lot, but what I do know for sure is that life will eventually put dog poo into a paper bag and light it on fire on your porch, ring the doorbell, and run off. Life is not good or bad. It just is. There are not even good or bad days. There are just days where sometimes good stuff happens and other days . . . well, not so much. This pilgrimage is steeped in beauty and brokenness.

There's no straight line from A "bad" to B "good." The line doesn't exist. This journey we're on promises to bring its share of immense pain *and* indescribable peace. That's why I loathe the "health and wealth gospel" teachings—if you can even call it that. Show me a person who ONLY has great days, and I'll show you a person in complete denial of reality.

I'm all for thinking positive thoughts and <insert your hip, spiritual-sounding quote here> or whatever. But there comes a point in your life when you will realize that life is happening all around you. Sometimes we get rotten lemons thrown at us in a non-stop barrage of WTF moments, while other times we take those lemons and say, "Fuck it," and throw them in a blender in hopes of making a somewhat palatable lemonade cocktail (or mocktail, depending on your situation). I spent so much of my life thinking I was broken and I could be fixed if I just had _____ or if I just did _____ or if I just met someone who would make me whole. I have no idea where I got the idea that life eventually would be free from pain.

Dear reader, do you want to hear something super depressing? It's commonly said that "We cannot learn without pain." Well, crap.

The more years I have under my belt, the more I've come to believe that saying was right. Life hurts sometimes, and we don't like it. And if you're anything like me, I tend to opt for the path that makes it hurt less . . . you know, fast-acting pain relief like emotional eating, binging on food or alcohol, or fill-in-the-blank-here with your vice of choice. There's a deep pain no one wants to feel. Or if it's not a pain, it's a deep ache for something different, something more. It's our soul's way of craving magic and miracles.

Yet, all our shortcuts are dead-ends. Every single last one of them. In the words of the wise Fat Bastard, as heard on the critically acclaimed (probably should've won a Nobel Peace Prize) *Austin Powers*, "I eat cuz I'm unhappy and I'm unhappy because I eat. It's a vicious cycle."[3] That it is, Fat B, that it is. Please tell me I'm not the only one who can relate to his wisdom?

I suppose the basic-yet-badass question is this: How are you and I going to choose to respond to all the bags of shit life leaves on our doorsteps from time to time? How are we going to deal with the inevitable existence of crisis, trauma, loss, tragedy, etc. that will continue to appear in our lives? There's a shortcut path that leads to more and more pain; then there's the path that eventually leads to peace and acceptance—which is hard to choose.

Why wait for the long, arduous marinating process that will eventually result in a soul's ability to move through life in a peaceful, strong manner (despite what crosses our path), when I can go to the pantry, grab a family-size pack of M&M's, and eat those until I'm sick? When I can go to the liquor cabinet within seconds and pour a drink? When I can pick up my phone and scroll for hours to (temporarily) forget how infuriatingly painful everything so often seems?

THE CHOICE IS OURS, LIKE IT OR NOT

I'm not saying there's anything bad with those choices that may involve addiction. I have zero problems with the act of eating, drinking, smoking, scrolling, whatever. Where I have a problem is when I notice myself grabbing my phone instead of a journal where I could benefit from writing some shit down. When I pour a drink instead of getting curious about why I'm so irritable. When I eat an entire plate of brownies, knowing what I really need is to be held, loved, and genuinely listened to.

Lord knows I prefer the quick fix. But I've got four decades under my belt, which gives me enough proof to know how that option will continually come up empty. It will always leave me wanting more. That's why I need ALL the chips at my favorite Mexican food spot. In a world that seeks to force us into a non-stop cycle of needing and chasing after more and more and more—the latest gadget, the newest smartphone, this season's purse, the newest car, etc.—let's be rebels. Let's start learning to be okay with less.

MORE IS MORE, BUT MAYBE NOT THE KIND OF *MORE* YOU BARGAINED FOR.

I promise that you and I are not going to die because we have last year's smartphone or last year's SUV. We'll also be okay if we don't end up having that third or fourth drink. The problem is that our minds are out to get us. My brain assures me that I *absolutely* 100 percent need to have a Whataburger egg and cheese taquito every morning on my way to work, a $15 cup of coffee and 3 cake pops at Starbucks every single day, and at least 30 minutes a day obsessing over the latest news on *NPR*.

BUT—and this is a bigger but than the one behind me—here's what my soul and spirit and heart crave: Peace. Acceptance. Freedom from stress, fear, and pain. Relief from overwhelm. A moment to myself. Solitude, and also times of being surrounded by those who love and support me. I want abundance in my life. Something to break through the monotony and routine. I long for wholeness and wholehearted living. Patience. Contentment. And ultimately, unconditional love.

Love will meet you wherever you are. Love has the power and the ability to meet you when you've eaten all the kids' Halloween candy. Love meets us in the darkest of alleys and the brightest of sunsets.

LOVE WILL FIND YOU IF YOU LET IT.

I still battle my vices and addictions. I may always. But at least now I have the awareness to know why I jump into familiar, addictive waters. I am now able to realize when I'm slipping into old patterns. We have the empowered choice of continuing on in our addictions or making a different choice, opting instead to love ourselves, parent ourselves, reach out to a Higher Power, or do whatever it is that makes us feel less alone, less scared, and less broken.

Kurtz and Ketcham go on to write that addiction enters because we fool ourselves into believing that whatever we're addicted to (drugs, booze, food, your phone, social media, biting your nails, pills, obsessions with people, or fill in the blank) will heal us. Unfortunately, it's those very vices that send us wallowing in a shame spiral. And we already know how problematic shame can be. Terrence Real writes, "An addict needs shame like a man dying of thirst needs salt water."[4]

THE DOUCHEY DUO STRIKES AGAIN: TEAM G&S

I want to touch base with you about something before we move on. Be on the lookout as vigilantly as you can for the dastardly duo of guilt and shame, as written about earlier. Remember, it's the guilt and shame that keep you and me stuck. This douchey duo keeps you in a state of drowning and repeating the same unwanted behaviors over and over (and over) again.

I took my kids to a wave pool recently, and my five-year-old kept getting slammed by the waves. He'd bob up and down fearlessly, trying to keep his head above water. But the huge waves would come and send him back down.

That's what guilt and shame are waiting in the wings to do to you. We're the five-year-old in the wave pool, except instead of a wave pool, it's the middle of the ocean in the darkness during a colossal storm. If you want to know why you stay in your addiction, we need only ask team G&S. Their favorite pastime is to make you feel like shit so you'll grab the very thing you think will help take that feeling away.

It's time for us to beat them at their own game. It's time we flip the script on addiction and show these losers who's boss. I know for me, I'm sick and tired of feeling controlled by my addiction. I want out. I want freedom—sustainable freedom. Yet, just as much as I want it, it eludes me often. I can write all day about this, and I hope it helps you in some way with your addiction battles. But the truth is that I'm still steeped in several addictions, even now.

The next thing I'm about to tell you is something I most definitely don't want to share. I'd rather keep it hidden in the shadows. At first blush, it might not seem like a big deal to you, but I assure you it's a huge deal to me. It's a vice I've battled for three decades. There have been seasons of freedom from it, but those have been few and far between. I've been to therapy about it, read incessantly about how to overcome it, and even tried hypnotherapy to treat it. These treatments would work for a little while, but then I'd just go back to it. Time and time again. The root: anxiety and stress. The addiction: picking my cuticles.

As I write this, I'm questioning my theory about the value and freedom in searching for a gift in the midst of addiction, even if that gift is trapped deep below the Earth's core. As that anxiety comes up for me, I pause and sit with it.

This awareness is also a gift. Why can I confidently say, for example, that my addiction to biting my cuticles has been a gift? You may vehemently disagree with that statement, and that's completely okay. I encourage disagreement and pushback. The more you get curious about your reaction as you read, the better you'll get to know yourself and what makes you tick.

I have the audacity to propose that addiction has the potential to be a gift because it's my warning signal. When I find myself yet again choosing an addiction and falling back into old, unwanted patterns, that's my wake-up call. Why am I messing with my cuticles in the first place? That's my first clue to look deeper and see if I can find the root that's producing the (spoiled) fruit of cuticle picking. My addictions have also become my greatest teacher, just like the pain I write about later on in the book. Our addictions can be the grackle that keeps dive-bombing our heads, or we can get curious and allow our addictions to be the canary in the coal mine.

Look, if we want to believe something badly enough, we'll find a way. If we want to live in denial about our own addictions and pretend they're not there, it might work for a while. But eventually, there comes a point when you must ask yourself the tough questions and tell your right brain to quit believing the bullshit your left brain is feeding it. There will be a moment in our lives, and many of us have already experienced this, where we cannot NOT hear and see the canary. How long will we ignore what our addictions are trying to tell us and teach us? How long will we stay in our own cages, like those birds, and continue to inhale and exhale, all the while filling up our lives with toxicity? No wonder the canaries were caged! Are you caged? I am, but at least I'm aware of it now.

I'VE GOT BOTH HANDS IN MY POCKET

I was a very anxious child growing up. Through no fault of my parents, I was obsessed with perfection. I had an image in my mind of how things *should* be, and when they weren't, it caused me major stress. I always bit my nails growing up. I don't even have any memories that *aren't* plagued by my gnarly nails. When you might have been rebelling through beer and cheap cigarettes, I was sneaking away in a corner to bite my nails. I knew it was bad for me. I knew about the germs and all the other terrible things that could befall me due to this addiction.

Yet, I persisted. I couldn't stop. I didn't really care to stop. Biting my nails was giving me some sort of benefit. It was something I could control . . . or so I thought. Then, as I got older, my fingernail and cuticle biting needed to go into the closet. I kept getting in trouble for messing with my nails, and I don't blame my parents for trying to figure out ways to help me stop. Instead of stopping, I just went into the cuticle closet. This is like the gay closet but for cuticles. You can find them at IKEA (I'm pretty sure).

I knew that at some point, I would HAVE to keep my dang fingers out of my dang mouth. My Sunday School teacher once scolded me for my vice and said, in the most obnoxious Southern bless-your-heart tone, "You know, sweetie, no man is gonna wanna put a ring on a finger that looks like it's been in a meat grinder." I think I was eight years old. Little did she know that no man was going to want to put a ring on my finger because my fingers and I are super gay. I remember being filled with so much guilt and shame, wondering if I'd be an old, single spinster-maid at age fifty, hanging with my hedgehog, sitting by the fireplace in an old worn rocking chair, and biting my nails off and spitting them into the flames.

So, I had to hide my vice. I had to keep the fingers as far away from my mouth as humanly possible. I was too little to understand addiction, and there was no Google to help me read up on solutions to my problem. The shelves full of *Encyclopedia Britannica* I had access to in my childhood home certainly didn't have a damn thing to say about *Dermatillomania*, the term that I'd learn about much later in my adult life.

Because I wanted to keep my fingers out of my mouth, but still wanted to feel the sensation of making something smooth that didn't feel smooth to me, I started picking my cuticles. Apparently, this addiction or disease or whatever TF you want to call it is strongly associated with one's intense desire (read: obsession) to experience smoothness with touch.

Do you pick at your face when you feel a pimple or mess with a scab that you know you should leave alone? Do you obsess over a picture that isn't perfectly affixed to the wall or demand that your room look a certain way? Though I've not been formally diagnosed with OCD, it appears that I am quite prone to feeling the urge to make everything associated with my skin, fingers, and cuticles smooth. If I feel a hangnail, GOD FORBID, we are going to war. I could be sitting in a client meeting fidgeting with my fingers and notice a rough nail. It will bother me the entire appointment until I'm able to do something about it.

You know what's sad? I consciously and intentionally hide my fingers as much as possible. And I have A TON of guilt and shame around it still, even though I've made so much progress and growth in this area. As I'm sitting here typing this chapter, I am conscious of my cuticles. Sometimes, I realize I'm obsessing over the lack of smoothness on my fingers, and other times I don't even realize I'm picking. Anytime I felt stress or anxiety as a child, I would mess with my fingers. It was my way of reacting to whatever stressor may have been present at that moment. Some habits are just that—habits. But other habits (like this one of mine) are full-blown addictions.

As I got even older, I started to realize how much energy I was spending trying to hide my hands. The more I hid myself (moving deeper and deeper into the closet in hopes of ignoring my sexuality and hiding my truth from everyone), the more I realized I had to hide my hands. I didn't want to let anyone see my fingers, all swollen and bloody. I had a real problem on my hands. Pun intended, per usual.

But instead of judging it, like I'd done my entire life, for the first time I got curious about it. I wanted to know WHY. Why couldn't I let a random piece of skin roam free without feeling the need to pick it? Why did everything affiliated with my skin have to be smoother than Adele's voice? Why did my "willpower" continue to elude and fail me? Why did I keep doing it even though I hated everything about it?

The answer: because I needed to. Picking was and still is serving me a purpose. There's something about it that makes me feel a release. It hurts, but that physical pain takes my mind temporarily off the emotional pain I simply cannot deal with at that time. It's a shortcut; it's not sustainable; I know that. Yet, I keep doing it. This is one of my addictions I haven't yet fully overcome.

Everyone, repeat after me: PROGRESS, NOT PERFECTION. Now say that eighty-five times until it sinks in.

WILLPOWER IS A JOKE

What became an obsession with an unwanted pattern turned into an obsession to control the unwanted pattern. After years of trying this approach, I was frustrated to learn that the control-the-picking-in-hopes-of-changing-the-behavior obsession was the very thing that kept me chained to that behavior. I thought that if I just had enough willpower, I could do this. What is wrong with me that I'm forty and still don't have normal-looking hands? I can't even step into one of those strip mall nail salons without feeling judged and scorned by the people who work there.

Once, in college, I finally got up the courage to get a mani-pedi. The pedi was dreamy, and I was instantly best friends with my nail tech, Melissa. But then Melissa transitioned me to the manicure chair. She took one look at my hands and stared at them for longer than should've been normal, then glared at me, and snarled back to my hands. She started talking to her friend Shannon in an Asian language I didn't understand.

I was mortified. They were snickering and laughing, which I can only assume meant they were mocking me. And rightly so. My fingers were not normal, and everything she did to them hurt. The cuticle ointment and whatever else she put on my bleeding fingers caused me intense pain. Begrudgingly, she continued with the manicure and finished. My nails and fingers looked okay, but I didn't even notice because I was drowning in a shame spiral that I thought this woman had forced me into. It's always fun blaming someone else.

But that didn't last long. It was mere moments before I started the song and dance of blaming myself, then hating myself, and judging myself. Guilt and shame were waiting outside the nail place ready to attack. And I let them. Giving in to their antics caused me to go right back to picking. It really is a vicious cycle.

The longer I've been alive and struggling with this addiction, the more I realize I have to tackle this 12-step style. I've admitted that I'm powerless over my addiction to picking my fingers and that my life (in this area) has become unmanageable. I've come to believe that a Power greater than myself can restore me to sanity. I've decided to turn my will and my life over to the care of God as I understand Him/Her/Them/Universe/Love Intelligence/Source/Whatever TF . . .

I've made a fearless and moral inventory of myself. And the 12-step list goes on and on—powerfully. I am a huge fan of AA's program and the corresponding steps of Al-Anon. Yet, despite the power and beauty of these steps and their obvious success in the face of addiction, I continue to pick.

But what's different—instead of beating myself to a pulp about it, I walk myself through a process of awareness, acceptance, and then action. When I notice I'm picking or about to pick, I notice the cue that sets me going: I start feeling for smoothness, and if I identify something that isn't smooth, I respond accordingly. I'm trying to break the cycle so that before I start picking, I ask myself if I'm nervous, anxious, bored, tired, hungry, or is it something else? How is this potentially serving me? What am I getting out of this addiction and how the hell can I get out of it? Not forever, not even for this week, but just for today.

People in 12-step programs are always talking about "one day at a time," and rightly so. But some days, ladies (and gents, non-binary, etc., you are all welcome), it's one minute at a time. It's one-foot-in-front-of-the-other time. It's "what's the next right thing?" time.

TAKE YOUR POWER BACK (AND KEEP IT)

Throughout the course of some good therapy and meds, I came to realize the finger picking is only there as an expression of me not being *fully me*. I want to stop the picking, but I can't. It's almost as if I'm compelled by something to keep picking. And then I realize I am. Guilt and shame compel me to continue repeating the patterns and pursuing addictions. So then, my focus shifted from my fingers to the real culprit: guilt.

There is guilt inside of me and inside each of us. We are giving our power away in small and large doses. Each time I take on guilt about whatever, be it how I'm too much of a mom to be a good advisor or too much of an advisor to be a good mom, it's there. It wants to be taken on. Guilt is powerful. And now I see it. I see guilt for what it is. I go so far as to accept it. I accept responsibility for how I've participated in and perpetuated this situation.

The moment you and I take responsibility for our actions, angels are celebrating all around us because we are finally taking responsibility for feeling guilty and seeing how that guilt is trapped in our energy field. This process of self-forgiveness is the answer. I must forgive myself for the guilt and for punishing myself because I feel I don't deserve this.

Can I get an amen? Has anyone else in the crowd felt this way? I will take you to church.

You and I cannot be in our full power if we keep giving it away.

Take your power back. And I don't mean in some superficial women's empowerment way. I mean in the deep gutters of your gut kind of way. Take it back. There's no way to love unless you have your power and love for yourself. We have to stop giving it away like it's worthless, like some dirty penny on the street.

This pattern, whatever addiction or habit may be ruminating in your mind as you read this, may have started early for you. And the guilt keeps it going, which is why this has followed you into all your relationships and has seeped into almost every area of your life. I don't know the answer for you; though, I believe there's an answer for each of us that is specifically crafted and designed for our situation. Maybe for you, it's a 12-step program, or maybe it's running or fishing or walking around the mall like the retired ladies do in their unnaturally white sneakers.

Let's start listening to our own canaries so we can learn more about those coal mines. I hope that in hearing my story, something is unlocked within you—something that leads you to ask new questions, even if you don't know the answers right away. Sometimes knowing what questions to ask is a good enough place to start.

Break It Down for Me

- Addiction represents a desperate attempt to fill a spiritual vacancy with material items, substances, or experiences.

- Despite the illusion, whatever we're addicted to isn't going to be the quick fix we were hoping for. It's about as useful as thinking that duct tape will fix a gigantic crack in a dam.

- Addiction is fueled by a belief that something outside of ourselves can fix whatever feels wrong with us.

- The gift of addiction can be found through the journey of recovery and self-awareness. It can be a powerful catalyst for growth and transformation.

Chapter 3

THE GIFT OF ANGER

"I wouldn't have to manage my anger, if people
could learn to manage their stupidity."

**—a meme I found on the internet whilst
searching for "funny angry memes"**

"Roy, I mean, you used to run like you were angry at the grass.
You'd kick the ball like you'd caught it fu$king your wife,
for Christ's sake. But that anger doesn't come out anymore
when you play. But it's still in there. And I'm afraid of what
it's gonna do to you if you just keep it all for yourself."

—Ted Lasso, *Ted Lasso* (S1, E7)

There are a lot of things that make me angry. Toward the top of the
list: burpees. Recently, I was in a kickboxing class doing burpees for
what felt like decades, and I started down a rabbit hole in my brain.
Who was the first person to do a burpee? Did some dude jump up to
the sky during his exercise routine and then decide, "You know what,
this isn't good enough. I need to go as high as I can AND THEN throw
myself on the ground. Reach up for the sky, and down to the floor.
Heck, let's kick out the legs for some extra fun!" And why the name?

I couldn't help myself this morning. I *had* to research the origin of burpees. I was drawn to a *Men's Journal* article about the "badass history" of burpees. Invented by some douchebag named Billy Bob Burpee. His real name was actually Royal, ya know, for ROYAL pain in my ass. In the 1930s, he dedicated himself to "figuring out a simple, fundamental concept: How to determine a person's physical fitness."[1] Yes, Mr. Royal pain-in-my-ass Burpee decided he needed to invent an exercise that could test the physical capability of humans.

Burpees make me so angry.

Call it a pet peeve, call it anger-inducing things about life that drive you batty, call it whatever you want . . . but usually, it's something that makes us want to take a cheese grater to our forehead. While I'm not going to ask you to do burpees, I am going to challenge you with more of a *mental* exercise.

WHAT LEAVES YOU LIVID?

Think about something that makes you livid, boiling with anger, and downright P.O.'d. Now, once you feel that anger rise up in you, sit with it. Don't judge it. Don't try to make it go away. Sit with it. Just like we did with fear, invite it to the table. Zoom out, as if you're flying up over yourself, and begin to notice what you're feeling.

What is the feeling and thought after you let yourself embrace anger? Are you judging yourself? Did you just punch a hole in your closet door? Are you unaffected by the anger? Notice what's coming up for you. You don't have to do anything. Just be aware.

I want you to also consider how long the anger has been there. When you feel rage bubbling up within you in response to a certain triggering situation, see if you can find a situation that may have produced similar anger or rage from your childhood. For example, you know the people who pop off in anger relatively easily when someone cuts them off in traffic? Maybe it's you, or maybe it's your best friend or romantic partner. We all know someone who will go from zero to a hundred in a matter of nanoseconds when someone upsets them in traffic. Why is that? Is it because they were cut off in traffic when they were a child? Doubtful. Most of the time, it's because the act of getting cut off in traffic brings up rage and anger related to something completely *unrelated* to traffic—usually something from the past.

If you have road rage and instantly feel your blood boil when someone cuts you off, you may feel deep down that other people don't care about you. Maybe the action of getting cut off reminds you of how you weren't seen as a child, like you didn't matter. Or maybe your mom always cut people off in traffic, and you hated your mom. There are many reasons why people have road rage, and it can usually be traced back to a mountain of unresolved rage and anger from the past.

"STOP JUDGING ME!"—ANGER

Most of us tend to view anger in a negative light, due to our experiences with what anger can lead to. The effects of anger can hurt people, sure. But anger in and of itself isn't hurtful, and it doesn't need to be. Anger can actually be there to *help* us if (and only if) we can channel it properly without bringing harm to ourselves or others.

There's a reason we get angry about what happens in and around us. Just like addiction wants to be the canary in the coal mine, so too does anger want to be on our teaching staff. The more we can become aware of our anger, its origin, and where it takes us, the more we can learn from it. Think about what you tend to get angry about. If you look hard enough, it's usually about something you're not okay with. Anger can be a necessary fuel, just as important as oxygen. Anger is the warning signal that lets us know something isn't quite right.

How can we begin to identify the feelings of anger and *not* judge it? Understanding how best to channel anger is crucial. There's magic in learning to allow anger to teach us valuable lessons that no other emotion can.

This change in my mindset didn't happen overnight. It was a long process of separating the *emotion* of anger from the collateral damage anger tends to lead to.

GRANNY: THE *LEAST* ANGRY PERSON I KNEW

Her name was Patricia, and she was REGAL in every sense of the word. Growing up, my granny was my best friend, confidante, cheerleader, and the type of woman I dreamed of becoming. She had class in a way I'd never seen and haven't seen since. My favorite picture of her is from eons ago where she is mowing the lawn in heels. You read that right. Mowing the lawn. In high heels. A few years before she died, she gave me her favorite strand of pearls. I wear them to this day and feel her presence each time I have her necklace on.

Granny was also one of the meekest and mildest humans who seemed to glide through life effortlessly with unbelievable poise. She always seemed to have it all together, yet she never took life too seriously. Granny and I would sit on the bed and eat coffee ice cream while watching cartoons. She let me eat mac and cheese for breakfast, AND she let me swim in my jeans.

Later on in life, Granny battled dementia and Alzheimer's. Every year, I lost a little more of her. My visits with her used to be filled with thought-provoking conversations where she would call me her iridescent light and look at me with those big, beautiful eyes. As the visits continued and the years went by, my love for Granny grew as her awareness of the world around her diminished. It was painful to watch. If you've ever loved someone with dementia, you know exactly what I'm talking about.

In the last year of her life, I went to visit Granny at a little home she was staying in. I had the remarkable privilege of spending time with her by myself, just me and her. That day when I went to visit her, I couldn't get close enough to her. She had the type of energy you'd want to be enveloped in. I sat next to her while she sat quietly, almost lifeless in her vintage chair. This was the first interaction I would have with Granny where she was completely out of it. She wouldn't make eye contact. We struggled to connect. It was excruciatingly painful, especially since our conversations up to that point had been so fruitful and profound.

After several valiant attempts at forcing a connection, I finally gave up and let go. I stopped trying to talk to her and stopped trying to get her to talk to me or even see me. In my surrender, I decided to simply lay my head against her chest right next to her heart surgery scar. She was such a strong, resilient woman even in that weak moment of near unconsciousness. As I lay on her chest, I was heartbroken and angry. I couldn't have hated the disease of Alzheimer's more than I did at that moment.

In a split second, love broke through with the fierceness of the sun having the audacity to shine bright on the cloudiest of days. As I lay there silently grieving with my head on her heart, I heard the most beautiful, life-giving words come from Granny's mouth, heart, spirit, and soul. These were not weak words said in a soft tone. She spoke with such strength and grit that it left me stunned. With all clarity and confidence, she said, "**I love you!**"

Those were the last words I would hear Granny say. She passed away shortly after my visit, and her memory lives vibrantly in my heart and life.

GRANNY GETS PISSED

Despite all the sweetness and serenity of my grandmother, she had a temper. I remember a specific instance from when I was probably eight or nine years old. We were at my brother's soccer game, and I had ridden with my grandparents. I can't remember all the details, but my granny was madder than mad when we got out of the car. She was fuming and pacing around the field as if she was looking for a lifelong sworn enemy. We were probably late or couldn't find the soccer field, but either way, my meek and mild granny was mad AF. I'll never forget the moment she raised her voice and said, "WHAT THE HELL?" I was stunned. She wasn't saying this *to* anyone or *at* anyone. She was simply upset at the world in general, it seemed.

Looking back, I have so much more appreciation for that moment. My granny never let me see her angry side, though I now know she had a temper. But in that moment at the soccer fields, she let it out. She didn't hurt anyone. (She wouldn't even hurt a fruit fly.) But she let it out and refused to keep it in. I still don't know what was bothering Granny that day. But I'm thankful I had the opportunity to witness her tiny, seemingly inconsequential outburst.

I remember thinking as a child: *if my granny gets angry, then maybe that means it's okay for me to get angry, too.* Not sure where I learned this exactly, but growing up, I was programmed to fear anger. I was terrified of the anger emotion, and I would get extremely uncomfortable when I saw anger, felt it, encountered it, experienced it, gave into it, was on the receiving end of it, etc. But that day at the soccer game, Granny's anger didn't make me uncomfortable at all.

Though it took me decades to realize this, Granny's outburst encouraged me and made me realize that the emotion of anger isn't bad. Emotions aren't bad or good—they just are. Some emotions can lead to bad actions, as we know, but anger in and of itself is not the enemy. Granny handled her anger like a champ.

Am I encouraging you to go and yell "WHAT THE HELL" in front of your kids? No. But I am encouraging you to shift your perception of anger. We need a major paradigm makeover in the area of anger.

That day, my granny's anger was a gift, though I didn't understand the power of the gift until recently. But let me tell you this, I've experienced quite a bit of anger and rage from others, and there was no gift to be found whatsoever. Even in the most painful moments when I was personally impacted and damaged by another's anger and rage, looking back I am now able to see some hidden treasures.

JESUS GETS SUPER PISSED

Before I completely throw myself under the bus in the next few chapters, I have to give some airtime to Jesus. Yes, the Jesus who seemed to float around based on the stories I heard in church growing up. The kind, gentle Jesus who befriended lambs and had a daisy tucked behind His right ear. The Jesus who asks us to "turn the other cheek" and "love God, love people above all else." The mild-mannered, empathetic Jesus who wept with His friends when their friend died, who was born in a feeble feeding trough fit for a cow, not a king. The Jesus who rode in on a donkey just to make a point about humility. Let me tell you about this Jesus and the time He got royally pissed. Because if feeling anger is good enough for Jesus, it's good enough for me.

Jesus was hanging with His boys and went to Jerusalem one day. When He entered the city, everyone started freaking out, wondering who this man was. I guess whoever was MCing at the temple that day explained to everyone, "This is Jesus, the prophet from Nazareth in Galilee."

According to the NLT Bible (*New Lindsey Translation*), Jesus ignores the MC's intro and heads straight to the entrance of the temple courts. These temple courts were like if a present-day church was in a strip mall packed with people trying to make a buck off selling stuff. This pissed Jesus off real, real bad.

Listen to this drama—in His anger and utter disgust, Jesus starts throwing shit everywhere. I'm not kidding! He aggressively knocks over ALL the tables of the money changers and the chairs of the people who were selling doves and pigeons. He cleaned house and kicked out all the people in the temple who were selling and buying things. I like to imagine Jesus as if He was a bouncer at a nightclub and last call already came and went. While He's driving all these folks out of the temple courts, He is recorded by witnesses in real history as yelling this:

"It is written: 'My house will be called a house of prayer.' But you are making it 'a den of robbers.'" (Matthew 21:13)[2]

Then (once Jesus had drained the swamp) something magical happened. Blind and lame folks came to see Jesus at the temple, and He *healed* them. This really ticked off the religious leaders of the day, who were livid as they witnessed these miracles.

Sometimes the breakthrough of healing happens after you've allowed the emotion of anger to move through you in a way that doesn't hurt you or others. Throw a plate on the ground, go to a rage room and bash an old washer with a crowbar, beat a pillow with a plastic bat, or attend a kickboxing class. Do whatever you have to do to stop all the anger and rage stuffing. You can try and push it down for as long as you're able, but that anger will come out somehow, someway—and it's usually sideways.

This temple throwdown needed to happen. Jesus got mad because something wasn't right. And He felt like throwing tables over was the right reaction to that feeling of ire which whispers softly to us, "Something is wrong here."

THAT ONE TIME AT SUMMER CAMP (YIKES)

One summer, after my freshman year of college, I went to Missouri to be a camp counselor. What happened at the summer camp was a clear moment where I realized, "Something is wrong here." I'd heard about an extraordinary inner-city camp where kids from all over would come have the time of their lives, and I knew I had to be a part of that magic. I applied and got the "job." I was eighteen, about to turn nineteen, and mostly unaware of the world around me. Though I'd been through a lot and seen a lot, it seems I was really clueless at that age.

Because I loved basketball and coaching basketball more than almost anything, I had the privilege of being the basketball coach at camp. Most of my campers had attended the school of hard knocks throughout their lives. These girls were badasses. The older girls intimidated me, but not in a fearful way. I was in awe of how strong these campers were despite the horrific circumstances they came from. These were young women who had no interest in taking any shit from anyone, especially not a goody-two-shoes girl from Texas.

The first week, I was assigned to be the camp counselor for the sixteen- to seventeen-year-old girls. By the first day, I'd already had a large, linebacker-esque, eighteen-year-old camper come at me. As she tried to put her hands around my throat, the other campers pulled her off me. She was angry because I took the contraband I'd found in her pillowcase. I couldn't blame her, and I wasn't upset. I was really just thankful to still be breathing.

Summer camp was going smoothly until one hot day in June. Like I did every other day, I arrived early at the basketball gym and prepared the court for class. In about five minutes, I'd have the best and the brightest ballers at camp. They were so much better than me. These girls were players. Tenacious, aggressive, and strategic.

Despite my best efforts to teach technique and basketball basics, each practice and game turned into streetball. No rules. No refs. Rampant fouls. Imagine *Fight Club* but with balls. Some days, it would get so rough I'd have to step in. As if I was actually going to do anything . . . my chances of running a marathon were better than my chances of playing referee to these high school inner-city ballers.

On that excruciatingly hot day in June, about halfway into basketball "class," one of my campers triggered me in a way I'd not been triggered before. Shalene had a temper, and I'd been warned about her by the camp director. She came from the projects in Chicago. She was sixteen but looked twenty-six and had both emotional and physical scars. We connected almost instantly when we met. Most counselors handled her with kid-gloves in hopes of avoiding any potential incident that might set her off. But I didn't get that vibe from her. I felt very comfortable with her and felt like in another life we may have been long-lost sisters.

During our basketball period, Shalene aggressively elbowed a camper on the opposing team. I called her out and raised my voice to give her a warning that if she did it again, she'd have to sit out. What happened next still feels like an out-of-body experience. She looked at me with the sassiest (and also the saddest) eyes and mouthed off to me. I don't even remember what she said exactly. But she spoke to me in such a way that it triggered something deep inside me. Her words, her approach, and the way she directed her rage toward me dug up a seed that had been subconsciously planted deep down in my soul.

Without a single thought, and in a split second, I grabbed a nearby basketball off the ground, picked it up, and violently threw it right at her. The ball crashed into her stomach and left Shalene doubled over.

The whole incident lasted maybe five seconds, but it had a lasting impact on every person who was there that day.

I lost my shit.

This was not premeditated. I was not expecting to ever do something even remotely close to that. It just happened, and I "came to" after it was too late. In that tiny moment, my own rage shot out of me like a rocket. I didn't even realize what had occurred until I saw Shalene's face. Betrayal, fear, and disappointment were written all over it. I'd fractured any sense of trust I'd built with this young lady. It's a miracle she didn't react and come straight for me.

To this day I have no clue how she showed such restraint. Did she feel sorry for me? Was she stunned and paralyzed? Did someone hold her back? I don't know. There are definitely some gaps in that day, memories I can't access. But I do know that I took my anger out on my favorite camper that day.

I, the Christian camp counselor who was supposed to be a woke, empathetic, and trustworthy leader, had launched a basketball at a sixteen-year-old camper, hitting her in the stomach and knocking the very breath out of her lungs.

> Anger is a sadness that had
> nowhere to go for a very long time.
> **—UNKNOWN**

Anger is a powerful emotion. It can be both beauty and beast. My Bible teacher used to remind me about how Jesus said, "Be angry, but do not sin."[3] I'm certain I was angry and also sinned that day. I lost control. But did I really have it in the first place?

I think *control* in this sense is an illusion. Kurtz and Ketcham write, "Seeking to control what cannot be controlled destroys precisely what we are trying to control."[4] I hadn't learned to control my anger or tame the beast. I hadn't attended anger management courses nor had any reason to. I didn't know I was prone to rage, and I was just as surprised by what happened that day as Shalene was. We were both shocked but for different reasons. Soon after I noticed Shalene doubled over trying to catch her breath, it hit me like a hurricane. What on earth had I just done? I became flooded with guilt and shame. I got completely caught up in the shame spiral tornado and had a minor panic attack.

Thankfully (though, I certainly wasn't thankful at the time) the executive director of the camp was nearby and saw the whole thing go down. She was a powerful woman named Portia. What she lacked in height she made up for in wisdom and respect. She ran over to check on Shalene and then walked over to me. Then she approached me and quietly said, "Please come with me."

With my head hanging low in shame, I followed Portia to her office. The short walk from the basketball court to her office felt like a half marathon to my downtrodden soul. I kept playing the scene over and over again in my head, and I couldn't fathom or process what had just happened. Not only did I lose control, but I also lost the respect of all my campers. I betrayed them. I became what I feared most.

The truth was, I never had control in the first place. In hindsight, I realized I'd simply stuffed the anger inside me and refused to let it come out in a healthy manner. Instead of being aware of my anger and rage, I shoved it deep, deep down and swept even the smallest appearance of anger under the heaviest, most durable rugs. Because I hadn't dealt with my anger in healthy ways, it came out sideways. Turns out I had zero tools to help me understand the power of anger and its importance. I had no grid for my own rage and the seed that had been growing, unbeknownst to me. So, I snapped. And I didn't realize it until after it happened.

With all the gentleness she could muster, Portia asked me to sit down. She shut the door and looked at me lovingly, which completely threw me for a loop. She could've yelled at me, fired me, sued me, pressed charges, or chosen to respond in a variety of ways that would've handed down a punishment of epic proportions that I deserved. But that's not what she did. At all.

Portia chose curiosity over condemnation, love over lashing out, and seeking to understand over subjecting me to unrelenting chastisement. She chose to respond with grace. As I sat on that couch (terrified of what all this meant), I experienced mercy, not malice. Freedom, not fear. Hope, not hostility. Somehow, the camp director was able to see me with God-eyes. She didn't look down on me, the out-of-control almost-nineteen-year-old camp counselor who had just chucked a ball at a camper. She didn't see what I saw.

Portia saw a young woman buried in pain, self-doubt, and trauma. She saw a hurting heart that had long been denied the much-needed gifts of self-love and acceptance. She saw past the big, cheesy smile I always felt pressured to keep on my face no matter what. She saw through me, to my soul. Her approach allowed me to experience the love of my Higher Power in a new way. Portia had the wisdom to know that I was beating myself up enough and what I needed was grace, love, mercy, and help. I needed to be seen and heard. My rage-induced outburst was a cry for help. Portia heard my cry.

To be clear, I was sufficiently disciplined, and the camp handled the entire incident beautifully. I begged Shalene for forgiveness, and she graciously extended it to me. We both grew as a result of the situation, though I wish it hadn't happened in the first place. Well, that's not actually true. I'm glad it happened because seeing my rage spew out that day was a gift. Had that not happened, I'm not sure I would've realized how much anger I had buried deep within me. I guess what I'm saying is, I wish I hadn't chucked the ball at her. Maybe at the ground, a wall, or a bush—but not at Shalene.

Either way, it happened. And I'm better for it. But how?

SEEING MYSELF WITH NEW EYES

That day in Portia's office, I saw myself with new eyes. I answered the loud wake-up call and started to accept what this meant. Awareness (as you'll hear me say over and over again) is the key to the magic of growth. I became aware of my rage and unresolved anger that day. Little did I know at the time, but that moment was a major breakthrough for me. I started a journey of getting curious about why something like this could happen. I learned so much about myself as I embarked on the journey of self-discovery into my rage and anger.

Turns out, I had let my fear of anger paralyze me. Growing up, I saw anger as my enemy, and I would go to great lengths to ensure I never allowed myself to get angry. Well, that's not how anger works. I wasn't controlling my anger or trying to curb its impact on me and the world around me. No . . . I was stuffing my anger so far down that I didn't even know it was there. For years, I unconsciously chose to bury the triggers and whitewash the tomb of my heart's rage in hopes that it would go away.

That's not really how emotions work, I've come to find out.

It's been said that emotion is energy in motion. When emotions get trapped, bad things happen. Not to oversimplify it, but it really is that straightforward. Think of what happens when you shake up a champagne bottle and then pop the top off. The champagne doesn't just seep out gently and slowly. No! The champagne starts exploding and pouring out. It has to go somewhere, and it can't go back into the bottle.

How many of you have rage trapped deep inside? Are you aware of it? What does that rage look like when it comes out? Are you letting it out in healthy ways, or does your rage cause damage and pain to yourself and others?

It's time we notice the anger (especially if it's hysterical anger), increase our awareness about why it's there, and ask it what it may be there to teach us.

NEVER WASTE A TRIGGER

What makes you absolutely livid? Think about that question for a few minutes. Usually, you'll find some wisdom at the bottom of that question's answer. One of the best pieces of advice I ever received was, "Never, ever waste a trigger." We need to stop demonizing our anger and internalizing our rage. We have to find healthy ways to become aware of our anger, acknowledge it, ask ourselves why this reaction is coming up for us, and get curious.

If we don't find productive ways to address (and allow ourselves to move through) the anger, it will always come out sideways.

We must give all our big, intense feelings and emotions time. As we commit to being responsible for our emotions, understand it will take time. Building a habit of asking yourself how you can honor your feelings and emotions while working through them takes as much (if not more) time than it took you to learn the habit of denying your feelings in the first place.

The next time the feelings hit, prioritize the pause and remember that you can't wish these feelings away or change them on the spot. If we attempt to do away with the feelings we perceive to be "bad," then all the emotions on the spectrum will be done away with. Emotions and feelings are there to guide us into something that we need to learn. When you notice something is coming up for you as a result of a situation or interaction with someone, understand that it is most likely an old wound rising up, crying out, begging to be addressed and healed. You and I can *and must* do that healing work on our own. This is where the true growth opportunity lies.

But don't take my word for it, take this nugget of wisdom from Ted Lasso as it relates to people who push our buttons:

I gotta say, man, sometimes you remind me of my grandma with the channel hopper. You just push all the wrong buttons.
—TED LASSO[5]

Break It Down for Me

- Give your undivided attention to every single thing that makes your blood boil. Inquire within and avoid judgment.

- Anger is a necessary warning signal that tips us off to the reality that something isn't right.

- Never ever (ever ever!) waste a trigger. Stare it in the face and face it head-on. Otherwise, it'll come out sideways. Like hurling balls at kids.

- Anger is a natural emotion (neither good nor bad) that everyone experiences from time to time. If Granny and Jesus can lose their shit, then so can we. Let's try to do so in a productive manner, though.

NEVER
EVER
WASTE
A
TRIGGER

Chapter 4

THE GIFT OF HUMILIATION

"You are blind to reality, and for that, I am most proud."
—**Moira Rose,** *Schitt's Creek* (S2, E2)

Moira Rose: "Who put a picture of a ghost on my desk?"
Roland: "That's the sonogram of our baby!"
—*Schitt's Creek* (S5, E10)

I was just out of college and was about to perform in front of a large room of 300 or so people, mostly made up of my friends and peers. I was standing with a large set of double doors right behind me. I had my guitar on and ready to go because I was about to be introduced. Just before the introduction, I saw a dear friend I hadn't seen in a long time. I just HAD to express my sheer excitement at seeing her, so I proceeded to throw my arms up and jump back so as to say, "HI, OH MY GOSH, I'VE MISSED YOU! Look at HOW MUCH I've missed you!"

Before I knew it, I had accidentally fallen back into the set of double doors. Crashed into them would be a more accurate description. The gigantic doors swung open, and the intense momentum sent me flailing back into the other room, where a large couch broke my fall. I flipped over the couch, my legs went up in the air, and I came crashing down on the other side. As my legs returned to the ground (thanks to gravity), they landed on my guitar and cracked it, snapping the neck almost entirely off. I can still hear the cacophony as I type this. Crashing sounds, a very upset guitar, and I messed up my shoulder pretty badly too.

Everyone was cracking up. I was mortified but would never show it. I composed myself, stood up, and raised both of my hands to demonstrate my victory over the moment. People cheered and continued laughing. I was just trying not to cry.

The show must go on, so I borrowed someone's guitar (who happened to bring theirs that day) and did a full set—playing through the excruciating shoulder pain and emotional wounds.

I'm extremely clumsy, so I have a dozen stories very similar to this one.

Speaking of embarrassing moments while singing in front of people, let me tell you about Wynonna Judd. I'm OBSESSED with Wynonna and have been since I was a little girl. In fact, hers was the first concert I ever went to. I was seven.

Brynn and I went to hear her in concert a couple of years ago. Going to her concert as an adult was incredible. She performed at a small venue in San Antonio, and we had great seats. The moment she started singing, my heart fell out of my butthole, my stomach had butterflies, and I was filled with excitement. After about the third song (and my third glass of wine), I couldn't help but make my way up to the very front row directly in front of the stage.

Everyone was sitting, so I knelt down. Yes, I was kneeling at the altar of Wynonna. I was looking cute, too. I looked up at her as if she were Jesus Himself coming down from the clouds. Her hair was bigger than ever, and her voice was crystal clear. I was doing a fairly decent job of remaining calm, but then the band started in on "No One Else on Earth." As she hit her first note, I stood up from my kneeling position, stood in front of her (directly in front of her), and raised both hands up in the air as if someone in the venue had just scored a touchdown. I was blocking people's views, but as they witnessed the vigor and unbridled passion that fueled my fandom, they let me be.

During the instrumental break, she looked down at me and said, "You don't know this song" in a harmless teasing manner. She then said to the larger group, "Y'all don't know this song!" as if to tempt us. Well, I couldn't take it anymore. I yelled the longest run-on sentence ever yelled in my very best chest voice, "I know the song I know the song I know all your songs I love you you are the most talented woman ever I am so happy to be here!"

Wynonna—moved by my passion—bent down and handed me her mic. You read that right. She. Handed. Me. Her. Mic. Without skipping a beat, I grabbed the mic and turned around to face the adoring crowd. They were rooting for me, almost as if to say *This is your one shot! Don't screw it up!* I wasn't going to screw up. I was MADE for this moment.

But then, I screwed it all up. Turns out, I was so incredibly nervous that I ended up humiliating myself in front of God, Mary, Joseph, all the other disciples and angels, Wynonna, her band, MY WIFE, and all the concertgoers. Y'all, **I sang the wrong words**. I messed up the lyrics. LYRICS that I have been singing since I first heard Wynonna's tape back in the '80s. Did everyone notice? I honestly didn't care. Yes, I felt humiliated, but my vocals were on point (though Brynn later told me rudely that I was "a bit pitchy"). I handed the mic back to Wynonna and resumed my kneeling position. The show was magic.

Once Brynn and I returned home later that evening, I got a text from my friend who is close family friends with Wynonna and who hooked us up with the tickets in the first place. Here's what the text said:

Lindsey, hope you and Brynn had fun tonight. Wanted to let you know that Wynonna and I are on her tour bus and she's listening to your latest album right now. She loves it and thought you were fabulous out there!

So, *what* was the gift that I mined out of this particular story of complete and utter humiliation? Wynonna. That's what. That's who. Wynonna is the gift.[1]

THE HUMILIATION OF BEING ODDLY DIFFERENT

If you're a straight female and you're reading this, you most likely experienced butterflies in your stomach when you crossed paths with a boy you liked during your formative younger years. That wasn't my experience. My butterflies accumulated only upon encountering a girl I liked. Growing up, I didn't have the language to speak about what I was feeling. I'd never even heard words like gay, bisexual, lesbian, or transgender. In middle school, I knew that my friends made fun of our coaches, but I never really understood why. I always loved my coaches, and they always loved me.

I channeled my aggression on the court, and it made me a force to be reckoned with. I'd join in on the gossiping and judging that my friends hurled at one coach in particular. At the time, I didn't know what exactly we were making fun of her for, but I wanted to join in so I wouldn't seem too different from my girlfriends. Finally, I got up the guts to ask my best friend Veronica to remind me, "Why are we making fun of Coach again?"

That's when I realized for the first time that I never wanted to be the subject of anyone's ignorance, ridicule, and homophobia. Veronica explained that we almost had to make fun of her because she's "one of those women." After inquiring further, it became clear that Coach was a homosexual.

At seventeen, I spoke a sentence to myself that would change my life forever. Let's go back to that time and unpack the story of me coming out to myself.

MY FIRST *REAL* GIRL CRUSH

In high school, when most of my female friends were going to parties, drinking wine coolers, and doing who-knows-what with boys, I was your typical goody-goody church youth group leader and teacher's pet. When they started having sex, I was leading a Bible study on purity and challenging my peers to sign *"true love waits"* purity commitment cards that could only be found in the back of their teen study Bible.

Right around the time I started to realize I REALLY wasn't similar to my friends who were girls, I met someone who would make me feel as though all the butterflies in the world had come together to attend a butterfly convention inside my body. I had just turned seventeen, and she was about to turn eighteen. One grade separated us, but virtually nothing else would.

As I'm sure you've already noticed, I have changed some of the names and details of people in my life whom I write about in this book in order to protect their identity and respect their privacy. We'll call this new friend Bonnie.

The second I met Bonnie, something clicked. I couldn't explain it, identify it, or even remotely put my finger on it, but whatever it was, it was extremely real and intense. Bonnie and I quickly became inseparable best friends. I *felt* the way about her that my straight girlfriends would *speak* about the boys they were crushing on. At the time, I had no reason to think it was anything other than a soul connection between two high school girls who loved Jesus. But looking back, it was clearly a codependent nightmare. Bonnie, as I'd come to find out (quite painfully) later, was and is straighter than an arrow. She may have been a gorgeous, flirtatious arrow, but she was a straight, 100 percent hetero arrow, nonetheless. The friendship quickly turned into a friendlationship.

Each time I would find myself being attracted to her, thinking about her, or wanting to be near her, I would find a way to justify and condone whatever I was feeling. By that time, I believed being gay was a sin. I was subconsciously filled with so much self-hatred and internalized homophobia that I wanted nothing to do with gay people. I could see it in others and condemn it in others, while completely ignoring the little gay girl trapped inside me, cowering deep within the back walls of the closet.

But one night would change everything.

Without going into too many details out of respect for (and fear of) those who may be reading this, I will share some of the highlights, or in this case—lowlights.

Coming Out to Myself First

Bonnie and I were having a sleepover, which had become a recurring thing. We'd been best "friends" for months, and our connection deepened rapidly. We went from casually holding hands in the car to cuddling in a way that wasn't typical for two girls who were just best friends. The closer we got, and the more physical our interactions got, the more I purposefully didn't think anything of it because, to me, I was OKAY as long as there wasn't *obvious* gay stuff going on—like kissing or whatever lesbians do.

In my delusion and denial, I believed we could be in love and physical without crossing that line into gayland. I had subconsciously drawn a line in the sand, a boundary for what was okay and what was not. For me, with Bonnie, the line was kissing on the lips. I realize now how ridiculous this was.

I could fully enjoy my interactions with Bonnie now that I'd drawn my invisible, dumb line in the sand. Turns out, I was lying to myself. There was no line. That line sailed off long before this humiliating night that would alter the course of my journey into gayness.

As Bonnie and I cuddled in the same bed, things got pretty hot and heavy. We didn't kiss, but we were getting a bit handsy. Right before I thought that surely I couldn't fight the temptation anymore and I absolutely had to kiss her, her mom walked into the room and knew something was up. We froze awkwardly, trying to act like we were just working on a group science project or something like that—you know, like you do late at night, in the same bed, in high school . . . with the lights off. I was stunned because Bonnie's mom was terrifying in that moment. I thought, she's either going to kill me or I'm going to jump out this second-story window and begin my new life as a paraplegic with no friends and whose ex-best-friend's mom now spends her time working at the church secretly plotting my ultimate demise and death.

Somehow, I left the next morning unscathed, except very much scathed emotionally. I was mortified. No one ever spoke of that night, and I was forbidden to continue my friendship *or whatever it was* with Bonnie. Her mom would have none of it. Probably for the best, honestly. I was way too immature to be in any type of relationship.

Something had broken inside me, as I'd realize many years later. Despite how horrifying that experience was for me, it was instrumental in my life and in the painful journey that would become my reality for years and years. It was that night that I finally came out to myself. I admitted to myself that I was gay. In fact, my exact words were, "Shit. I think I'm a lesbian."

I'm incredibly thankful her mom walked in when she did because it stopped us from doing something we couldn't come back from: actually kissing. Though I'm sure Bonnie and her mom hated my guts from that moment on, that's when I started to realize how much I needed to start loving myself. I had so much guilt and shame from that night. I was embarrassed and wanted to crawl into a hole and never come out again. It was a painful start to my painful journey, but an essential start.

Coming out to myself at age seventeen was **as liberating as it was terrifying**.

It finally clicked. Oh, *this* is what other people feel like who are heterosexual and have experiences with members of the opposite sex. Sadly, this awareness that I was gay led me down a very dark path of self-hatred, diving deeper into anti-gay beliefs, internalized (and external) homophobia, and years of ex-gay therapy. I went from using prayer as a medium through which I could have conversations with my Higher Power, to using prayer as a weapon toward myself in hopes of praying the gay away.

I JUST HAD TO SIT THERE AND LISTEN

Fast-forward to the year 2008. After years and years in the closet, drowning in thoughts of self-loathing and shame, I experienced another severe humiliation. I'd come out to myself, but no one else knew about my struggles except my therapist and then-partner, whom I was secretly having a relationship with.

One of the leading evangelical Christian speakers at the time asked me to tour with her for a few events. I can't say much or share too many details for legal reasons, but let's just say she was big-time in the Christian circles. We'd teamed up to do a women's conference in a state that just so happened to have an anti-gay marriage ballot on the table. (This is back when gay marriage was illegal.) I sang a few songs before she got up to give her talk, which was usually encouraging and focused on inspiring her listeners. She was gifted and able to connect well with her audience.

Her forty-five-minute talk was filled with anti-gay, homophobic rants and raves. She was visibly angry when preaching about the abomination of homosexuality and that marriage is between a man and a woman—always, period, end of sentence.

The words she spoke pierced my heart. This was right when I was making the slow, painful transition from thinking I was going to hell because I was gay to struggling with reconciling my faith and my sexuality, knowing that I had been created by God exactly how He/She/They intended. I was making meaningful progress in searching for what God thought about my sexual orientation. I had stopped listening to what everyone else was telling me about what God thought, and I started searching for myself.

Originally, I'd set out to prove to myself, beyond any shadow of a doubt, that being gay was 110 percent not okay and 110 percent the worst sin ever. But what actually ended up happening is that I stumbled and fell into the arms of a loving Higher Power who held me through it all.

That's what made listening to the speaker that day extra excruciating. I wasn't hating or punishing myself as much as I had been. I was starting to learn to love myself, gay and all. Yet, there she was up on stage, preaching about how people like me had a one-way ticket to hell.

Even as I write about this moment all these years later, I can still feel it in my body. When I first started working on this particular experience in therapy, and I recalled this memory, I could feel it physically—and I felt completely paralyzed. I was inundated with fear as I worked through the PSTD caused by moments like the one that night.

The worst part is that I had to go up and sing one last song after her homophobic rant fest. I had to psych myself up for it because I felt nauseous. Keep in mind, at this point I was still in the closet and doing everything within my power to protect my secret. I wasn't ready to come out yet and lose everything. So, I swallowed a big gulp of saliva, prayed for help to get through it, and walked up on stage.

I could barely get through the song. Somehow I did, and then it was over. At that point, I promised I would NEVER betray myself like that again. I would never allow my voice to follow a voice like hers. It seemed so ironic; the reason I'd gone into full-time ministry was that I wanted to spread hope and love. And yet here I was, sharing the stage with someone whose mouth was spewing hate and judgment.

HERE'S YOUR SIGN

I sometimes like to daydream and imagine what it would've looked like that day at the women's conference and what it would've felt like to walk up on stage, take the mic, but not play my guitar and not sing anything. What if I had just spoken from the heart about what I was really feeling? What would I have even said to these women? I desperately wanted to scream into the mic: "What you just heard isn't the Truth!" They would've run me out of that venue faster than you can say BIGOT.

I remember feeling so torn that night. A member of the local church had the audacity to come up to my hotel room to see if I needed anything. She had a yard sign in her hands and asked if I wanted to "take it back to Texas." Upon seeing the yard sign with a blue man and a pink woman on it with the words "1 man 1 woman. Vote NO on Prop *whatever*," I tried to hide my disgust and politely declined. I've blocked the sign out of my memory, but I'll never be able to block out what it felt like to be on the receiving end of a political sign that intended to rob folks just like me of the right to marry whomever they love and want to spend the rest of their life with.

Here's the thing with humiliation: sometimes it's there to help us learn something deeper about ourselves that we might not yet have awareness about but desperately *need* awareness about. I felt humiliated during the entire weekend at that women's conference because I was in the thick of my identity crisis. Deep down, I was blinded by a fear I had of feeling conflict *within myself* as I questioned my identity. If I wasn't a full-time touring artist, speaker, and singer, who was I?

You see, I've now hit upon a recurring theme that has been the background music of my life up to this point: questioning my identity. Not understanding it, and all but full-on fighting against it. I was either too girly or not girly enough. Too athletic or not athletic enough. Too nice or too bossy. Too much or not enough. And that constant dissonance reverberated like an echo chamber deafening me to the sound of truth. Who was I really, and who did I want to be? More importantly, who did I *not* want to be?

Done with Denial

I sure as hell didn't want to be that person who forces herself to walk up on stage after a homophobic sermon. I remember distinctly thinking after that event: *I don't want to lie anymore about who I am.* I don't want to continue to deny very real parts of who I am. I don't want to be a person constantly fighting with herself. A person caught in the crossfire of living for me and the life I believe God has called me to live versus living for others who want to write an entirely different story about me and my life. The reason I continued to put myself in these compromising, life-numbing situations was because I was too afraid to face the conflict I knew would arise if I questioned my true identity.

TRAVEL TOWARD THE TENSION

We are all made up of so many different parts. There's not one singular part that defines us. Imagine seeing a dog and calling it a kidney just because the dog has a kidney. Maybe that's an oversimplification, but you get where I'm going with this. You and I are human tapestries, woven together with unique colorful threads, pictures, designs, and aspects we aren't even aware of yet. We shouldn't have to hide parts of ourselves. Can you imagine staring at the *Mona Lisa* and seeing a small sticky note covering one of her eyeballs?

All those years in the closet did so much damage. Turns out, my brain was trying to protect me because it thought I needed to be protected from the internal tension and struggle that constantly plagued me. I have many parts to my identity (in no particular order): female, wife, mom, gay, daughter, sister, friend, Christ-follower (sometimes), wealth advisor, singer, artist, dog lover, performer, coach, educator, cheese enthusiast.

We all have a list. But within my list, there was undeniable dissonance. I never in a million years thought you could be gay and be a Christian. I thought I had to choose. If I loved God, how could I be gay? If I accepted my identity as a lesbian, how could I love God?

I once saw a huge water fountain that had a vibrant fire within the water. Yes, water and fire coexisting in a magical world where the water didn't put out the flame. It was bizarre but such a helpful word picture. My search for wholeness went to the next level when I stopped trying to protect myself from the tension I was feeling. Instead, I got curious about it and began slowly working through it, thread by thread.

My brain tries to steer me away from tension when that's actually where my heart and spirit want and need to go. Did I want to re-live that moment at the women's conference during PSTD therapy? No. But I knew it would benefit me. Through doing the work, and focusing on progress, not perfection, I was eventually able to gather up all the tiny, shattered pieces of glass that were scattered across the floor of my life.

When we experience a painful emotion like humiliation, a piece of us splinters off. It takes work to heal from those wounds in hopes of becoming whole and wholly integrated. Our spirits want the freedom to fully express themselves just as much as we need the freedom to fully show up and participate in our lives exactly as we are. **Exactly as we are.**

Try to love someone for exactly who they are, metaphorical (or literal) warts and all, and see what happens. A shift happens when we begin to love people regardless of where they happen to be in a given moment, versus loving them with the underlying intention of getting them to be who we want them to be for our own purposes.

Anytime I sense fear, humiliation, or any of the other topics we're diving into throughout this book, I ask the fear (in this specific example) what it is. What's the root? If you can't locate the root, the next best place to look is the fruit. See what the root is producing, and then work your way backward.

Sometimes I even talk to fear. What are you here to teach me or show me about myself? What do you look like?

TAKE BACK THE DAMN PEN

Embarrassment is a powerful emotion, and it comes with its own set of underlying hidden gifts and challenges. Deep down, we all fear humiliation. It's paralyzing; no one wants to be humiliated.

When I came out (or was outed, depending on your interpretation), I was absolutely mortified. I wasn't prepared. I was outed publicly before I was ready to take that step. But in that humiliation, I developed really thick skin. I realized most of it was smoke and mirrors. What others thought of me and still think of me to this day is none of my business. One more time for those in the back: what people think of you and me is none of our goddang business.

Each time I beat myself up after being embarrassed or humiliated in some way, big or small, I was inadvertently and unintentionally trying to extinguish my spirit. Each time I ignored the fear beneath the embarrassment, I was betraying myself. I was too steeped in my shame to allow my spirit to be fully free. It was as if I was bringing a firehose to a tornado in hopes of squelching it. Think of your spirit as that fire within the water fountain.

My encouragement and challenge to you is this: the next time you become aware that you are embarrassed or feeling the fear of embarrassment, take a moment to breathe, pause, and ask your spirit to be present with you and that fear. When I have done this in the past, I continually receive one central message—that I'm really afraid of my spirit being fully expressed. I've made myself smaller all these years because I was too scared to let my spirit fully express itself in and through me. In a world where people tell you you're too much or too hard to love or too *whatever*, get curious about that. You have a much better idea of who you really are than they do. Don't let anyone else write your story for you. Take back the damn pen and get to writing.

Don't forget to forgive yourself for the guilt and shame you may feel about not fully expressing your spirit, for trying to quelch it. You did the best you could, just like I did. And now that we know better, we can do better and be better.

Spend some time thinking about what has caused you to feel humiliated or embarrassed in the past. Don't rush the process. Dig in, and try to find one nugget of wisdom to see if that fear has something to teach you. If you're embarrassed when you don't always have the right answer, why is that? Who are you if you don't always have the right answer? How do you feel about that person? Or maybe it's with parenting, when your kids embarrass you in public like mine often do. What are you scared of? Being judged by the PTA moms? God forbid you brought a pre-packed grocery store brownie container to the luncheon!

THE SILENT EMBARRASSMENT OF TRAUMA

The root of the fear of embarrassment can unlock some pretty cool awareness if you let it. Maybe you've experienced severe trauma, and you feel embarrassed about that. Maybe deep down you've been believing the lie that you were the cause of that trauma, which makes it very personalized, as though it only happened *because* of you.

Let me tell you with all the force and fierceness I can muster: YOU didn't cause a damn thing in the trauma you may be calling to mind as you read this. When we personalize and internalize our trauma, our whole identity *becomes* the trauma. And the trauma *becomes* our identity.

But it doesn't have to stay that way. In fact, it *cannot* stay that way if we want to move from surviving to thriving in spite of and despite the experience.

Here's the deal, folks: we need to begin to understand that our humiliation isn't what we thought it was originally. It wasn't about us; it was about our *perception* of ourselves. Once we can understand that and see it from a different perspective (this part takes A LOT of time), then you and I will find that there's surprisingly no reason for us to feel humiliated anymore (though, we may still go to great lengths to ensure we aren't humiliated).

Remember: first the mind changes through reframing and then the behavior will start to change. You'll see . . .

Break It Down for Me

- Humiliation helps us learn something deeper about ourselves that we don't yet have awareness about.
- A piece of ourselves splinters off when we experience humiliation. Healing from being humiliated causes a major shift in our awareness and perception.
- Most humiliation is rooted in a fear of not being able to fully and confidently express ourselves.
- Humiliation isn't what we initially thought it was. It's not about us. It's about our perception of ourselves.

I
LIVE
FOR
AWKWARD
MOMENTS

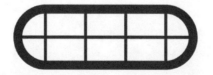

Chapter 5

THE GIFT OF TRAGEDY

"There are only two ways to live your life.
  One is as though nothing is a miracle.
  The other is as though everything is a miracle."
  —commonly attributed to Albert Einstein

If I've said it once, I've said it literally 100,000 times: I do not believe in a God that causes bad things to happen. But I DO believe in a loving God who is powerful enough to cause goodness to arise out of the most tragic of moments. The end doesn't justify the means. Meaning, the gift doesn't justify the tragedy. The treasure *informs* the tragedy, and the gift reflects the pain. If there weren't gifts hidden in every painful moment, then our memory of those moments would be pure darkness—void of any peace or joy.

In my own tragedies and in the stories people have shared with me, I've found that tragedy brings up painful memories but also purposeful ones. Someone can tell me about their family dog dying, and I can automatically see myself lying next to Gabby, our fifteen-year-old golden retriever, while the hospice vet gently put her to sleep. A type of sleep I had to explain to my five-year-old was the kind of sleep you don't wake up from. I could get stuck in that tragedy, but the gifts that came out of it give new purpose and meaning to what happened the day Gabby went to doggy heaven to see alllll those puppies that tragically died in the movies, traumatizing me when I was younger. Here's what happened.

A few months back, I was meeting with a client who was struggling with the same excruciating decision concerning her elderly dog. She knew he was in pain, and it was probably time to start planning for her fur baby's quality of death, just like the quality of life she'd been passionate about creating for her four-legged kid. We kept in touch since this was so near and dear to my heart. Finally, she reached out and told me she felt like it was time. I was able to give her the name of the wonderful organization specializing in at-home hospice care for dogs that provided a caring vet who came to our home so we could give Gabby the best-case scenario as it relates to her quality of death.

My client reached out to the organization and was able to create a painful, yet beautiful experience, saying goodbye to her pup in a manner that made everyone feel the best possible way about something that would forever leave an emotional scar on her and her family. Now, when I'm flooded with memories of Gabby (just yesterday I called out for her even though she's been gone for months now), I'm also reminded of how I was able to help my client with an impossible decision. I'm sure you all have a story like this if you think hard enough.

Have you been through something tragic in your life that enabled you to sit with someone else experiencing something similar? There is nothing quite like confiding in a friend who has been through a similar situation as the one you're in. You know the difference. If I go through something painful and talk to a friend about it who has never experienced anything like it, that feels one kind of way. But when I spend time with a dear friend who has been through a similar struggle or battle, there's a magical, unspoken understanding. You see them, and they see you.

It's similar to how I feel when I meet someone who is a parent of twins. (If you're reading this and you parented twins, you know what I'm talking about.) When I find out someone had twins, yes two newborns at the same time, I feel connected to them instantly. *Oh*, I think in my head, *YOU know how it feels to never sleep for a year, to listen to well-meaning people giving unsolicited advice—"Just get them on the same schedule!"—and YOU KNOW how it feels to change 134,102,340,103,401 diapers in one day. In. One. Day.*

I FEEL LIKE TRAGEDY IS THE WORST (ME TOO)

If you've been through a tragedy recently, or maybe you're even in the midst of one as you're reading these words, don't waste it. Tragedies are already the worst. It's going to suck and hurt and make you feel like the bleeding may never stop. And it may never stop. You will never feel the same post-tragedy. The wounds will turn to scars, but the pain won't ever go away. The pain just gets different.

But what if your experience of that pain can provide a safe space for someone else who may be going through a similar pain? When I'm able to speak light and hope into someone's life who may be reeling from tragedy (even if it's much different from my own tragic experiences), it redeems the tragedy for me in a tiny way. A tiny shred of light can bust through the heavy blanket of darkness and grief, even if only for a moment.

Tragedy brings with it the unique opportunity of meeting someone right where they are. Have you experienced this? Maybe you've shared your personal struggles with someone, a close friend, a family member, or maybe a therapist. And when they say "Me too" . . . it's that feeling. The feeling that maybe I'm not completely alone in the universe after all. This is one of the reasons the Me Too Movement was *and is* so incredibly powerful. Knowing that other women have been the victims of sexual violence in its many forms gives other women hope and comfort that it's not just them. There are more women out there who can understand a little bit—and maybe a lot bit—about what they've experienced.

Here's a bit of helpful background about the Me Too Movement, since this seemed to get lost through the viral #metoo hashtag in 2017.

It did *not* start in 2017, with Alyssa Milano's tweet, "If all the women who have been sexually harassed or assaulted wrote 'me too' as a status, we might give people a sense of the magnitude of the problem."[1]

While I do feel that we all owe Alyssa a debt of gratitude for fanning the fire for this movement, it wasn't Alyssa who built it and spent years and years sparking the flame and tending to the embers.

The Me Too Movement was founded in 2006, by survivor and activist Tarana Burke, a strong Black woman who exudes excellence and power. She writes: "When your life is forever changed by sexual violence, where can you turn? . . . In those early years, we developed our vision to bring resources, support, and pathways to healing where none existed before."[2]

WHAT ARE THE WORDS YOU NEED TO HEAR MOST? ME TOO.

As I pored over Tarana's website, I was moved by this story about Heaven. Tarana shares that the Me Too Movement started in the deepest, darkest place in her soul during her time as a youth worker.

While working with Black children and children of color, she'd seen everything from broken homes to abusive or neglectful parents. That's when she met Heaven, who proceeded to share an excruciating story about the abuses she'd suffered at the hands of her mother's boyfriend. Tarana listened to the little girl until she couldn't take it anymore. In the middle of Heaven's story, Tarana had to cut her off and direct her to another counselor who she thought could "help her better."

Heaven felt rejected, and rightly so. As much as Tarana loved her, she was unable to tell her that she could feel her pain. Tarana goes on to share, "And as I stood there, I couldn't even bring myself to whisper the words circling my mind and soul: 'me too.'"[3]

Whether the tragedy is sexual or otherwise, knowing we're not alone gives balm to our hurting souls. Like aloe on a fresh sunburn, learning that someone else has experienced pain similar to yours can breathe new life into your pain. In my life, I might ask: What if I could lessen the pain of someone else who may have come out and had a painful experience? What if I meet someone who is battling with addiction, guilt, or shame? What will I say when I listen to another's cries about witnessing someone's death in front of them? Or—fill in the blank.

I SEE YOU IN YOUR PAIN

In a general sense, we all have a Me Too moment. You've most likely been through something tragic. And you may very well meet someone, even if it's just *one* person, who might be going through something similar or who may have already come through to the other side. Imagine looking into their eyes and saying, "I've been through something similar. Here's what happened to me and here's how my life has changed as a result."

These Me Too moments tend to come when you least expect them. Maybe you'll cross paths with someone at your local park. Maybe it'll be your next Uber or Lyft driver. Maybe your mom will confide in you about something painful that occurred in her past. Keep your ears open to it. Keep your heart sensitive to it so you don't let the moment pass you by. The pain you've experienced from *your* tragedy can make someone else dealing with a similar pain feel less alone and overwhelmed in the midst of *their* tragedy. May we try and meet those moments like this:

"I see you in your pain. I can't perfectly empathize with your exact pain because all pain is unique to the person experiencing it. But I still see you. I've been down a similar road. I've walked in similar shoes. I've been in a similar storm, but maybe in a different ocean."

Did you notice what I didn't say? This is crucial, and I don't want you to miss it. What I didn't say was, "I know how you feel."

We have to stop using that phrase, effective immediately. Just because you may have gone through a divorce, you don't know exactly how someone feels who may also be going through a divorce. Just because your friend had a miscarriage and you had one too, doesn't mean that you know truly how she feels. Our pain is as unique as our tragedies.

I met a woman recently who shared with me that she'd lost her husband who was her best friend of thirty-five years. Even though it was ten years ago, she explained feeling like it had just happened earlier that day. Out of curiosity and care, I asked her what her greatest challenge was ten years after his death. She told me emphatically, "I hate when people say they know how I feel, even if they've also lost their spouse. I can't stand it. Because they don't. No one knows exactly how I feel, and just because you've lost someone doesn't mean you fully understand my pain."

That hit me deep. Just because we've been through something similar doesn't mean we know exactly how that person feels. "Me too" sounds different from "I know how you feel"—as it should. Fight the urge to utter those words when you are connecting with someone over a shared experience. While we can appreciate how someone feels and imagine what it might be like to walk in their shoes, we can't physically walk in their shoes. Those are their shoes, and we have our own.

Just because my son puts on my size ten high heel boots to pretend to be Mama Lindsey (as he adorably calls me), Atticus doesn't know what my life is like. He wasn't there when I spilled red wine on those boots at a karaoke bar in Kansas. He doesn't know how much my feet hate me when I walk more than five minutes in those boots, no matter how fabulously fashionable they are. But when he looks in the mirror, he cackles because in *that moment* he feels like what he thinks I might feel like.

We will never really know what someone is going through, because we weren't there when that person experienced their first major wound or injury. John Bradshaw writes, "The wounded inner child is filled with unresolved energy resulting from the sadness of childhood trauma. One of the reasons we have sadness is to complete painful events of the past, so that our energy can be available for the present. When we are not allowed to grieve, the energy is frozen."[4]

There is an unspoken magic that happens when we begin to bring a new perspective to the purpose of tragedy. When I started to reframe my brain and how it thinks about tragedy, I began learning more than I ever thought possible. The more present I am with my own tragic experiences, the more present I can be with others who are in the throes of their own tragic moments. The more sadness I can let out, the more healing I pursue, and the more my healed heart can support those in desperate need of healing.

TRAUMA TEACHINGS

If we were able to better understand the purpose of trauma, then we would have a better chance of thinking differently about trauma, as if it wasn't just all *bad*. (To clarify: I am NOT saying that the end purpose justifies the means of trauma . . . or that trauma exists to teach us a lesson. I'm simply stating that we can start to heal from our trauma when we start to identify a gift or purpose that came out of the trauma.)

I no longer believe the traumatic events in my life were sent by some grumpy old white dude with a beard, living in the clouds, to punish me or hurt me. I now see trauma as an inevitable part of life that can have a purpose based on my paradigm shift. I now see trauma as a way to get to harmony. My journey to wholeness, harmony, and healing wouldn't have been possible without the traumatic events I've experienced and most likely will experience in the future.

We just can't see this when we're in the midst of active trauma. During a traumatic event, we shatter. Parts of our soul and spirit splinter off. We shut down areas of our brain to survive. But we can ask our spirit to call these shattered, splintered pieces back where they can be healed and integrated again into our lives. It's not that we've been in denial about trauma, it's that we've been trapped in unawareness. It is our choice whether to bring new awareness into the light so we can look at it and get curious about it.

I wonder if one of the reasons you and I hold on to our trauma response is that we felt someone else should've done that for us in our past. Someone else should've responded for us, saved us, and made it all okay. But, because no one did this for us (or we perceive no one did this for us), we subconsciously feel we must hold on to both the trauma response and possibly even the trauma.

Ukraine's Kids Are Not Okay

Think of a child growing up in crisis. I'm thinking of all the little kids suffering at the hands of Putin's war in Ukraine. These children know something is wrong. They can feel it in their bodies. But they also know innately that their parents have the ability to love them and make the bad feeling go away. Kids tend to believe their parents can fix it and make it right so that they can feel better.

However, in this sense, it's bigger than simply making these kids feel better. It's more like these kids need a major shot of love and divine protection in order to feel okay. Even then, they most likely won't actually *be* okay. There are a lot of kids trapped in the middle of this war who won't be able to get this shot of love. These kids may grow up holding on to the trauma they are experiencing now and holding on to their trauma responses. Why? Maybe some of these children will feel the need to unintentionally hold on to it so that everyone around them will see that SOMEONE, somewhere should've intervened. Someone should've protected them. Why wasn't anyone there to love me in such a way that would take this pain away and make all the bad feelings go away?

Logically, as these kids get older, they'll realize that those who vowed to love and protect them did the best they could with what they had at the time. But emotionally and psychologically, the tragedy of what they've had to go through will alter the way they experience life. Despite their parents' best efforts to love and protect them, many of these children will be damaged for the rest of their lives.

I grieve for these kids, and I grieve for all kids who grow up in trauma, crisis, and tragedy. I pray they are being held by Divine Love and that one day, sooner rather than later, they will feel the spirit give them that gigantic shot of love, which can produce a flood of all those same exact feelings that they should've gotten from the people who were supposed to protect them and keep them safe. Only the spirit can do this work, and it truly is miraculous work.

Parents Are Incapable People

Maybe you were one of these kids I'm writing about. Maybe you didn't get the love and protection you needed from the people in your life whose job it was to make sure nothing bad happened to you. And then, maybe something bad *did* end up happening to you.

There is a love and a spirit who desperately wants to connect with you and give you that divine shot of matchless love so you can heal and someday truly let go. Spirit has the power to collect all the splintered, broken pieces that the world has scattered throughout our lives. We can move from a place of *dis*integration to complete integration and wholeness. I would argue, we *must*.

Love is asking us to be present with our feelings that surround whatever has caused the splintering in our lives. The more present we are, the more we cry out for help, which leads to deeper levels of wholeness.

There will come a time when you can look back on your childhood and realize you no longer need your parents (or caregivers) to do the things for you that you wish they would've done when you were little. In most cases, they would've done those things if they *could* have. But they were incapable. They, too, had trauma fragments from their childhood experiences that left them feeling as if their lives were stolen and spirits splintered off. They couldn't do it for you even if they'd wanted to. This isn't an excuse, but more of an explanation for why us parents keep screwing up our kids.

BREAKING THE CYCLE (EVEN IN OUR BROKENNESS)

The work of wholeness is ours alone, but we're not alone all by ourselves in it. We were meant to do this *for* ourselves by trusting and honoring our spirit—and *The* Spirit. Since the beginning of time, fragmented parents and caregivers have been raising kids who will inevitably become splin-tered and fragmented, too. The cycle will continue—until it doesn't.

This is where you and I can become cycle breakers. We can either give up and give in to a life where we are basically human trauma responses, simply responding to other people's trauma, or we can begin the brave work of healing ourselves so we can inspire healing in others. Profound wisdom is unlocked when we begin to realize that we're all having trauma responses to each other's trauma. This concept alone has made all the difference in many of my friendships and relationships.

I hear a lot of people these days joking about PTSD. I've been guilty of it too. But I want to caution us. Post-traumatic stress disor-der is real and can sometimes feel more real than the actual trauma that preceded the disorder. There's a reason why my friend who is a war veteran cannot attend a fireworks show. He knows he's hearing fireworks. He knows logically that the firecracker lighting up the sky isn't enemy fire. However, deep inside his soul, he feels the trauma of the gunshots, and his ears still ring with the sounds of war. If we look hard enough, the majority of us have our own version of PTSD.

According to the Mayo Clinic: "Post-traumatic stress disorder (PTSD) is a mental health condition that's triggered by a terrifying event . . . Symptoms may include flashbacks, nightmares and severe anxiety, as well as uncontrollable thoughts about the event. Most peo-ple who go through traumatic events may have temporary difficulty adjusting and coping, but with time and good self-care, they usually get better.." Without the proper treatment, though, the symptoms can get worse and last months or even years.[5]

You'll notice: "with time and good self-care . . ." I'm no doctor, but I've found it takes A LOT of time and A TON of GREAT self-care. In this book, I share with you a detailed account of a traumatic experience I had in my twenties. Ever since then, I cannot drive by an accident or see someone on a motorcycle the same way. Even though I've done a ton of work and therapy and processing on this one expe-rience, it forever changed me, and I have legit PTSD from it. It's the first thought I have when I see someone on a motorcycle. It's the first thought that rushes into my brain anytime I see an accident, an ambulance, or a helicopter airlifting someone.

Tragedies physically change our brain chemistry. Tragedies can also physically change our heart chemistry. The gift in all of this talk of tragedy can be something as simple as relating to others in pain. The more aware I become of my own experience with tragedy, the more I can be aware and present with someone who may desperately need to share their tragic experience with me.

In case you're still struggling with how to be present with someone in the midst of their own tragic pain, here's one last example of how NOT to approach the situation. Exhibit A: Last week, my son (at five years old, mind you) came up to me and said, "Knock knock." Trying not to sound annoyed because I've heard one trillion knock-knock jokes that are rarely (if ever) actually funny, I mustered up the obligatory response, "Who's there?" To which my son responded in a manner completely void of emotion, "Gabby's dead."

Yeah, that's *not* how you do this thing I'm writing about.

How does one segue from the family pet dying to a completely unrelated inspiring Bible verse? Well, I suppose I just did.

We read in Psalm 40:1-3:

I waited and waited and waited for God.

At last he looked; finally he listened.

He lifted me out of the ditch, pulled me from the deep mud.

He stood me up on a solid rock, to make sure I wouldn't slip.[6]

THE DROWNING THAT DROWNED ME

While it happened over fifteen years ago, June 5th might as well have been yesterday. What occurred that day will never be lost on me, because that day marked the beginning of the end of my simple, blind faith that saw God as a mere genie who honored my every request. Kind of like a holy Santa who nodded to my every prayer with a grandfatherly wink or a savior who would always come to my rescue. The God of "if you do A, I will do B."

After all, God came to the earth to be poor, beaten, and ridiculed to make sure I was happy, right?

That day started like any other day. I was working as a camp counselor the summer after graduating from high school. This was always the highlight of my summers.

. . . and then I came to know a sixteen-year-old named Brandon, who wasn't even a camper at the summer camp.

With our cabins resting on the water, my campers and I prepared to enjoy a "free swim" lazy afternoon when I noticed a boy and his friends swimming across the lake toward us. Despite my tough don't-you-dare-do-that! act, they continued making their way over. While there were three boys horsing around that day, my eyes stayed on the one whom I'd learn later was named Brandon. The boys began pretending like they were drowning, hoping to entice us to jump in, going under for a bit, coming back up for air, and then laughing.

But then, Brandon went under and never came back up. Finally, I realized the joke was over.

I leaped out into the water and franticly looked all over for him . . . all under for him . . . all around for him . . . but nothing.

During my failed search, the camp director arrived in his boat, jumped into the water, and was able to locate Brandon. Together, we dragged him up into the cabin, surrounded by onlooking campers. I grabbed the boy's leg, surely leaving an imprint, as I prayed harder than I had ever prayed in my life while they gave him CPR.

The entirety of my faith up to that point had convinced me that all would be well. I was taught that if I just laid hands on him and asked for this miracle, it would take place. This is the God of Resurrection we're talking about here. I had zero doubts.

Even though Brandon had been underwater for an unbelievably long time, I knew. I trusted. I believed. I had faith. I prayed, knowing with an unbending confidence, begging God, and yelling, "SAVE HIM. SAVE HIM. SAVE HIM."

At that moment, amidst my picture-perfect unshakeable faith, the nurses who had arrived on the scene stopped doing CPR.

But even then, my faith would not be tested. Minutes went by.

No more mouth-to-mouth. No more chest compressions. I persevered with prayer. More minutes passed, and I had to physically be removed from the cabin. I watched in unspeakable disbelief as the paramedics went into the cabin and emerged with a body bag.

It was then that my faith in the God of my understanding passed away with Brandon. The year that followed was filled with guilt and self-hatred. Why didn't I jump in earlier? It was all my fault. That year, I waited and waited on God to move into my broken, hopeless life. I needed God, but I sure as hell didn't want the old God of my understanding.

Then, on a mountaintop in Missouri, in the summer of 2001, I heard an audible holy whisper that saved my life and faith.

| **IT'S NOT YOUR FAULT.** |

That's the day I met God anew and opened myself up to whatever and whoever that meant. As you read the words of Psalm 40, what do you do when you wait and wait and nothing goes as (you) planned? Why is waiting for God so incredibly hard? Is there a moment in your own life when you began seeing God in a new way?

Because of that defining moment with Brandon, I spent a good part of two decades fearing water if someone was swimming nearby. I became hyperaware anytime I was near water and people were in it. I went from loving the water and enjoying every moment to being a hypervigilant, self-proclaimed lifeguard for every scenario. Kid's birthday party at a pool? I've got this. Even if an actual lifeguard was present, I still kept watch.

Remember that scene with Melissa McCarthy in *Bridesmaids* (the best movie on the planet), where she is convinced that she's sitting next to an undercover air marshal who must need her assistance with keeping watch over the plane? That's how I was.

Casual group of people floating in the lake? I was there. Ready at any moment to jump into action. I was like an overbearingly awkward

Baywatch actress who hadn't quite mastered the whole "sexy run on the beach while tossing hair" thing. And if I was around kids, my eyes were glued to those children. If you saw me at a public pool, you might think, *Who's the creepy lady watching all the kids swim?* That was me. I prefer the term CAREFUL over creepy, but tomAYto, tomAHto.

POOL PARTY REDEMPTION

Pre-Covid I was at a kids' swimming party with my children.

This birthday party was different from any other I'd been to. It was terrifying. And then it became a profound teachable moment for me.

There were probably ten or so kids in the pool. Parents were socializing, and everyone was having a good time. Everyone except . . . well, me. It is impossible for me to relax when I'm by a body of water with children swimming in it. I noticed a three-year-old boy walking down the pool steps with no floaties, and he didn't know how to swim. Something inside encouraged me to keep watch. A few seconds later, the child stepped off the shallow part and went completely into the water. He couldn't see that the shallow part had an end, and he went straight down. His mom had looked away for only one, maybe two total seconds. This was NOT a parenting fail in the least. This WAS about to be a freak accident.

Because of what happened with Brandon when I was seventeen, my eyes were glued to the little boy. As soon as I saw him step off that shallow shelf, I leaped toward him and scooped him out of the water. The child was visibly upset and low-key traumatized, but thankfully unharmed. Parents exchanged those "damn—that was close" glances with each other. We knew that could've gone down much differently than it did. Would the boy have been okay if I hadn't been watching him? I honestly have no idea. His mom was right there, so I'm sure she would've noticed and saved the day. But it all happened so fast, and it was VERY quiet.

I learned a valuable lesson that day. Brandon's drowning did not purposefully happen when I was seventeen so that I could save a boy from potentially drowning twenty years later. Brandon drowned that day and died right in front of me. That moment changed the way I would relate to water and people (especially kids) swimming. If it weren't for my experience with Brandon, I wouldn't have had my eyes on the little boy that day at the birthday party and most definitely wouldn't have noticed anything when he walked into the water.

That was the day I realized that **sometimes shit just happens**, for no reason. But *in* those tragic moments, there *may* be a gift that is born inside you that you may not see come to fruition until many years later. There was a seed of vigilance planted in me the day Brandon died. That seed has been growing inside me ever since. I was able to scoop the boy out of the water at the birthday party so swiftly because I had played similar scenarios over and over again in my head since Brandon's death. I never wanted anyone to drown in my presence again.

FLOWERS BUSTING THROUGH CONCRETE

Gifts are hidden treasures buried deep within us when the unthinkable happens. You may not realize the gift until decades later, and I guarantee you it will come packaged in the way you least expect. On the other hand, you may never see the gift or uncover the beauty that can come from ashes. For every traumatic situation I've seen good come out of, there has been a handful of other situations where I've yet to see any good come from it at all. Who knows if I ever will.

Regardless of whether or not I get to actually witness the gift and find that buried treasure, I know that nothing is wasted. Somehow, some way, good will come from this. I can't explain it, and I can't prove it. Plus, I know I could list a litany of traumatic experiences and tragedies for which no silver lining seems to exist.

Why do bad things happen to good people? This is the billion-dollar, age-old question. The way I see it, bad things don't happen to good people. Bad things just happen. Sometimes bad things are happening to bad people, and other times bad things are happening to good people. I don't believe that bad things go around like a gang of thugs looking for good people to destroy. It's true what the bumper stickers say: SHIT HAPPENS.

But I've come to believe that there are tiny treasures buried deep down in the muck and the mire. Maybe we'll see them; maybe we won't. I'll tell you this though, there are few greater miracles in life than having the privilege of witnessing even one tiny buried treasure making its way to the surface of our consciousness. Those treasures don't *negate* the pain of the trauma or tragic experience, but they do lessen the excruciating pain just a tiny bit.

When I look at a flower that has rebelled against the concrete jungle in which it lives, I focus on the power of the flower to grow and bust through concrete. I don't focus on the concrete and say, "Oh good, this resilient flower has now made me feel great about the concrete that has paved over paradise." I can still see the concrete for what it is. The flower growing despite an acre of surrounding pavement attempting to suffocate it simply makes me appreciate the flower's audacious journey.

I can't believe in a God who chooses one kid to drown while choosing another kid to live. Can you? I grew up thinking God was a pick-and-choose master. Growing up in church, I witnessed huge groups of people in prayer chains who would fervently pray for Person A to be healed from cancer. I watched a separate group of people pray for their loved one, Person B, who also had cancer. The prayers were just as fervent and the faith just as strong. Yet Person A died of cancer, while Person B was miraculously healed and spared.

Why do some die of diseases while others are spared? Do school shootings happen for a reason? I can think of a thousand occurrences where if someone told me, "Well, you know, everything happens for a reason," I would respond with a swift throat punch while whispering, "Well, you know, everything happens for a reason—including that throat punch."

Though I'm not fully past my fear of someone drowning in front of me, I've done enough work in therapy over the years to know that I do have control over acknowledging and observing the trauma and recognizing its impact on my life. Though I don't know much about it, I do know that EMDR (eye movement desensitization and reprocessing) trauma therapy made all the difference in the world when I was finally ready to take the box off the shelf where I had neatly packed away the drowning experience. With the help of my therapist and the safety of the EMDR process, I now have a completely different perspective on that summer when I was seventeen. I see it with new eyes, which would've never happened if I didn't choose to be brave and open myself to the reality that it was time to work through that trauma.

GOD'S NOT A PUPPET MASTER

Are you ready to start fully participating in your own life, even when life feels like the worst? It's not easy, and it may be more awkward than the first few steps of a newborn giraffe, but it'll be worth every uncomfortable second.

Unless you want to completely waste your life, join me on this journey of intentionally plugging in. It's time to sit *all* the way down, love. Tragedies are an integral part of life—no matter who you are, where you come from, or where you've been. I hope you'll challenge the tired old lie that God is the culprit to blame for all the bad things that happen in life. I can't believe in a God who causes horrific things to happen. But I DO believe in a Higher Power who can and desperately longs to bring forth goodness and mercy and hidden gifts or treasures out of every one of those tragedies.

In God's economy, nothing is wasted. No trauma. No tragedy. No loss. Nothing. Nothing is wasted.

As a parent, when something terrible happens to one of my kids, I am vigilant in my pursuit of finding a way to mine some goodness from the pain. I conspire with God/Higher Power/The Universe to find some shred of goodness that may be right around the corner from the bad. It doesn't mean that I'm sitting on my parenting bench thinking of ways I can cause bad stuff to happen to my kids so that I can also be the author of the goodness that may come after it. I'm a selfish human being who is extremely flawed. So of course, I can *only* believe in an all-loving God who magically plants gifts within the tragedy.

If you still believe in a punishing God who causes terrible things to happen, I hope you will challenge that perception because it's a lie.

God isn't a puppet master. We are humans who have free will. That free will *can* and *has* and *always will* lead to terrible things happening in life and in the world. Never underestimate the power of a tragedy. Sometimes the greatest, most profound treasures are born out of the depths of tragedy. I suppose this is why I've heard the following wisdom a hundred times in the rooms of Al-Anon:

I NO LONGER KNOW THE DIFFERENCE BETWEEN A TRAGEDY AND A MIRACLE.

Break It Down for Me

- Tragedy is an experience shared by all of us. It can create an opportunity for deeper human connection and empathy as we seek support and comfort from others who understand what we're going through.

- Not *everything* happens for a reason, but even the worst tragedy can serve a purpose that infuses the tragic experience with new meaning.

- The work of wholeness is ours alone, but we're never alone on the journey.

- If you keep putting one foot in front of the other, you soon will come to believe that a life exists where you will no longer be able to differentiate between a tragedy and a miracle.

I
ENJOY
LONG WALKS
TO THE
COUCH

PART TWO

"The most difficult aspect of transition is not the outer
changes; it is the inner reorientation. Transition is a
psychological process, not a logical one, and the transition
points in our lives are natural opportunities to reorient
ourselves in response to the shock of change."

—William Bridges[1]

WELCOME
TO THE
SHITSHOW

Chapter 6

THE GIFT OF REJECTION

"Never let the bastard get you down."
—Moira Rose, *Schitt's Creek* (S3, E7)

"Can't make a good soup. Can't do a handstand
in a pool. Can't spell the word 'lieutenant.'
There's a lot of can'ts in my life right now."
—Leslie Knope, *Parks & Recreation* (S1, E11)

Rejection is horrific. Most of us (if not ALL of us) go to great lengths to avoid any semblance of rejection—at all costs. But in many cases, especially in my case, rejection has been paramount to putting things in perspective and keeping me on the right path.

This didn't happen overnight. It has been a process that continues to this very day. The work is in reframing our thinking about rejection. What is rejection, and what is it most definitely NOT? How can we approach rejection with new eyes and ears, while not taking things so personally? Most of the time, a situation that leaves us feeling rejected has very little to do with us. Some of the greatest lessons I've learned have come from sheer, unadulterated rejection. Before we learn how not to take everything so personally, please allow me to flip that phrase on its head.

ACTUALLY, YOU *SHOULD* TAKE IT PERSONALLY

Yes, you read that correctly. I know you've heard your whole life *not* to take things personally. But the same world that discourages us from taking things personally is the very world that has conditioned us to blame everything on The Other. We need to take a step back from looking at other people and anything that exists *outside* of ourselves and go internally, especially when feelings of rejection come up.

In the rooms of various 12-step programs, you'll hear the words "Let it begin with me." Instead of diagnosing the root of our emptiness, we tend to place blame or worse, play the victim. I don't think humans are born with a victim mindset. I think it starts as a tiny seed that's planted early on. By the time we realize what's going on and that we've fallen into this victimization trap, it's already grown into a gigantic tree.

Don't get me wrong, I know many of you reading this have literally been victimized. That's a different thing entirely. I'm not negating or trying to explain away the abuse and trauma you may have endured in your life. What I'm speaking of is our tendency, especially as women, to give in to the victim mindset.

We all have a little bit of this in us, and it's that very mindset that saddles us with rejection baggage. Instead of trying to silence it, I welcome the thought now. I become aware of what I'm thinking about, and I get curious. I take a deep breath and acknowledge the thoughts and feelings. Go deeper within yourself. **Take it REAL personally.**

When you do, you'll usually find that expectations are at the root. **Expectations are future resentments.** Now that I'm aware of that truth, I immediately diagnose my expectations. Awareness starts with thinking about what you're thinking about: the pursuit of metacognition. Rarely, if ever, are we mindful in every moment. The good news is that's something we can change over time.

From Mindlessness to Mindfulness

So, how do we move from meaningless, automated living to a life where we are fully participating and aware of our thoughts and feelings? How does mindlessness—filled with yesterday's recycled thoughts—become mindfulness?

You simply need to become aware and then be fully present with whatever you've just become aware of. It's Step 1 in the 3 A's I've learned through my 12-step work.

- Awareness
- Acceptance
- Action

In that order. You don't have to DO anything right now. Just become aware. And NEVER waste a rejection trigger.

BEING THE OUTSIDER

A dear friend of mine recently asked me to answer a few questions for her podcast. As I started brainstorming how to answer these questions with complete authenticity, I was surprised by what I started to write down. I'd like to share it with you here because I think this is a common human condition: feeling left out, which is simply another side of rejection.

All the Feels

Being on the outside of a group feels like home. It feels normal because that's how it's been for the majority of my life. I don't say this as a victim. Quite the opposite. I say this as someone who knows herself and has awareness about where I've been in life, where I've come from, and where I am now. Growing up, I never really felt like I belonged. I always felt different. I grew up in a loving home with incredible parents who always made me feel like I belonged, so I assign zero blame to them. It genuinely felt like it was in my DNA. I wasn't just on the outside looking in, I was on the outside obsessing over whether the *inside* people were looking at me *with judgment*. In high school, I was finally able to admit to myself that I am gay. That intensified the feeling of being on the outside of a group and internalizing that rejection. And then, much later in my adulthood, I learned that I am on the spectrum. Initially, this was a HUGE surprise, but then it became something that helped me make sense of the world, *my* very odd world. Regardless of the why, I could never shake the feeling of being inexplicably "other."

Finding Comfort on the Fringes

When I'm wallowing in despair—in those darkest valley moments of rejection—I begin to believe all sorts of things about myself. They aren't new beliefs; they're old beliefs that are still somewhere down deep inside me, bubbling up to the surface and sounding something like this: "You don't belong, and you've never belonged, have you? You are unworthy. Unwanted. You don't matter. You *are* a reject, so you should probably just shut up, shut down, and shut everyone and everything else out including the light." There's nothing quite like feeling left out that fuels the fire of those old tapes burning everything in their path. I start to question whether I'm going to ever "belong" anywhere.

As I've gotten older, I've come to realize I'm comfortable on the fringes; but why? Why do I prefer to be right outside the gate without ever walking through it when it opens?

After graduating from college, I went into full-time ministry. I've never felt more on the outside than when I was in ministry. Being gay and in the closet while touring the country and singing songs about God in churches that were openly anti-LGBTQ+ will do that to you. Every day, I was compromising myself. I had dishonored and rejected myself on so many occasions.

And then, recently and slowly over the past few years, it hit me. I've felt like an outsider because **I am an outsider**. And I'm finally learning to be okay with that and accept it. The gift, the hidden trea-sure for me, has been found in those moments of feeling rejected. Turns out, there's peace in the fringes. I have faith in the fringes, and I know where I belong when I'm there. You see, I needed to understand what was really going on when I felt this way. I needed a paradigm shift in my thinking and perception of belonging and how I interact with being rejected.

The Longing for Belonging

The day I stopped trying to fit my square peg into life's round hole was the day I set myself free from living as if there were only the two options: square peg or round hole. I made the decision (and have to remake the decision sometimes throughout the day) that I want to live as if there is no peg or hole.

When I experience feelings of rejection, that's a key indicator to me that I need to get curious about that feeling. What is it that I'm really looking for? The more awareness I gain from looking inward, the more freedom I have from the tyranny of trying so desperately to belong and avoid rejection at all costs. I already belong because I *am*. I belong to my God. I belong to myself. I belong to love.

I wonder how many of us feel like we are on the outside looking in because we feel that way within our very own selves. Until we find a way to allow the outside and the inside to sit down together at the table, we won't get anywhere. It's not an either/or proposition; it's both/and.

And sometimes rejection is the very thing that leads to belong-ing. Think of it this way: My dogs have always hated being in their crates. I don't use crates anymore because one time my dog Whiskey spent a few hours destroying the strongest crate I thought ever existed. He chewed and moved pieces and parts and somehow completely destroyed the crate. Yet, when the door of the crate is open while I'm home, he loves going in there.

What changed? His *perception* of what's actually happening in any given moment. When I let Whiskey out of his crate, he may feel like he's finally free. But guess what? He's still inside the house—which is essentially just a really big crate. (That's why they want to bust out running straight through the front door whenever it opens even the tiniest crack.)

REFRAMING REJECTION

What if, just for today, we thought about the concepts of *rejection* and *belonging* differently? What if we turned these concepts on their heads? We will never feel like we belong anywhere until we acknowledge the deep sense of belonging that exists within each of us. The work is in marrying the two internally—bringing those opposing realities into alignment. That will unlock our ability to know we belong, regardless of whether we're feeling rejected and dejected on the inside or outside of any given situation, group of people, or reality.

You belong because you *are.* Our sense of belonging can't come from someone else or some group or anything outside of ourselves. And don't worry. This isn't selfish thinking. This is self-awareness and rigorous self-honesty and love.

Having an internal belief that you belong with love *because you are love itself* will bring a sense of peace and strength to feelings of rejection. There is hope for us yet, especially in the midst of our reactions to those moments where my square peg doesn't fit into a round hole.

"Square peg in a round hole" is an idiomatic expression that describes the unusual individualist who could not fit into a niche of their society.[1]

The metaphor was originated by Sydney Smith in "On the Conduct of the Understanding," one of a series of lectures on moral philosophy that he delivered at the Royal Institution in 1804–1806:

> If you choose to represent the various parts in life by holes upon
> a table, of different shapes,—some circular, some triangular, some
> square, some oblong,—and the person acting these parts by bits of

wood of similar shapes, we shall generally find that the triangular person has got into the square hole, the oblong into the triangular, and a square person has squeezed himself into the round hole. The officer and the office, the doer and the thing done, seldom fit so exactly, that we can say they were almost made for each other.[2]

What if, instead of running as far away as possible from being even remotely considered as The Other, we instead intentionally volunteered to be The Other? Think about it. If we make a practice of volunteering to be The Other, we'll rarely—if ever—find ourselves alone, because we will be surrounded by other *Others*.

THE RUBBLE OF REPUDIATION

The gift of rejection can be found in the very sense of not belonging. Feeling left out is actually where the answer lies. Each time we feel left out, we can get curious about why we feel that way. What need isn't being met? Is there codependency involved? Are you looking to your spouse to make you feel that sense of belonging? Are you hoping that next job, relationship, or group will bring you the belonging you've been craving since you were a child?

You won't find it there. You won't *find* it anywhere because it's already inside you. The work is in uncovering what's been piled on top of the inherent belonging that's been robbing you throughout your life. Wake up to the gift of rejection—feeling left out and left behind. Go inside, and let it begin with you.

I'm trying to train my brain to think this thought as soon as I become aware I am struggling with feelings of rejection or frustration: *I'm about to learn something new.* Every time I've found myself sitting atop the rubble of repudiation, I'm met with a fresh supply of character-building and learning. When I can finally muster the strength to stand up, dust the rubble off, and make my way down the mountain I've made out of a molehill, I inadvertently end up on a learning journey.

MY (ALMOST) ADVENTURE IN STARDOM

I've experienced rejection so often in my life that in my present-day life, I see it almost immediately as something that's happening *for* me, not to me.

In December 2019, B.C. (you know, Before Covid), an email ended up in my inbox from an extremely popular TV show that's been known to launch the careers of countless singer/songwriters. Normally, I delete spam emails right away, but something was different about this one. I didn't read it, but I also didn't delete it. I just kept it in my inbox.

Then, a few months later (still prior to Covid closing everything down), I attended a small church gathering to sing a few worship songs. It's one of my favorite churches—a place called Imperfect Faith Community in Austin, Texas, with a congregation as diverse as the colors in a bag of Skittles. After the service was over, a dear friend came up to me and told me about how he got a clear sense in his heart while I was singing and felt compelled to encourage me to audition for a world-famous talent TV competition whose name I cannot include in this chapter due to a very thick legal agreement I signed. It was the same TV show whose email was sitting in my inbox.

I immediately laughed off my friend's suggestion because who has the time, I thought. Despite being in the music industry for fifteen-plus years, I'd never tried out for any of the talent shows like *American Idol*, *America's Got Talent*, or *The Voice*. I never wanted to be *that* musician or singer who "made it" because of a television show. Despite it being a reality show, it certainly didn't feel real to me. It felt too easy. Shooting to stardom via a televised game show felt like a shortcut, and I believed I needed to pay my dues.

After my church friend motivated me to audition for the show, I sat on it for a few days and eventually opened the email I'd been saving for months. I figured, "Hell, what have I got to lose?" I clicked on the email, followed the steps to register, and thought nothing of it. Much to my surprise, I got an email shortly thereafter giving me details for the next steps. I can't go into much detail here, because of the fine print in the contract I signed in order to move forward with the audition, so I'll be vague.[3]

Within the span of a few weeks, I advanced to the next level and nabbed a slot to audition in person at a huge convention center. Brynn and I packed up the car, guitar in tow, and headed to Dallas. The lines were insanely long, and the waiting room was filled to the brim with dreamers. I'd never seen the show, so I didn't really know what to expect. But I did know how to BRING IT under pressure and was majorly looking forward to seeing what this was all about. I could at least show my kids how their tired old mama could still muster up the energy to chase her dreams. They were convinced I would win the whole thing. I am obsessed with their unapologetic confidence. No matter what transpired, I knew I would walk away with an incredible experience.

When my number group was called, we shuffled into the audition room. I had ninety seconds to show the judges what I was made of. This wasn't the TV audition yet, just the prelims. I was so excited and very nervous. I got up, did my thing, and sat back down. To show the versatility of my talent, I did a mash-up of three songs and played my guitar. Imagine "Ain't No Sunshine" meets "No Diggity" meets the rap from "Waterfalls." I felt really good about my performance, and the judges seemed happy. Everyone in my group got sent home, and we were told that we'd be receiving email communication with updates and next steps. Buttttt, I got held back, much to my surprise, along with a six-year-old drummer phenom.

I'd soon come to find out that I was going to stay at the convention center since I'd advanced to the next phase of the audition process. I hadn't eaten, I'd barely had any water, and I was tired of walking all around God and country in my very cute (yet very uncomfortable) boots. Also, I was wearing a dress. WHY ON EARTH was I wearing a dress? It was cute, sure, but also very uncomfortable.

Brynn was elated to find out I'd advanced to the next round, and we were able to reunite. We waited and waited, and then someone important looking came up to me. I knew she was important because she wielded a clipboard AND an earpiece. She motioned for me to follow her. I surely would've followed her anywhere. We went on quite the journey through the convention center, with twists and turns, wading through throngs of people. There was a WIDE variety of talent at this audition. One dude was blowing balloon animals out of his nostrils. Another guy was doing something terrifying with knives, and there may have been a small flame involved. Some little people were practicing an impeccable pyramid. One elderly woman just kept kissing her border collie on the mouth while it spun around in circles.

My clipboard earpiece guide led me to a promising hallway where I sat and waited some more. Finally, my name was called. I headed into what appeared to be a great hall of some sort. There sat the two women judges/producers from my initial audition. In their intimidating British accents, they explained that they loved my mash-up and loved reading the story I'd written in my audition packet. I probably over-shared, but again, what did I have to lose? Also, not one person on this planet has ever accused me of being concise.

The two women asked me to sing something else. A former boss of mine once told me that no one can ever *put* me on the spot because I *LIVE* on the spot. So, I was ready. I started singing my favorite a cappella version of "His Eye Is on the Sparrow" circa 1993, from the movie *Sister Act 2*. I channeled the very best of my idol Lauryn Hill and sang my heart out. At one point during that song, I had a crazy vision. It was so crazy that I fear sharing it here, but to hell with it.

During the last half of the song, I had a vision of the huge white walls opening up directly behind the two women who were intently listening to me sing. As the walls opened, I saw a sea of people—thousands upon thousands. It was as if I'd stepped directly into the halftime show of the Super Bowl. And *I* was performing. The vision gave me full-on goosebumps from the tip of my head to the bottoms of my feet. My face was tingling. It was bizarre, and I felt like I was standing on holy ground. This happens quite a bit when I sing, especially when I'm singing from the very depths of my soul, which was created to sing. It was magical and terrifying all at the same time.

As soon as I finished the song, the walls closed back up. The judges were misty-eyed and provided encouraging feedback. They asked me to share more about my story with them, which I did. After we talked for a while, they said that I had "a story the world needs to hear." Interestingly enough, this is the exact sentence that my friend from church spoke to me the day he emphatically told me to audition for this show. *The same exact phrase.* I started to believe that maybe this crazy thing just might happen.

I tried not to get my hopes up, but I also wanted to enjoy the adventure. I was instructed to leave the room and was met by my clipboard lady, who led me to another wing of the convention center. I filled out more paperwork and sat back down to wait some more. My name was eventually called, and Clipboard Clara continued serving as my audition doula to help me give birth to whatever this thing was that I was doing.

This walk was the longest, and my feet were screaming obscenities at me. I frantically texted Brynn so she could try to get to where I was going. Several security rent-a-cops tried to stop her, but she would not be deterred. Plus, she had all my snacks, so she had to find me before I fainted due to low blood sugar.

We finally made it to the next spot, and Brynn met me a few moments later. This time, I was sitting outside another large banquet-type room. After what seemed like hours, Clipboard Clara motioned me in through the door, where I would be met by a sight I'd only seen on TV. There was a stage, a fancy backdrop, cameras, and important-looking people staring at their computer screens. After a short, awkward welcome, I started singing.

I sang my little heart out like it was the last time I'd ever use my vocal cords again. At one point, it truly felt like an out-of-body experience. It was as if I had made my way up to the ceiling and was looking down, observing what was happening in that huge room with those large lights. I couldn't let myself think of what was actually happening because I didn't want to psych myself out. So, I just kept singing. After one song, the important-looking people asked me a few questions which I answered with obvious nervousness. I sang a few more songs and felt really good about my performance. The leading lady at the long table with the Hollywood-looking glasses said I could leave. Apparently, I was just standing there awkwardly, frozen in disbelief that I'd made it this far. She had to instruct me to get the hell off the stage.

I walked out of that room knowing I'd given my very best and quickly realizing how seriously I needed to pee since I'd been holding it for who knows how many hours. I wanted so badly to make it to the next round that would take me to a different part of the country. I wanted it so badly. It wasn't that I wanted to be famous. I wanted a platform from which I could bring hope to the hurting and light to those meandering in darkness.

WHY ALL THE GREEN LIGHTS?

It was about a month later, after weeks of checking and refreshing my emails to no avail, that I finally received the email from the show. It was short and to the point. And damnit, my reaction to the email revealed that I'd definitely gotten my hopes up. It informed me that I'd *not* been chosen to advance to the next round.

Sure, I was bummed and sad. I felt a deep sense of rejection. But I was also thankful in a way because, in hindsight, there's no way in hell I could've left my job and family for the range of time required for me to stay in a faraway place for the taping. Making it on the show would've most likely derailed several important components of my life, and no show was worth that.

So why did I go through all that? Why did the lights continue to turn green and doors swing wide open? Why the vision of throngs of people listening to me? Why the positive feedback from the judges? Why the feeling of excitement and the subsequent awareness of passion that had been reignited inside me? I went from feeling the spark to seeing the flame to watching a fire extinguisher eliminate the flame. I didn't advance to the next round, but the flames were not *entirely* quenched. There were still embers giving off light and heat.

After sitting with the feeling of rejection and learning from it, I accepted it. I accepted the fact that this entire experience unfolded exactly as it needed to. From start to finish, I learned a ton and found that I still have that deep, intense desire to sing and share my story with as many folks as possible who will listen. This is why I'm thrilled to share these QR codes at the end of each chapter. I long to share my songs with the world.

Getting the rejection email didn't make me doubt my worth or gifts. It didn't lessen my passion for singing and speaking and sharing my story. The email simply informed me that *my* path wouldn't include *this* show. I was able to hold the acceptance and my sadness in the same space.

Just because my vision wasn't going to come to fruition in this TV show didn't mean I wouldn't eventually have the opportunity to sing or speak in front of a crowd of people someplace else at some other time. I've made peace with the rejection, and now I'm incredibly thankful for it.

In her blog *Black Girl Musings*, Nicole writes:

REJECTION REMINDS YOU OF WHO YOU ARE.

She goes on to say, "How much different would we see ourselves if we viewed rejection as an opportunity to remember that [we] are enough without the opportunities, people, or jobs we have tricked ourselves into believing we need in order to feel worthy?"[4] . . . She goes on to say that who you are and what you've done are not the same and that rejection can remind us of this. She reminds us not to listen to the nasty voice inside our heads.

REJECTION IS THE NEW REJUVENATION

Rejection doesn't just automatically remind me of who I am and whose I am. Rejection HAS THE POWER to remind. The power to renew and re-invigorate our spirits. Rejection need not be wasted because it's FULL of possibilities and unique opportunities. Merriam-Webster defines the word "rejected" as "not given approval or acceptance."[5]

This is precisely why the power of rejection is so essential to our lives and personal growth. We humans with our big egos need to periodically be reminded of the feelings that result from *not* being approved of or accepted. Too often, my life was plagued with an obsession for approval and acceptance from people and organizations wholly outside of myself. That pursuit left me feeling empty and disappointed because it was never enough. When one person would reject me (in my perception), it took away any joy I'd had from a previous person accepting me.

We need to be reminded of rejection. Our pride desperately needs to get a healthy dose of rejection from time to time to keep us humble. Not always being accepted and approved of forces us to look inside ourselves for sustainable, lasting, and REAL approval. We are already approved of. We are wholly accepted by the One who made us, even when we're sleeping and especially when we're screwing up. Before we do anything with our lives, there is an underpinning of God's unconditional love and acceptance found in the foundation of this life we're building.

I've been rejected, resented, repositioned, refused, and repudiated. Yet, I now stand taller than I would be standing if all my dreams had come true.

ALL THE WHAT IFS

What if I had gotten married in college to the nice Christian man who adored me and had no idea he was about to marry a Goldstar lesbian who never intended to have sex with a man—ever? I'd probably be miserable and trapped in a sham of a marriage with a few kids wondering why their mom is always drinking vodka and watching reruns of *The L Word* in secret.

What if I'd made it on the TV show I auditioned for? I would've left my family at the worst possible time when they needed me the most. I would've left my clients in a lurch, clients who depend on me for sound, objective financial advice. Our hedgehog would go into a deep depression because I'm the only one who tends to him.

What if I had taken the record deal I was offered in college by a major label that wanted to sign me (but only if I'd lose thirty pounds and stop singing songs about "religious stuff")? I'd have majorly compromised everything I stood for at the time.

What would my life look like if I continued rejecting myself and denying an integral part of how God divinely created me instead of coming out and walking in my true power and spirit-ordained freedom?

The various roads of rejection *in* my life have led to the roads *of* my life that I desperately want to be on. What about you? What are your What Ifs? Isn't it possible that your experiences with rejection, too, have led to even better experiences and outcomes in your life? While you listen to the song and color your little heart out, reflect on your What Ifs. Follow the path to the end for each circumstance where you were rejected in an impactful way. See what comes up for you. This may help you reframe your thinking about rejection in the future because it will happen again.

Break It Down for Me

- Rejection is a major blow to the ego, but it also tends to put things into perspective and help us get right-sized with ourselves and our spirit.

- Never forget that expectations (no matter how noble or sensible) always lead to future resentments.

- Ironically, rejection can be the very experience that unlocks a feeling of belonging.
- Rejection reminds us of who we are deep down when everything else is stripped away. It is nothing short of a unique opportunity that should never be wasted.

NOT
TODAY
PATRIARCHY

Chapter 7

THE GIFT OF UNANSWERED PRAYERS

"I'm eating egg whites and hoping the building will collapse."
　—Moira Rose, *Schitt's Creek* (S2, E1)

"Let's all go to bed and pray we don't wake up."
　—Moira Rose, *Schitt's Creek* (S4, E9)

Though I don't believe prayers go unnoticed or unanswered by God, I do believe there's a reason we sometimes don't get what we ask for. As I look back on my life, most of my pleading and begging to God in prayer didn't pan out the way I'd wished it had—at the time. But in hindsight, I have clarity that those "unanswered prayers" were a huge gift.

Time to challenge ourselves when it comes to prayer (whether you pray or not). First, let's establish a working definition of "prayer," so we're all reading from the same sheet of music. Prayer, to me, is communicating with the Universe/Higher Power/Love Intelligence/Insert Name Here. I wonder if we can learn to pray in a way that isn't the tired old genie-in-a-bottle strategy. Is there any hope for us to see prayer in a different, non-religious way? I would argue *we must*.

It's not about asking for what we want, it's about having an open and honest daily dialogue with God (as we understand Him/Her/Them/Etc.), sharing anything and everything in those prayers. Do we have a shot at letting go of our desires and letting go of outcomes? Trusting that no matter what happens, somehow, we'll be okay? As hard as it might be for you to read this, and as hard as it may be for me to write about this, I'm afraid I have no choice.

Here's the greatest gift I've ever received in the area of prayers that didn't go my way. Let me tell you about my dark night of the soul; the night I spent on the floor of my bedroom in tears, drenching the carpet, begging God to kill me in my sleep if He wasn't going to wake me up heterosexual.

Once when I was in college, in the depths of depression due to my being in the closet, I wanted to die. I didn't want to kill myself, but I did want to die. I wanted the pain to stop. I was engaged to a good Christian man who was crazy about me, but just one tiiiiiny little problem: I was in love with my best friend. My very straight, female best friend. Despite my best efforts, I couldn't make my heart love this man. And I couldn't make my heart *not* love my best friend. It felt like torture because, internally, that's exactly what it was.

One evening, after watching a movie, sitting between my fiancé and my best friend, I knew I was "supposed" to desire intimacy with *him*, but I only wanted *her*. This was despite years of trying to pray away the gay and dabbling in ex-gay therapy. The guilt and shame from decades of believing surely, I was going to hell, finally swallowed me up. While sobbing and blind to a way out, I prayed that God would take me in my sleep or wake me up straight. I knew I wouldn't survive another day wallowing in this torture. I wanted out.

I AM GAY *AND* GOD LOVES ME

Thankfully, God didn't grant me that very misguided wish. I woke up very alive (and still very gay) the next day, which served as the catalyst to begin my healing journey—a journey that would lead to the reconciliation of my faith and my sexuality.

In fact, I'm closer to God now than I ever have been. I want other LGBTQ+ folks to know they don't have to choose between being gay and having a relationship with God. For those of you who want to maintain your faith and honor your sexual orientation, I hope you will see my story as evidence that you *can* have both. I am gay, *and* God loves me deeply.

My faith is growing by leaps and bounds. I am more open-minded than I've ever been, and I honor others' journeys and opinions, even if I disagree with them. I almost don't recognize the college student who fasted every Thursday for a year in hopes of praying the gay away. What if God had made me straight and granted the wish I'd hoped and begged for over many years? I wouldn't have my three kids, my person with whom I'll grow old, a career I love where I know I'm making a difference in people's lives—so much of what makes me *me*. What if the ex-gay/reparative therapy had actually worked in forcing me to live a life void of love, dying single and sexually frustrated? Mercy . . .

I've finally and fully abandoned the misguided, harmful teachings of my past as it relates to fundamentalist, evangelical christianity. (I use a lowercase "c" on purpose.) I want to live a life like Christ did, 100 percent free of judgment and full of love. My hope is to bring hope to a hurting world. My dream is to inspire you to walk confidently in the way of your own dreams or discover your ideal life, possibly for the first time. I dream of a world where diversity, education, and inclusion are basic values of all humans, where anti-racism is the *norm*, and where racial equity is the goal we all strive for. I dream of a world where people learn to love themselves, and I hope to help create a culture and environment where people feel free to fully be themselves and embrace their own uniqueness and divinity.

We are all worthy. And I finally believe, *more than I ever have*, that I am worthy. I am worthy to live another day. So are you. Were you like me, raised by the teachings of the church to believe you weren't worthy? You were sinful and bad and in need of mercy? Well, I officially wave the bullshit flag on that (*cue song from Chapter 3*).

DON'T GIVE UP BEFORE THE MIRACLE

You may read this several times throughout this book, but it bears repeating: don't give up before the miracle. I gave up and wanted to die that lonely night in college. But God knew all the great things that were in store for me. There's really no way to use twenty-six letters to string together some words that accurately convey how grateful I am God said "HELL NO" to my suicide prayer.

If you're reading this and you've struggled with wishing you weren't here anymore, thank you for staying. I hope and pray you will keep choosing to LIVE. And even if you don't believe it's a choice in that dark moment, *it is*. Even though my mind and body wanted to be done with life that night, my soul and spirit were fighting for me in a wholly other-worldly space. My spirit was interceding on my behalf and God's Spirit, that bottomless well of love, was covering me and holding me so close, as if we were one. And I believe we *were* . . . and are.

I love this passage in the Book of Romans about God's Spirit: "The Spirit helps us in our weakness. We do not know what to pray for, but the Spirit intercedes on our behalf with divine groanings—too deep for words. And the One who searches hearts knows what the mind of the Spirit is, because the Spirit intercedes for all of us . . ."[1] (Romans 8:26-27).

I'm so incredibly thankful that God's answers always hold more wisdom than my prayers ever did. I believe in a Higher Power who takes my ignorance and short-sightedness into account when dealing with me and my frantic requests.

As a component of our Covid-proof, viral, drive-in movie theater wedding toward the beginning of the pandemic, my then-future wife Brynn and I incorporated a gorgeous tapestry of one of my favorite Dalai Lama quotes: "There are only two days in the year that nothing can be done. One is called yesterday and the other is called tomorrow, so today is the right day to love, believe, do and mostly live."

One of my favorite books of all time is called *Happiness Is the Way* by Dr. Wayne Dyer. And it's not even really a book. It's actually a compilation of quotes from countless lectures given by the spiritual guru from the 1990s to the 2000s. If you have any reading bandwidth left after reading this book, you should check out that book. He shares a quote that has always meant so much to him, and it now means so much to me: "When you change the way you look at things, the things you look at change."[2]

What would our life look like if we placed our focus on today, instead of obsessing over our wants and needs of tomorrow? There is untold magic in moment-by-moment presence and awareness, where prayer is a *conversation*, not a Christmas list. What is it that you want to change? Or what situation or circumstance are you desperately hoping to see change? Think of how you are currently looking at those things. How are you seeing your first step and the larger journey? How do you see yourself on this journey, and what do you see when you start taking steps to walk confidently in the way of your dreams?

Every single experience you and I encounter in our lives has the unique possibility of expanding our awareness and opening our minds. Sometimes, the expansion is dramatic and sudden. Other times, the opening is a slow, arduous process, like waiting all day for roast beef to cook in the Crockpot (I know about Instant Pot, but it doesn't taste the same; I don't care what you say). Either way, the more mindful we can be of how we are seeing ourselves and the world, the more magic will start to come our way. The miracles and magic may not come in the way you would like or the way you'd imagine based on what you know about magic and miracles. These hidden gifts and treasures are typically found deep within a type of packaging you're not expecting.

GARTH BROOKS WAS WRONG

STILL, it never fails that anytime I hear the words "unanswered prayers" I am instantly reminded of Garth Brooks' song thanking God titled "Unanswered Prayers." I mostly get the idea, but it still rubs me the wrong way. I've come to believe there's no such thing as a prayer that goes *unanswered*. Here's my logic:

Let us consult the dictionary. "Prayer": a solemn request for help or expression of thanks addressed to God or an object of worship . . . also, an earnest hope or wish. "Unanswered": not answered or responded to. (Thanks, Captain Obvious.)

If my kids come to me with a request, even if I don't respond the way they want me to or desperately believe they need me to, I still hear them. We can still communicate openly about whatever it is they feel they need.

Once, when Annabelle was three, she begged and begged for hours with huge crocodile tears, "*MAAAAAAMA, PLEASE get me a baby tigerrrrrrrrrrrrrrrrrr*!!!" She begged and begged and begged and couldn't understand why I wouldn't do that for her. She felt betrayed and deeply wounded by my NO. She knows I would do anything for her, and that I want to do everything I absolutely can for her and her siblings. But dangit, I just couldn't quite make the baby tiger thing happen.

I mean, look, if I put my mind to it, and I believed that was the best thing for Annabelle, maybe I'd go find a way to make it happen. But lawd, I knew better than to give my three-year-old daughter a baby tiger who would grow up into a big tiger and eat our hedgehog AND her. No matter how much she would've begged for it, I wouldn't have done it. Not because I don't love her. Not because I don't want to give her every little thing her heart desires. But because, well, I think it's obvious.

This may be way too much of a stretch to compare my parenting and saying no to baby tiger requests with the way that God chooses to be in a relationship with me. However, I think you can see where I'm going with this.

I'm afraid many of you may have grown up the same way I did. I subconsciously thought God was basically an illuminated Santa Claus living in the clouds with a sheep-led sleigh instead of reindeer. It wasn't until much later that I learned the differences between a prayer, a wish, and a grovel or beg situation. When I was six years old, I asked Santa for space shoes that could help me fly. Somehow, I was convinced this was a real thing that had already been invented, developed, and sold at local toy stores.

And I didn't just ask Santa for these magical space shoes. I begged. I wrote letters. I did just about everything I could think of to pressure Santa into bringing these miracles down the chimney and into my life (read: guilt Santa into bending to my wishes). Surprise surprise, Christmas morning came and went. No space shoes. However, I should note that Santa got me YET ANOTHER doll, which I hated and threw out into the backyard where all my other dolls ended up. I never asked Santa for a doll, yet again and again I got the damn doll. Thanks, Mom.

Somehow, unbeknownst to me and by complete accident, I started to associate my perception of God with my perception of Santa. I wondered if a prayer was just like a Christmas wish, but instead of Santa, it's God—who I also thought lived in a fictitious place with a white beard, angels instead of elves, and spiritual gifts instead of actual gifts. I guarantee you, there are no magical space shoes at the North Pole OR in heaven. (Still very disappointed about this. Now, I have zero chances of flying.)

In hindsight, I'm grateful Santa never gave me the space shoes. I would've surely ended up in the hospital, like that time I was running as a small child, tripped on my sandals, ran head-first into my grandad's parked car bumper, and split my forehead wide open.

As I looked back on my wildly long list of Christmas wishes, I started to think back to my prayers. This was a fun exercise to reminisce on the prayers I would pray as a child—and I'd like to share it with you, followed by an invitation.

Here's an incomplete and hysterical list of ACTUAL prayers I prayed when I was growing up . . . and I don't mean ironically prayed. I truly wished and prayed for all these things:

- My earliest memory is begging God to bring a pet leopard into our home. I was so angry that we couldn't get one and I didn't understand "rules" about "wild animals."
- For almost an entire year when I was probably seven or eight, I would beg God to heal my eyes. Yes, I'm aware this is very strange. BUT I had A LOT of faith, and I've had horrible

vision since I was four. I prayed and prayed that God would heal me and give me perfect vision. Once, I even remember laying *my own hands* on my eyes in hopes of healing myself with the hands-on prayer technique I'd witnessed at a church camp.

- Around age ten, I begged God to help me dunk a basketball. This would be the path that would lead to my next fervent prayer, which was the one where I prayed to be the first female in the NBA. You read that right, not the *WNBA* (which wasn't around when I was little) but the *NBA*—you know, the league where only super tall, fast, athletic dudes are allowed in.

- When I was about four years old, I begged my parents to let me move to Africa where I would live off the land and help people who didn't have any food. They said no. Then I thought to myself, "Welp, anything is possible with God, so I'll ask Him." I begged God to somehow create a path that would lead to me living in Africa. Not later on in life, like as a missionary, but RIGHT NOW as a budding young four-year-old. *Crickets* No help from God or my parents whatsoever.

It doesn't take a genius to find the commonalities between childish wishes and child-like prayers. When you see God as a Spiritual Santa of sorts, the whole house of cards comes crashing down. Life doesn't work that way, but I know I don't have to tell you that. Sometimes people pray and their loved one gets healed from cancer. Other times, other people pray (with the same strength of faith and belief) and their loved one dies from cancer. It wasn't until ages seventeen and eighteen that I finally learned life doesn't work that way.

Just because I have faith and belief in whatever prayer I'm sending up to HP, just because I want something so badly I can barely see straight, doesn't mean I'm going to get whatever I asked for. We live in a world where *sometimes* we get what we ask for; other times, we get what we don't ask for; still other times, we don't get what we ask for. It's all a part of the process. I no longer believe in a God who picks and chooses whom to cure of cancer and whom to let die of cancer. He's not making a list. He's not checking it twice. He's not sitting up in the sky on some giant cloud playing a game of "heal from cancer, don't heal from cancer" like I used to play "she loves me, she loves me not" with flower petals.

Paul Selig says it best: "How could you believe that a Creator could favor one over another? How could you possibly believe that God's love is sanctioned—one is approved of, one is not? You are all perfect creations, you are all deeply loved, and the realization of this, truthfully, will and would transform this planet in a second if it were realized in its fullness. You are all loved. You are all perfect in your expression."[3]

Cancer, along with a boatload of other atrocities, sometimes *just happens*. As I'm writing this chapter, I've never been more aware of cancer than I am right at this moment. Last week, I found out my dad has cancer. Thankfully, it hadn't spread, and the doctors said it is 100 percent treatable with radiation. But still . . . you never want to hear the C word when it comes to someone you care deeply about. (The good news: Dad's treatment was a total success, and he is 100 percent cancer free!)

As soon as I found out, I found myself wanting to pray that God would heal my dad of cancer. But I was quickly reminded of my dear friend Carol who lost her battle with cancer many years ago. Same prayers. Different results. Prayer was never intended to serve as a spiritual bypass. It's not a Magic 8 Ball that will pave the way to getting what we want and living the life we've always dreamed of.

Look, here's the deal . . . I don't know what's best for my life. I may think I do, but I don't REALLY know. If I would've planned my life out, I wouldn't be anywhere near where my life actually is today. Today, I see prayer simply as a conversational tool. We make it way too complicated. How do you get to know someone in real life? You talk to them. You have conversations with them, and you get to know them. That's what I think prayer is. Here's what one of my heroes Brennan Manning has to say about prayer:[4]

- Prayer is first and foremost an act of love.
- The deepest desire of our hearts is for union with God. God created us for union with himself. This is the original purpose of our lives.

I believe having open lines of communication with your Spiritual Self, your Higher Power, your fill-in-the-blank is the secret to cultivating this union with God. And I've experienced first-hand how powerful prayer can be when I start seeing prayer as a conversation with Source and not a wish list to a mythical being in the sky. Changing our *perception* of prayer (be they answered or unanswered prayers) will change how we approach the whole experience.

THE PRAYER WITH THE WEIRD NAME

Have you heard of the Ho'oponopono Prayer? Weird name, but it goes like this: "I'm sorry. Please forgive me. Thank you. I love you." Serious true story.

Joe Vitale and Dr. Hew Len in their book *Zero Limits* described the journey of Dr. Len and the power of the Ho'oponopono Prayer (which we will call the Pono Prayer for ease's sake since that H word is very hard to say and type). Here's what they write:

"I had always understood 'total responsibility' to mean that I am responsible for what I think and do. Beyond that, it's out of my hands. I think that most people think of total responsibility that way. We're responsible for what we do, not what anyone else does. The Hawaiian therapist who healed those mentally ill people would teach me an advanced new perspective about total responsibility."[5]

Joe Vitale and Dr. Hew Len got curious about the concept of prayer. The book goes on to say, "I asked him to tell me the complete story of his work as a therapist. He explained that he worked at Hawaii State Hospital for 4 years. That ward where they kept the criminally insane was dangerous. Psychologists quit on a monthly basis. The staff called in sick. A lot of them simply quit. People would walk through that ward with their backs against the wall, afraid of being attacked by patients. It was not a pleasant place to live, work, or visit."[6]

Yet, this is where Dr. Len chose to spend his time. **Except he never saw one patient.**

The more I learned and read about Dr. Len, the more I realized the power of his process and the magical nature behind the prayers he prayed. He makes it clear that his work is not to heal anyone else, but *only himself*. Dr. Len focused on looking inward and walking the talk of "let it begin with me." In light of this, there really are no *unanswered* prayers.

Dr. Len was a psychologist in Hawaii who is known for curing an entire ward of criminally insane patients without ever actually laying his eyes on them. The foundation of his therapeutic approach was to pore over each individual's file. Once he understood the inner workings of the inmate's chart, he would then search inside himself to find commonality with each individual. Yes, this sounds completely insane, but keep reading.

Instead of placing his focus on his patient, he focused on increasing his awareness about his patient while also increasing his awareness about himself and how he contributed to whatever illness the inmate was struggling with. As Dr. Len committed to the work of healing himself, slowly and one by one, the patients in the ward began to heal as well.

So how the HELL did Dr. Len accomplish such a feat?

He utilized a Hawaiian healing process known as Ho'oponopono, a healing process even more unique than its name.

When other psychologists were spending their time, energy, and effort doing normal psychologist-y things, Dr. Len was hunkered down in his office, reviewing patient case after patient case. He spent his days reviewing the inmates' files in-depth and looked inward, working on himself primarily.

What happened next in the ward absolutely blew my mind. The more Dr. Len placed emphasis on working and improving himself, the more freedom and peace were experienced by the patients. Dr. Len tells Joe Vitale in his book that after only a few months of this internal work, the patients who were formerly shackled were given permission to walk freely. Patients who had to be heavily medicated were getting off their meds. And those who had "no chance of ever being released were being freed. I was in awe," the author recounts.[7]

You may be asking yourself the same question the author asked and the same question I asked when I first heard about Dr. Len, which sounds something like this:

Wait, WTF? What on earth did this dude do inside of himself that became a catalyst for change in these criminally insane patients?

When approached with this question, Dr. Len replied, "I was simply healing the part of me that created them."

Here's the gist of what he meant by this answer. "Dr. Len examined that total responsibility for your life means that everything in your life—simply because it is in your life—is your responsibility. In a literal sense, the entire world is your creation."[8]

Look, this is where Dr. Len almost lost me. I'm all about owning it, and I even tell my kiddos, "You mess up, own up." But this? This is far too far. I've done too much work on myself to start taking on other people's crap. I believe what anyone else does or doesn't do is none of my business and not my responsibility. However, I also see the point Dr. Len was trying to make with the way he lived his life both professionally and personally. **His mission was healing**. He understood that total transformational healing comes from within. And it all starts with taking responsibility for your life. Healing for Dr. Len and his utilization of the Pono Prayer translated into one thing: **Loving yourself first**.

You know that friend or neighbor you can't stand? Try this prayer I learned in Al-Anon: "Bless them, change me."

That's definitely a prayer that will be answered.

Don't get it twisted though—this doesn't mean we take on blame for other people's behaviors. All this means is that today I have the choice of taking total responsibility for my life and everything I'm experiencing in it. It's all there for me to heal or not to heal. That really is the question. If you and I are hell-bent on improving something about our lives, there's really only one place to start . . . inside each of us—taking it all very personally.

WHEN YOU LOOK,
DO IT WITH LOVE.

NOW IT'S YOUR TURN

Before moving on to the next few pages, take a moment and think about some of the prayers you may have prayed when you were a kid. What was your concept of prayer (if any) when you were young? Did you see praying as a form of asking a Santa-like God to do things for you and give you things? Or did you see prayer as a conversation between you and your Creator? Between you, the Beloved, and Love Intelligence aka God aka Higher Power aka whatever name you'd like to assign to your HP.

Write down whatever comes up for you. Think about one or two prayers that you fervently prayed and ended up not going the way you'd hoped. Did that "unanswered" prayer end up working out for the best? You prayed for one thing but got another. What was that experience like for you?

I saw prayer the same way I saw the rabbit's foot charm/keychain/trinket that was sold at the skating rink when I was a kid. If I prayed hard enough and had enough faith (and rubbed the rabbit foot into a tangled mat), surely my prayers would be "answered." And my definition of answered was "getting everything I want and ask for because I know what's best for my life."

Do I really though? I don't think so. I believe we're all just trying to do the best we can from day to day, choice to choice. I have no earthly idea what tomorrow holds, but I know Who is holding all our tomorrows with love and grace.

Break It Down for Me

- There may be a good reason we don't get what we ask for. Prayer isn't about getting stuff. It's about maintaining open lines of communication with ourselves and a Power greater than ourselves.

- Prayer is an ongoing, ever-present exchange of authentic communication between us and our Higher Power. In the words of Anne Lamott, "My prayers seem to be filled with 'Gimme, gimme, gimme' and 'Thank you, thank you, thank you,' with very little 'Wow.'"[9]

- Hold on. Don't give up before the miracle. It's coming, and be aware that you may not recognize it as a miracle.

- Our lives are our responsibility and ours alone. Peace can be found in knowing there is no instance in life when we are ever truly alone, despite what our feelings may lead us to believe.

Chapter 8

THE GIFT OF WAITING

"I would be pleased to RSVP as . . . pending."
—Moira Rose, *Schitt's Creek* (S3, E6)

"The best things in life are often waiting for you
at the exit ramp of your comfort zone."
—Karen Salmansohn, *The Bounce Back Book*

Waiting is as much a part of life as breathing. Many times, we are subconsciously waiting, which seems much easier than when we are consciously waiting and aware of that which we wait for. Trying to rush through times of waiting is like trying to press the fast-forward button on my favorite TV show that doesn't allow for rewinding or fast-forwarding because I was too cheap to upgrade the streaming service.

Whether we like it or not, it's in the waiting that we tend to grow the most. It's in the spaces *between* the notes where the truest of all music is felt. And it's in the space *between* the logs where the fire can grow. If we know waiting is an essential part of life, then the question becomes this: How do you and I make the most of our waiting season, regardless of what we're waiting for or whom we're waiting on?

When my daughter Olivia was six months old, she got very sick. We spent hours waiting on her test results from Dell Children's Hospital. Here's how we got to Dell in the first place.

My then-wife, Jenny (now ex-wife whom I'm grateful to successfully co-parent with), and I took Liv to the pediatrician late one afternoon. Based on whatever her doctor saw or noticed during the initial exam, our pediatrician strongly recommended that we go directly to Dell Children's. *Immediately.* When we asked why (trying not to completely freak out) the doctor responded with a long, confusing sentence of which all I heard was "lymphoma." LYMPHOMA?!

We ran out of there as fast as we could and headed straight for the children's hospital. Thankfully, my best friend Catherine was the charge nurse for Dell Children's Oncology Unit at the time and was able to get us right in. My parents met us there. My tiny little six-month-old was terrified, uncomfortable, and cold. The doctors and nurses placed her on the exam table and informed us that a catheter would be required. All of this was due to the blood work they'd seen for Olivia, which reported a dangerously low white blood cell count.

If you're a parent or caregiver of a small child and you're reading this, you know full well the pure angst that crashes through your entire heart, body, and mind when you see one of your littles in pain. There Liv was, helpless. The nurse looked at me and then at Jenny with eyes that said, "Okay ladies, who is going to hold this baby down while we administer this catheter?" Both Jenny and I fell silent.

Before either of us could speak up, my dad volunteered as tribute. "I'll stay with her, let the moms go out. They don't need to see this."

Jenny and I, along with my mom and Annabelle, left the room. We couldn't watch. Unfortunately, however, we heard every single shrill scream and shriek coming from my baby's mouth. I can *still* hear her screams as I type this paragraph. It's true what they say about how our bodies hold all our memories. I felt so helpless as she screamed bloody murder in that hospital room. My heart broke for Liv and for my dad. I don't know what I would've done without him that day. He stepped up in such a huge way. I didn't even realize how badly I needed him in that moment.

Once the catheter was placed, the screaming stopped a bit, but the crying didn't. Afterward, my dad came out to invite us back in so we could hold Liv and love on her. We waited and waited for what seemed like hours for the test results. I still have no idea how much time passed between the catheter placement and the doctor informing us of the good news. Yes, *good news*. I always tend to think the worst, prepare for the worst, but hope for the best. The doctor informed us that Liv *did not* have anything even remotely close to lymphoma. She was fighting an infection, which caused the low white blood cell count, and she would be okay and have a full recovery. Looking back, the gift in that moment was the experience of watching my dad show up in a major way for my baby girl and our family.

EIGHT MINUTES FROM HELL

Toward the end of 2019, my dad had emergency triple bypass surgery. I'll never forget the day my mom called to tell me. I rushed to the local heart hospital to be there with my mom and brother. Those moments are still quite a blur, but there are eight minutes that left a mark that will most likely stay with me my entire life. Allow me to paint the picture of what happened that day.

The surgeons told us that the surgery would take about three hours, and they'd send someone to update us throughout. My mom, brother, and I sat in the waiting room trying to talk about anything other than the fact that Dad was on an operating table, fighting for his life. Both his parents had major heart disease and several open-heart surgeries. I had a feeling my dad would be OKAY, and that felt nice. But also, with these types of surgeries, you never know what might happen.

The surgery had been in progress for only about two hours when a hospital worker came up to us. He was the patient care coordinator or something like that. (Super nice man with kind eyes.) My first thought was one of pure panic: "Wait, it's only been a couple hours.

It's too soon for them to be done. Oh God . . . " I would come to find out later that my brother was having the same exact thought, as well as my mom.

The man asked us to follow him to a different room where families could wait on the surgeon to give an update. We frantically gathered up all our belongings, snacks, and booze, looking like a couple of teenagers whose mom just busted them for snacking in bed and drinking underage. Mom looked very concerned. My brother and I were trying to be strong for her. No one said a word. We just followed the nice man through the hospital while he stayed eerily silent.

I was hoping or expecting some sort of, "The surgery was a success! Now, please wait here where the surgeon will give you an update along with other helpful information. Would you like some pretzels, perhaps a sparkling water while you wait?" But no. That is not what we got that day.

We were led to a room that had the words "Patient Consult" on the door. We walked in, and the room immediately felt cold and isolated. There was a small coffee table in the middle of the room with one item on it: a box of Kleenex. Hmmm, I thought. This doesn't look good.

Once we got settled into the room, the man left. I looked at my phone and the time was 4:47 p.m. There were no magazines with which to distract ourselves. No music to sway our minds away from the worst possible outcome. All I had was my brother and mom. And they were enough. I remember being so thankful that we were all together and we'd always be there for each other. I checked my phone again, it was 4:50 p.m. Then 4:55 p.m. Still nothing. I've never thought so many thoughts in such a short span of time.

There may be power in the waiting, but God knows all I felt in those eight minutes was sheer *terror and panic.* After eight whole minutes, which felt like an eternity, the surgeon opened the door and walked in. No one touched the box of tissues, and Lord knows we didn't want to.

Right as I was about to stand up and scream, "JUST TELL US IF DAD'S OKAY!" the surgeon opened his mouth to speak. I almost wanted to put my hands over my ears. I didn't want to hear whatever he had to say. And I knew once I heard it, I could never unhear it. Much to my surprise and complete AWE, the doctor shared with us the good news about how great the surgery went and that Dad would have a full and complete recovery. He said a bunch more words, none of which I heard, because my thoughts kept yelling, *HE'S OKAY, HE'S OKAY, HE'S OKAY.* After the doctor left our room, my brother, mom, and I all looked at each other in disbelief. We held each other, and there were definitely tears, but not the tears we'd expected to need the Kleenex for. Not one of us was expecting the doctor to have good news. Those eight minutes proved to be very powerful once I was able to process what all happened that day.

It was in those excruciating eight minutes that I began to make peace with whatever would happen with my dad. I knew I'd be okay (somehow) whether Dad died or lived. *Okay* would look all kinds of different ways, and I wouldn't be okay for quite a while, but I knew eventually I'd be okay. And I knew my brother and mom would also eventually be okay. We would lean into one another and grieve together. We would survive. After the first two minutes of total panic during the eight-minute wait, I surprisingly felt a sense of peace wash over me. It was as if God had laid a blanket of comfort over me and my family during those terrifying moments. I was given the gift of believing we would eventually be okay no matter what the doctor said. This was a gift because I knew it was miraculously given to me. I had peace and calm in my heart even though I was 99 percent convinced that I wouldn't see my dad ever again.

Those eight minutes of waiting on that cold afternoon in December of 2019 inserted a new level of strength inside me. I was faced with my greatest fear (losing my dad) but wasn't swallowed by it. My spirit felt strong, despite knowing I was about to endure the greatest battle of sadness my life would ever know.

| **NEVER WASTE THE WAITING.** |

Sometimes we wait for what seems like forever, and other times the waiting is unexpectedly short. Either way, the *people* we choose to have in our metaphorical waiting room are essential to how we experience the very wait itself.

| WHO'S IN *YOUR* WAITING ROOM? |

Who is in your circle of trusted friends and family? Do they make the wait more bearable or less? I wouldn't be the woman I am today without my waiting room people. Waiting can be the worst, but having the right people in our waiting room can make it *suck less*. Think about the people you allow in your life's waiting room, during those impossible times when you're not certain you'll ever see the light of day again. Did you catch the phrase "you allow"? Don't miss that. It's your choice. You and I get to choose whom we allow in our waiting rooms. Choose wisely. For we all know that life can feel a lot like the well-known law commonly known as The Erma Bombeck Law which highlights the mindset of "The other line always moves faster." And it really can seem that way. Some days the other line WILL move faster, and other days your line will move faster. If you and I spend most of our time and energy obsessing over the other line, we will miss all that the waiting seasons have for us.

What if, instead of escaping by grabbing our phones to mindlessly scroll, we did something more productive with our periods of waiting? When is the last time you allowed yourself to be bored? To sit and look at a wall instead of social media? Can you remember the last time you let your mind just wander *and wonder*? There is power in the waiting that I'm afraid most of us are missing out on. We've curated a life surrounded by distractions and ways to get our minds off those periods of boredom or waiting, and it's harming us.

What would our lives look like if we flipped the script on waiting and saw it for what it truly is? An *opportunity*. With a little bit of intentionality and creativity, waiting can lead us to whatever lies in store for us, sometimes just around the corner. Waiting can be wasted, or it can be wielded. It really is our choice. The next time you realize you're in a period of waiting (literally or figuratively), flip the script or throw out the damn script altogether and do something different. Our minds are begging us to let them wander again.

It's time we vigilantly *welcome* the waiting. There exists within each period of waiting a well so deep, filled to the brim with power, that we would be senseless to squander it. Donald Miller writes, "Most of us are waiting. We're waiting for something interesting to happen. And I think we're going to wait forever if we don't do something more interesting with our lives."[1]

Are you reading these words as you sit in a literal or metaphorical waiting room? I'm certainly wrestling with my own present-day waiting as I write these words. It's the most challenging period of waiting I've ever encountered in my life thus far. I wasn't planning on including any of this in the book, but after talking with Brynn and getting her blessing, I know that I *must* include it.

I'M READY TO GET OUT OF THIS WAITING PERIOD, THANKS

A survey conducted by the CDC in June 2020 found that almost 41 percent of U.S. adults reported struggling with mental health during the pandemic. It was 20 percent only *one year* earlier. Three in ten adults in the United States reported symptoms of anxiety and/or depression.[2] I'm one of those three and so is my wife, Brynn.

Toward the beginning of the pandemic, Brynn was diagnosed with anxiety. Thanks to our fabulous doctor, she started taking medicine that helped. Paired with consistent therapy, the medicine helped Brynn feel more like herself. But then, about a year later, we were met with a new diagnosis. While the anxiety had improved, both Brynn and I became aware of a much deeper mental health issue she was battling. After an extremely difficult and painful period of feeling as if our world was spinning completely out of control, Brynn was diagnosed with Borderline Personality Disorder. Since the majority of people have no clue what BPD actually is (and more importantly what it is *not*), allow me to explain using a metaphor.

Imagine being on a rollercoaster that never stops, so you can't ever get off the ride. Add blaring music on top of it coupled with people talking to you nonstop while you're riding and *already* feeling extremely anxious. Just as the rollercoaster brings you up and down at high speeds, BPD can cause intense and rapidly shifting emotions, leading to a constant sense of unpredictability and instability. Think: chaos internally and externally, *every* moment of *every* day. Just as a rollercoaster can be thrilling but also frightening and overwhelming, people with BPD may experience intense emotions that are both exhilarating and distressing. What may be a normal, mundane situation to you, could feel like total chaos and panic to folks struggling with this mood disorder.

Since Brynn received the diagnosis in 2021, we have clung fiercely to each other in what has become the hardest waiting room of all. We both experience this waiting in completely unique ways. For years, I've watched my wife struggle, give up, fight for her serenity, maintain hope, lose hope, strive for healing, give in to hopelessness, and everything in between. Watching the person you love—your person—battle a mood disorder she has very little control over is one of the most excruciating pains I've experienced in my life to date.

And yet, it is also extremely painful for Brynn. Imagine how she feels in this waiting. Imagine how disheartening it is for her to work toward healing in hopes of finding sustainable, lasting peace, only to find that BPD is ever-present. If we could press fast-forward on this healing process, we would. Unfortunately, there's no quick fix or magic pill. There is no cure, as of now. Medicine, therapy, and utilizing Dialectical Behavior Therapy (DBT) skills have been incredibly helpful, but we have a long road ahead.[3]

This mood disorder has wreaked havoc on our individual lives, our marriage, and our family, and it continues to do so. We have good days and bad days. Hard times and unforgettably beautiful times. Brynn is my wife and is also the person who causes me the most pain. I believe that's true for most of us—the people we love the most end up hurting us the most, and we end up hurting those we love the most. I love her with all my heart. And yet, I find it indescribably difficult to stay hopeful sometimes, especially when the waiting room seems to be our new normal. Loving and living with someone who has BPD comes with its unique challenges, as well as unexpected gifts.

Due to the challenges we've experienced over the past few years, I am becoming the woman I want to be. We are both growing by leaps and bounds. We are learning from past mistakes and finding new ways to endure and address the pain of mental illness to find healing and peace. I remember being in the rooms of Al-Anon, where people who'd been in the program for decades would say how thankful they eventually became for the alcoholic in their lives. This always puzzled me and caused me to raise my eyebrows.

But the longer I stay in this waiting room—waiting for Brynn to get better, waiting for the disorder to go away, waiting for past trauma wounds to be healed in hopes of a better tomorrow—the more thankful I become for the role BPD has played in our lives.

I know that might sound insane, and I get it. How could I possibly be thankful for something that has resulted in so much pain and angst? Because (whether I like it or not) it's this *very* waiting room and all I'm experiencing in this season of waiting that has changed me and continues to change me in profound ways.

We have so much to be thankful for. I would not be the person I am today without the experiences I've encountered over the past few years. I am more aware, more resilient, more accepting, more loving, more patient, and more committed to peace and healing than I've ever been in my entire life. As a result of all this exhilarating self-reflection, I've also found new character defects that need serious work.

To share one example, turns out I'm *not* a great listener. I thought I was, but I interrupt people constantly. I chime in too often when I need to keep my mouth shut. Now that I'm aware, I can choose a different path. The wisdom I've gained during this waiting season will be the very foundation upon which the rest of my life will be built.

Pain is the universal human language. It connects us to one another. No one's life is free from it. Pain does not discriminate. And it is in the very waiting that pain is amplified. It all comes up during those moments of waiting *to be healed*. I recently heard this on a podcast, and it hit me right between my eyeballs: "I don't believe things happen for a reason. I think you have to put reason to whatever happens."[4]

This waiting period may never be over, and I have to radically accept that. Brynn and I may always be forced to contend with this unpredictable mood disorder. Or maybe, just maybe, we will get to a place where her BPD is in remission, which is entirely possible. While BPD is considered a chronic condition with no cure, there are instances where people with BPD experience remission in their systems over time. We both believe this is possible and will always hope for this.[*]

UGH, THE AIRPORT
BAGGAGE CAROUSEL

I was at the airport recently waiting for my bags. Instead of looking at my phone to pass the time, I decided to let my mind wander as one bag after another passed me by. Bags come out of the chute and land on the conveyor belt. We all know how this works. The bags go round and round, waiting to be picked up by their rightful owner. If *you* don't step in to awkwardly separate the sea of people while repeating "Sorry, excuse me, sorry," no one else will grab your luggage. We have to make the move and grab our baggage from the conveyor belt.

The more I thought about this, the more I realized how this is my new metaphor for life. How often do we stand at the baggage claim of our lives, bored and staring down at our phones while the bags just keep going round and round? The baggage will keep circling back around until we retrieve it. Obviously, the "baggage" I'm referring to here isn't a suitcase or actual luggage. It's the baggage that you and

---

[*] 2024 update: I'm heartbroken and devastated to share the news that I filed for divorce this past September. I can't go into details for legal reasons, but suffice it to say I had no other choice.

I carry around with us everywhere we go. Baggage from our past, baggage that we are too scared to look at and deal with. We'd rather just watch it, be removed from it, and let it go round and round. We don't really have to pick it up, do we? Maybe someone else can take our baggage. Maybe the conveyor belt will simply stop spinning, and the baggage will disappear.

I've spent far too many years of my life waiting and waiting for the baggage to come back around. Occasionally, when I can't see the baggage, I assume it's gone. Maybe it's been taken care of supernaturally. Maybe it went back up the chute and back onto a plane. Either way, I understand it can feel too hard to acknowledge our baggage and finally, once and for all, take it off the conveyor belt. If we don't face and address and heal from the baggage, we are doomed to take it into our lives and into our relationships.

Think of your life and all your relationships as a conveyor belt. If you don't pick up your baggage and deal with it during the seasons of waiting, it'll keep circling back. It will show up in your relationships and in the very way you interact with the world. It keeps showing up because it *has* to be healed.

Speaking of luggage, think about the lengths we go to so we can fit more in our suitcases. We unzip the zipper, expand the luggage, and stuff as much as we can in there. Then, we go to Herculean lengths to close the suitcase. We will sit on it, lay on it, and recruit others to join us so we can close the damn thing.

Instead of opening the suitcase and bravely looking at what I need to address so I can begin healing, I stuff more in it, shut it, and stand on it, going to great lengths to close it and keep it closed. I don't want to look at something painful from my past or my present, thank you very much. There are some memories from the past that I'd be fine with never looking at again. For all I care, it can stay shut in that suitcase for the rest of my life.

But then life keeps happening, and more baggage arrives. Because we haven't dealt with prior baggage, our suitcases are filled to the brim. We can't just keep buying new suitcases into which we stuff the unresolved baggage from our past. That's no way to live. At some point, we have to stop. We have to step up, get the bags off the conveyor belt, get home to a safe place, and open it up.

If we wait our whole lives without acknowledging the baggage and eventually healing from it, we'll never actually live. We'll be stuck in some random airport watching the bags go round and round. Despite our best efforts and intentions, the bags won't go anywhere. They'll keep coming back until we deal with it. See what I mean about finding power in the waiting? What if I would've just grabbed my phone to scroll mindlessly through social media while waiting on my bags that day at the airport? I would've missed the realization about metaphorical baggage, and you would've missed the marvelous opportunity of reading these words about the crazy ways in which my mind can somehow find a deeper meaning in the mundane.

I sure as hell don't want to get to the end of my life with the realization that I never *fully* lived. I don't want to be the person who stands at baggage claim watching the baggage circling, wasting life away by failing to address it and find ways to grow from it. There's a time for *waiting*, and there's a time for *getting after it*. The true gift is found in the intersection of the two. As you experience your own waiting seasons, remember these words from Gary Ryan Blair: "You cannot afford to wait for perfect conditions. . . . Opportunities are easily lost while waiting for perfect conditions."[5]

Break It Down for Me

- Whether we like it or not, it's in the waiting that we tend to grow the most. It's up to us to make the most of our time in the waiting room.

- Waiting periods can cultivate empathy and compassion for others who are also struggling with challenges and waiting seasons in their own lives.

- Never waste the waiting. There is growth and self-discovery to be found as we learn new things about ourselves and our lives. We develop a deeper understanding of who we are and who we want to be.

- We get stuck and trapped in the waiting when we ignore the baggage that keeps coming up to be healed. Open it up, look at it, address it, and **deal with it to heal from it.**

Chapter 9

THE GIFT
OF TRAUMA

"It took me forever to conceptualize that
core wounds are sacred allies."
—Monika Carless, "The 2 Emotional
Wounds that Cut the Deepest"

"Trauma is a fact of life. It does not, however,
have to be a life sentence."
—Peter A. Levine, *Waking the Tiger*

"It is one thing to process memories of trauma, but
it is an entirely different matter to confront the
inner void—the holes in the soul that result from
not having been wanted, not having been seen, and
not having been allowed to speak the truth."
—Bessel A. van der Kolk, *The Body Keeps the Score*

Everyone's trauma may look different, and trauma shows up in
entirely different ways in each of us. There's no rule book or road map
when it comes to your specific trauma and mine. To this day, so much
of my past trauma still lives in my body, and it's my job, and mine

alone, to do something with it. The work of healing hurts because you're digging up old wounds. But if you and I continue to ignore our trauma and shove it down, it will be the poison that ultimately leads to our demise. Yes, it's that serious.

Look, I wish we could do the spiritual bypass here. You know the one: praying that God would heal you of the trauma. Or begging your Higher Power/The Universe to fix it all in one swipe. Delete the trauma. Reset all contents and settings. As far as I know, there's no trauma easy button. There's not a MasterClass or *Trauma for Dummies* that can tell us how to magically wipe away all the effects of our trauma.

The trauma that has occurred in our lives has taken its toll. For some of us, the trauma *continues* to take its toll. Some days, I feel like I'm driving on a Tollway of Trauma, continually getting charged all the tolls because it permeates every area of my life. Just last night, I was doing bath time with the kids. I was in the middle of washing Annabelle's hair. She asked me how my book was coming along. She's so cute, and I love when she asks me things like that.

I answered and told her the book was coming along wonderfully and that I was in the midst of writing a chapter called "The Gift of Trauma." She thought about that phrase for a few seconds and looked up at me to inquire further: "Mama, I don't remember finding any gifts whenever I was held underwater for all those minutes that one time at summer camp when I was little."

Wow . . . she nailed it. I mentioned one thing about trauma, and she's aware enough to go back into her memories and pull that from her very own past-trauma filing cabinet. I empathized with her and reminded her how terrible that was and how safe she was now. This situation occurred when she was much younger. A couple of kids were playing around in the pool, and Annabelle ended up getting held underwater for longer than typical comfort levels would allow. She was terrified. She survived, but it was clear that moment left a mark. It continues to affect her even now when she's swimming and playing.

All I can do in these situations is ask for wisdom. Take a deep breath, say a quick prayer, and proceed with caution. You never know when those hard-hitting questions will come. But I assure you, those questions rarely come at a good time.

As I rinsed her hair, I explained how it was okay that she hasn't found a gift in that traumatic experience. We talked through it and came through to the other side. I was able to recall a time more recently when she was held under the water at a swimming pool last year. Because of what had happened to Annabelle when she was younger, she knew exactly what to do. I was in the pool and watched this happen. As soon as I saw it, I swam right over to her, but she'd already taken care of the situation on her own.

I reminded her of that memory from last year and asked if she thought she was able to navigate that experience better due to what had happened when she was little. She thought about it for a moment and agreed that maybe there was a tiny gift there. She was ready and able to get out from under those kids last year because her survival instincts kicked in, and she wasn't going to let what happened when she was younger happen to her again.

She paused and seemed to like that answer. Then, I went on to explain a future potential situation: Well, what if in a few years, you're at school sitting next to your friend who looks really sad? What if she starts sharing with you how traumatic her afternoon was the previous day when her brother held her under the water in their swimming pool? She's depressed, scared, and giving into fear—replaying the trauma repeatedly in her head. This friend can't eat, can't sleep, and is having a lot of trouble. She's not been able to talk to anyone about it because she doesn't want to get her brother in trouble, and she doesn't want her parents to worry. What if, just maybe, you are able to share some empathy with her in that moment?

If you felt comfortable, you could look up from your peanut butter sandwich, look her in the eyes and let her know that you've been in a similar situation. You could share your story with her, which could help her process her own story. Your empathy and care in that moment, letting her know you've been in a similar spot and you're there for her if she wants to talk about it, could be exactly what she needs to begin processing what happened and heal.

Annabelle seemed to latch on to this possibility. She sat silently for a few moments pondering the topic of trauma and quietly asked a question: "Mama, do ALL traumas have gifts?"

Insert record screeching sound here

Wow, I thought. What a powerful question from someone so young. I didn't want to be overly Ted-talkee, or too-positive-vibey, and I wanted to be honest with her (as I typically try to do). I paused to give myself some time to answer and finally said three of the most powerful parenting words on the planet: **I don't know.**

THE TRAGEDY OF THE HIT-AND-RUN

As Annabelle and I continued bath time, we discussed how another trauma hit our family hard and also brought us gifts.

Late one night in the summer of 2007, my then-secret-girlfriend Jenny (and now ex-wife) and I were driving home after leading a worship event out of town. I was in the passing lane on a four-lane road going the speed limit—40 mph. In my rearview mirror, I saw a dark SUV approaching *extremely* fast. Within seconds, the SUV had passed me in the right lane, going about 80 mph. It was a residential road, and I couldn't fathom anyone going that fast. As he flew by, I said to Jenny, "That person is going to kill someone." And unfortunately, I was absolutely right.

As he passed us, he sped through a red light in the distance. I saw him hit something, as indicated by his brake lights, which showed the vehicle briefly swerving out of control. However, the brake lights were only on for a matter of seconds before the driver—who would turn out to be a reckless, teenage drunk driver—sped up and continued on his destructive path.

Instantly, I saw something lying in the middle of the road—rather, *someone*. Someone who would become so important to me, I can barely describe it with words. Someone whose family would soon become *my family*. Upon realizing it was a person lying in the road, I stopped the car, blocking traffic, and Jenny and I got out of our vehicle as fast as we could. She called 911, and I ran up to the motorcyclist. He was a young man, wearing a motorcycle helmet, lying there eerily still. His clothing was tattered, and he was unresponsive. I looked ahead about two blocks, and there lay his motorcycle. It quickly became apparent what had transpired.

The dark SUV had struck this young man from behind, knocking him off his motorcycle and sending him and his bike flying through the air. This young man—as we found out later from his parents—was Private First Class Thomas Smith. He was in the Army and had recently gotten back from serving overseas. I will never forget his sweet face. He was unconscious and bloody, his motorcycle jacket torn to shreds.

I remembered from my first aid courses that you're never supposed to move someone who may be at risk for head or spine injury, and you're certainly not supposed to remove a tight motorcycle helmet. Yet, I wanted so badly to remove his helmet, start to administer CPR, and hopefully save his life like I wasn't able to do for Brandon, the boy who drowned when I was seventeen.

But there was something we could do while we waited on EMS. After calling the police, Jenny came to where I was singing to Thomas, and we prayed over him. I continued singing over him with a trembling voice as we waited for help. I couldn't help but obsess over the reckless driver of that SUV. Who would hit someone and then speed on?

I wanted justice so badly I could scream. In fact, all I wanted to do was scream, but I felt that singing would be more comforting to Thomas in those moments. Jenny was able to identify the general description of the SUV, which she shared with the cops. But the car was going much too fast to record the license plate. We don't see a lot of justice in our world, so when we do, it resonates acutely because deep down I think we all hope to see justice served. And it was.

It turned out, the SUV's license plate *fell off* upon impact with Thomas's motorcycle. While the police were surveying the area, asking people around if they'd seen anything, a young policeman walked up and said, "Is this what you're looking for?"

The cop held up the *actual* license plate from that SUV. Within twenty minutes, the police had found the driver. He was speeding on another highway, trying desperately to escape from the scene—*and from himself*, most likely.

Though I was thrilled to hear that they'd caught him, I was filled with intense grief as I thought about the young man whose name I didn't yet know. The paramedics prepared the young man to go in the Life Flight helicopter and be flown to the nearest hospital. I hoped for the best but prepared for the worst. Meanwhile, the cops made Jenny and me sit on separate sides of the road—because we were the only eyewitnesses and they didn't want us comparing notes.

We found out later that the testimonies we gave that night played a crucial role in convicting the perpetrator. I remember being scared in the police van—answering questions about a trauma I was still reeling from, my heart racing, my mind spinning out in a million different directions. Who was this man? Does he live close by? Do his parents know?

The drunk driver was arrested that night and was eventually given a twelve-year sentence. He was recently released, which haunts me from time to time if I'm not vigilant about that thought process. I do fear retaliation, which is why I've changed some details to "protect the innocent" as they say in the 1950s TV show *Dragnet*.

I saw zero gifts in this traumatic situation at first. I didn't *want* to look for any. I also didn't have the slightest clue or grid for the concept of any good coming from something THIS bad. Finding something good in this bad situation felt like it might minimize everything that happened. In a weird yet understandable sense, I wanted to suffer.

Then, about a week after the accident, Jenny's mom saw Thomas's parents on the local TV news, talking about what had happened to their son. Soon after that, Jenny's mom reached out to his family and told them about our involvement that night. His parents asked to meet us, and we made our way to the house Thomas grew up in, the house that he left for the last time on the night of the accident.

Shaking, I rang the doorbell. His parents greeted us with the kindest smiles, and as soon as we walked inside, we embraced. No words were spoken, but lots of tears fell. We hugged, and from that moment on, we've been family to the Smiths.

To this day, my kids call them Oma and Opa. In addition to all the remarkable ways they love us, they've stepped in to fill a void that existed (and still exists to this day) between my kids and Jenny's parents, who *would've been* incredible grandparents. I say "would've been" because upon our coming out to Jenny's parents in 2009, there's been little to no relationship due to their unsupportive beliefs about gay people. Oma and Opa were first in line to volunteer as surrogate grandparents.

The Smiths asked Jenny and me to attend the funeral, which we wouldn't have missed for the world. Not only did we have the honor of sharing with them that their son didn't die alone—that we were there right beside him, praying with him and singing over him—we also got to share that integral part of the story with the standing-room-only crowd at his funeral. Being able to look his parents in the eye and assure them that their baby boy was peaceful in those last moments and didn't die alone, has impacted us all more than I can accurately explain. It reminded me of meeting Brandon's mom for the first time. Her first words to me were, "I want to look into the eyes of the person whose eyes were the last my baby saw."

WE DON'T "GET OVER" DEATH (WE CAN GET *THROUGH* IT)

Oma and Opa are still close family to this day. We've been on adventures together, experienced holidays together, and always celebrate their son's life. I'll never forget attending a grieving group with them and about ten other couples who had lost their children. What I heard in that support group is something I'll never forget, and something I want *you* to never forget. The group moderator asked a general question to all of the parents, and it was this: What is your greatest fear at this point in your loss and grieving journey?

Every single parent answered almost identically, which I paraphrase here:

I fear the moment when people will stop talking about my kid. When people will stop asking about him or talking about him like he's no longer here. I know he's not physically here, but his spirit feels so close to me. Occasionally, if I'm lucky, he visits me in my dreams, and we can spend time together. But no matter what, I fear that my kid will be forgotten someday by this cruel world that just keeps on spinning as if my kid didn't die well before his time. And I never want that *forgetting* to happen. I lost him once, I can't lose him again to the reality that over time, people will stop asking about him, talking about him, and thinking about him.

If you are walking alongside someone who has experienced great loss in the death of a loved one, please remember this. People NEVER simply *get over death*. Death isn't something to "get over." We do eventually move *through* it, and some moments are easier than others. They say that time heals all wounds, and maybe that's true. But the scars can sometimes feel just as painful as the original wound. It's time that we start being as intentional with *grief days* as we are with our friends' and family's birthdays and anniversaries.

At a work conference, I heard a speaker whose perspective on grief and loss blew my mind. Her name is Amy Florian, and she's an expert in working with people who are grieving. Her husband, John, died in a car accident, and her life got flipped completely upside down.

I typically multi-task when I attend virtual conferences, but when Amy spoke, I sat completely still, hanging on to her every word. She talked about something called "marker days." She also talked about *grief* support, not just *death* support. Once the casseroles stop coming and the phone stops ringing, people are left with only their grief. However, this is when we need each other the most.

During her talk, Amy challenged us to do better than simply responding with "I'm sorry." That's powerful and empathetic, yes, but Amy thinks we can go above and beyond that by allowing people to do what they need most—to tell their story. To paraphrase Amy's talk: Instead of focusing on yourself and saying something like "I'm sorry," we need to remember the overriding principle of grief support—that what people need most in those times is to tell their story. It's how we make it real. When something bad happens, we want to make it NOT real . . . but one of the ways we make it real is to hear the words come out of our mouths . . . Instead of saying something about ourselves, ask good questions that invite the grieving person to tell the story. Grieving people are hungry to talk to anyone who is willing to listen to them. Follow their lead, and they'll let you know if they don't want to talk.[1]

This perspective translates perfectly into the area of trauma support. I am not a therapist or counselor, but I know that telling and writing about my trauma stories has been the catalyst for my healing. The more I hear myself speak the words about whatever trauma I'm explaining, the more I witness in real-time how I am a survivor and worthy of not only surviving but eventually thriving, and the more the light gets in and touches those dark crevices of my soul.

LIDS ON LIDS ON LIDS

We need to stop with this obsession that humans should somehow miraculously "be strong" in the face of trauma. The most compelling sign of a resilient individual is someone who can be vulnerable. Do you know how much energy it takes to shove down all the feelings that trauma has caused and continues to cause? To hide your true nature and feelings about whatever has happened to you? To keep the skeletons in the closet? It not only requires a ton more energy, but it prolongs and amplifies the suffering.

I want you to imagine a boiling pot of water. Imagine you're getting dinner ready for the kids and you're making spaghetti. Now imagine the water starts boiling, but instead of putting the noodles in, you grab a lid for the pot. You put the lid on the boiling pot of water. It boils over. So, you grab another lid and put that second lid on top of the first. You continue to add lids. Water keeps boiling and overflowing, making a mess of your already messy stovetop.

This is the scene I see when I think of stuffing down unwanted feelings. We need to go up to the stove, find the knob that corresponds to the burner, and turn the heat down a bit. In this scenario, awareness = turning down the heat. No number of lids would stop a pot of boiling water from boiling over while it's on the highest level of heat. Each time we try to ignore our trauma and the lifelong effects that come along with it, we are ignoring ourselves. Real bravery is finding a way to get to a place where you can safely work through past trauma—ideally with a trauma specialist or therapist of some kind. EMDR worked wonders for me.[2] The more we stuff, the more sideways everything will come out later. Trauma, grief, loss, pain, etc. will find a way to emerge from whatever box you've so neatly tried to tuck it away in.

Remember my story in the chapter "The Gift of Anger" about chucking the basketball at the kid at summer camp? That's exactly what I mean. That's what sideways trauma looks like. So, *how* do we find this elusive gift that trauma may have to offer us? One way I know for certain is to **work through it** if and when you're ready. I've cried a lot of tears with Thomas's family over the years. Did finding the gift of Oma and Opa make the trauma less traumatic? *No.* However, feeling the love I have in my heart for them and seeing the love in my kids' eyes when they see them makes the painful effects of the traumatic event a tad more bearable. It doesn't *redeem* the trauma, but it does *reframe* how I see and experience the trauma then and now.

Is There a Gift in Every Trauma?

Back to Annabelle's question as to whether gifts exist in *every* trauma: I still have no clue. The optimist in me likes to believe that it's true and possible, but I can't say for sure. What I can say for sure though is this: It's worth looking. And there's no hurry.

What I've found, and I wonder if you'll find this to be true as well, is that gifts can come across my path even when (and especially when) I'm not looking or searching. It's when I'm open and willing that I tend to find the tiniest of treasures buried deep in the trauma rubble.

Maybe the trauma is still too raw to even think about any of this—and that's okay, too.

Be mindful of how you respond when someone you know and trust asks you how you're doing and how you're dealing with the loss, whatever the nature of the loss may be. Do you respond, "I'm fine"? If so, consider this acronym that Amy Florian shared with us at the conference: F-I-N-E = Frightened, Insecure, Neurotic, and Exhausted. It's 100 percent FINE to NOT BE FINE. Never forget that. Fuck "fine." It's time for some good ol' fashioned *vulnerability*.

But only when you're ready . . . don't push it and don't rush it. Let it happen. Let it flow. Find the help you need, whether that's EMDR, meditation, therapy, reading, journaling, etc. There's no one-size-fits-all approach to healing and moving trauma through your body and soul. But there *is* one way (or many ways) in which *you* individually can begin to heal in your own unique way and in your own time. There's no going back to normal.

What is normal anyway? Did it ever really exist? I don't think so. Life is one way, and then something happens, and life is never the same. THAT, my friends, is normal. Change is normal. Grieving a loss is normal. Not being OKAY is normal and should be celebrated and honored. Hold space for all of it.

> There are losses that rearrange the world. Deaths that change the way you see everything, grief that tears everything down. Pain that transports you to an entirely different universe, even while everyone else thinks nothing has really changed.
>
> **—MEGAN DEVINE**[3]

Maybe it's time we stopped trying to get *beyond* the trauma. Maybe it's time to pull our emotional sleeves up, get our courageous hands dirty, and **get beneath it**. If we don't, we will live the rest of our lives with trauma trapped inside each of us, and us inside of it.

HARD-WIRED FOR THE F WORDS

Throughout the past few years, my perception of trauma has completely changed, and the entire concept has been flipped on its head. I'm not saying I LOVE trauma now, nor am I saying that trauma is great and everyone should join in the fun! Quite the opposite. I'm simply saying that I now see trauma with new eyes—a new perspective and deeper understanding of the power of trauma.

Once I began to understand the role that guilt and shame play when it comes to my feelings about trauma, the world broke open for me. For the majority of my life, I've carried around heaps upon heaps of guilt, feeling shame for how I've responded to trauma and the ways in which I've tried to survive. But the truth is that it's human nature to want to hide our trauma.

We're hard-wired for fight, flight, and freeze—so we shouldn't be surprised by how we respond to fearful situations that threaten our sense of safety and security. Sometimes, the victim mindset in me wants to stomp her feet and yell, "This isn't fair!" I want to be able to express my feelings and feel all my emotions fully, but I don't want to hurt anyone. I want to be honest with myself about how I feel, but what if all those big feelings completely swallow me whole?

Anytime someone or something triggers us, it's rarely about *them*. As much as it pains me to say, it is more about you and me than we may think. We all know it'd be much easier to focus on someone else's issues instead of having to worry about our own. But that's not realistic nor sustainable. It starts with rigorous self-honesty. We can lie and present a total façade to others, but it's much harder to deceive ourselves for a long period of time. The work is to tune in to that part of us that is yelling about how unfair life is. Embrace the little child inside you who is throwing a fit. There is a very good reason she's throwing a fit. Don't waste that fit.

Tune in to that part of you that knows what she wants but doesn't feel like she can have it. We need to become okay with expressing our thoughts and feelings *to ourselves*. This isn't something that just happens. I've spent decades feeling things I was never really aware of.

I could always tell you exactly what everyone around me was feeling (thanks to being a type A empath), but I could rarely express what I was feeling.

If you also struggle with this tendency of being hyperaware of what others are feeling and experiencing while being mostly blind to your own feelings and emotions, I'd encourage you to ask the following question and possibly journal about it:

Why are you not allowing yourself to **be honest with yourself** about how you feel—how you *really* feel? Is there something that's preventing you from processing what you're feeling? What is prohibiting you from fully experiencing these feelings and emotions in your body?

CONSIDER MY PROCESS FOR PROCESSING

I'd like to share what tends to help me in these situations of pain and panic when I'm triggered and having big feelings bubble up. I start by becoming aware of the feeling. Then, I identify the feeling and ask my heart, "What's the best way for me to process this feeling?" I feel it fully in my body, no matter how long it takes. I usually ask for help in allowing myself to feel this fully in my body.

Next, I ask myself where the feeling is currently living in my body. Said another way: "Where do I feel this feeling or emotion in my physical body?" There's magic in this mindfulness, and there's immense peace on the other side of practicing awareness of what's going on in your body.

Maybe for you, it's the feelings of fear and guilt that come from your own run-ins with trauma. Or maybe you feel so much anger and rage that you physically can't handle feeling all of it. There's no *one place* it's living because it's systemic and seems to be running rampant throughout the entire body. That's okay, too.

After taking the step to identify *where* this feeling is manifesting in your physical body, it's time to fully acknowledge the feeling and stare the emotion directly in the eyes. Sometimes I'll even say out loud, "I acknowledge this fight/rage emotion in me, and I understand that it's coming from my trauma and showing up as a trauma response. There's a reason I want to kick a hole in this drywall." Then, I look for the guilt and shame because they're always there. Once I locate that dynamic duo, I also acknowledge the guilt and shame I'm feeling for wanting to kick a hole in the wall. Or maybe I've already kicked the hole in the wall, and I'm feeling guilty about that.

THIS is the core of everything. Whether your trauma response is fight, flight, freeze, or a bad case of the fuck-its (or a combo of all four), you won't have to look too hard before you find guilt and shame swirling around those trauma responses. My rage and anger in those moments are tied to the fight response. My debilitating fear that leaves me feeling paralyzed is tied to the freeze response. I've found that there's always a little bit of freeze in my fight. Feeling paralyzed is the freeze. Or maybe for you, it's all about the flight. All you can think of doing is running as far away from the pain as possible whenever you get triggered or experience trauma.

WHO INVITED PITY TO THE PARTY?

I've written a lot about guilt and shame, but there's a third culprit who mustn't get away without being noticed and called out. This one's name is Pity. You know the one: feeling sorry for yourself or others. After this trauma response loop is triggered, I sometimes float into the land of pity. I start to feel sorry for myself and all the pain and trauma I've experienced in my life. Or if I notice a trauma response in a loved one, I find myself feeling sorry for them. Allow me to share a hard truth with you that I have learned recently.

Whenever I'm feeling sorry for someone else, it means I'm feeling sorry for myself, too, in some capacity. Let me clarify.

You can feel bad for someone and have pity on them like you would if you saw a toddler drop his ice cream on a germ-infested floor. That's not the kind of pity I'm talking about here. The type of "feeling sorry for" or "pity" feelings I'm referring to are those with the "well, bless her heart" energy. Some of you who didn't grow up in the South may not fully grasp the point I'm attempting to make. I call it the "bless your heart" back-handed insult shrouded in a façade of concern and care. You've heard it before, I'm sure.

It's when a seemingly polite person tells you some juicy gossip about their niece who is bow-legged, smells bad, and appears to have zero life skills. No matter what Karen says about her niece, she believes that if she follows the statement with "well, bless her heart," then anything goes.

When I feel this pity, I am actively and unconsciously giving away my energy. I become aware of the guilt and shame I feel about feeling that way. I then work to forgive myself for the guilt and shame I experience as a result of feeling sorry for myself or another person. When I pursue self-forgiveness and rigorous self-acceptance, the energy and power come right back to me. The energy knows what to do.

If I truly feel pity for someone, I'm giving them a part of who I am, in a sense. It's not necessarily wrong to feel *sorry* for someone, but it becomes problematic when we're not yet aware of why we're doing this. Why are we feeling sorry for this person or ourselves, for that matter? Do we believe they need us to heal them and rescue them? Dissect the pity to ensure it's coming from a place of compassion and empathy, not patronization or condescension. I used to think people needed saving and they needed me to do it. I've since broken this Messiah Complex stronghold, but the residual effects remain.

The more I try to spend my energy on saving and rescuing others, the less energy I have left to rescue and save myself.

Denying the existence of our trauma responses of fight, flight, and freeze and simply hoping they will go away eventually is the very reason our trauma responses seem to be getting worse over time. If I bury flight, it will come out sideways all wrapped up in fight or freeze. Let's take rage and anger, for example. Getting rid of the rage is to acknowledge it. Move. Be aware of the other feelings of trauma that come up as a result of whatever is triggering you.

Imagine you're playing whack-a-mole at an arcade. Feelings and trauma responses can be a lot like the moles that keep shooting up after we've whacked other ones down. The same thing happens with our fight, flight, and freeze responses to trauma or triggers—they just keep coming back up.

When the mole of anger and rage comes up, I don't have to stop it or try and beat it down with a mallet. My job is to simply become aware of what I'm feeling and try not to punch a hole in the door. Get curious to see if there's an opportunity to be found in this trigger and subsequent response. Each situation where we get triggered is an opportunity for us to practice awareness, acknowledgment, acceptance, and then action. Take a breath when triggered. Pause. Breathe. Ask for help. Put the mallet down. You may have to practice this numerous times a day. But stay with it, stay in the moment, and be present with whatever you are feeling.

YOUR MISSION (SHOULD YOU CHOOSE TO ACCEPT IT)

The next time you feel the twinge of fight, flight, freeze, or fuck-it, I encourage you to be present with the emotion. Remember that it most likely has to do with trauma. Forgive yourself of any guilt and shame that resulted from these trauma responses. Pay attention. Start asking yourself what the trigger, trauma, or trauma response is there to teach you. Consider what will be most appropriate for you and healing for you so you can be ready the next time the trauma comes up and shows itself. How will you respond so you can avoid falling into the same reaction patterns?

All of this is coming up to be healed, and it will keep coming to the surface until healing is experienced. It's not a one-time thing, unfortunately. Sometimes I practice these principles numerous times a day. It's okay. You *are* okay, even if you're *not* okay. We don't have to freak out and completely lose our shit (though I know it feels like that's the only option sometimes). Trauma responses will surface without warning, and we can't control them. We can find peace and acceptance in knowing these responses are coming up and happening to *help me let go* of the residual effects of the trauma. The medicine can be found in tuning into these feelings. The medicine and subsequent breakthrough *is* the gift.

If you feel it's a safe time to do this, and you're in a relatively healthy safe space mentally, I encourage you to write some thoughts down as they come to your awareness. Consider jotting down whatever comes up for you as you read the following questions:

- What did you feel in your body as you started reading this chapter?
- How does your body feel now, and what does it need?
- Have you yet noticed a gift hidden in any of the traumatic events in your life?
- Do you have unresolved trauma that still needs work and healing?
- Are you willing to do the work? What fears are coming up for you?
- Write about what comes up as you read the following two quotes:

> "Traumatized people chronically feel unsafe inside their bodies: The past is alive in the form of gnawing interior discomfort. Their bodies are constantly bombarded by visceral warning signs, and, in an attempt to control these processes, they often become expert at ignoring their gut feelings and in numbing awareness of what is played out inside. They learn to hide from their selves."
>
> —Bessel A. van der Kolk[4]

"Trauma is personal. It does not disappear if it is not validated. When it is ignored or invalidated the silent screams continue internally heard only by the one held captive. When someone enters the pain and hears the screams healing can begin."

—Danielle Bernock[5]

Break It Down for Me

- You may never find a single gift buried under the rubble of your specific trauma, and that's okay. Keep the door open for the possibility anyway. It may surface when you least expect it.

- We don't ever get over trauma, but with help we can eventually move through it.

- Drop the whack-a-mole mallet and pot lids and get to work when you're ready to start the journey of healing.

- Our bodies hold all of the trauma that has happened to us, which leads to a feeling of a chronic lack of safety. Respond with curiosity and commit to unlearning how to hide from ourselves.*

*Disclaimer: I wrote this song when I was in the thick of evangelical Christianity. Please don't let that ruin the overarching theme of the song. When you hear the words "Jesus, where would I be without your sovereignty?" feel free to automatically translate to whatever may more appropriately align with your faith tradition and beliefs. I *used to* believe Jesus was in control of *everything*, calling the shots. My spirituality has evolved past that earlier sentiment, and I no longer believe that ultimately every single thing that happens is a result of God's divine, sovereign will. However, I still wanted to include the song because it has been so impactful to me and so many others. If I could rewrite it, I might sing, "Love, where would I be without your grace and peace."

Chapter 10

THE GIFT OF LEAVING

"What now? Do I leave everything behind and move to some random island to be with the love of my life? Because I did that with Harry Styles in England and it was, like, too rainy."

—Alexis Rose, *Schitt's Creek* (S6, E8)

"Some cause happiness wherever they go; others whenever they go."

—Oscar Wilde, *The Duchess of Padua*

Here's the thing about leaving: we've been taught that we have to leave in order to go somewhere new. Some may even say that leaving is bad or has a negative connotation.

I used to think this too: if you left, it meant you were scared or let fear get the best of you. I always felt so bad for the kids whose parents left them. "Leaving" was never associated with anything positive. Leaving can be excruciating, especially as you get older. But every end is essentially a new beginning. Out with the old and in with the new, we've all heard it said. If you've ever left a job or unhealthy relationship, you know what I'm talking about.

In my experience, I've come to believe that leaving is actually the *most* challenging part. Once you've made the decision to leave, those first few steps to whatever new horizon you're headed toward make the subsequent steps much easier to take. I think that's true with most—if not all—things in life.

There's a difference between *leaving* in the sense that you are escaping and running away from something, without anything to run to, and *leaving* in the sense that you are leaving good for *great*. Said another way, you are walking in your power and boldness to leave something or someone that no longer serves you and your vision for your life. You may be leaving a construct or paradigm of thinking. Either way, there comes a point in all of our lives when we know it's time to get the hell outta Dodge.

Disclaimer: Please resist the urge to use this chapter as justification to leave a situation that you might not actually need to leave yet.

I believe we'll each come to a point where we know deep in our gut that it's time to leave an abusive marriage, a dead-end job, a toxic group of friends, a Bikram yoga class, a conversation that's going nowhere and simply inflicting pain, the shame of the closet, the comfort of a life you've falsely constructed to keep you from taking any risks and experiencing failure, and so on. When you reach that point, where you know in your gut it's time to move on and transition from something to something else, and you know you're not simply running away from the first thing, but you're running TO something that will lead you further down your path to wholeness, that's when the rubber meets the road.

No matter where you are in your journey, leaving should *never* be taken lightly. Deciding to leave (regardless of what or whom you're leaving) is an excruciating decision when it comes to the stuff of life that really matters.

And the danger is that in this move toward new
horizons and far directions, that I may lose what I have
now, and not find anything except loneliness.

—SYLVIA PLATH[1]

I WOULD KICK YOU IN THE TEETH

In the middle of my junior year in high school, during a ride in the car, my dad told me we'd be leaving Midland, Texas, where I'd lived my whole life, and moving to Austin for his job. I hated everything about that car ride. I was in the backseat directly behind my dad, who was driving me to soccer practice. He said, "Lulu, what would you say if I told you we are moving to Austin?"

What I said was something I never thought I'd ever say to anyone, much less my dad. I blurted out, "I would kick you in the teeth." Not my best moment. I was filled with so much anger. I was about to be the starting point guard on a 5A public school basketball team, just another step on my journey to play for the Texas Tech Red Raiders. That was my dream, and it all got crushed in the car that day.

I didn't end up kicking my dad in the teeth, and we did end up moving to Austin. All I knew about Austin was that everyone there was a liberal Democrat, people walked around topless, and they worshipped a local legend named Leslie, a man who dressed up in women's clothes and wore a thong. (It is worth noting that I shared a pizza with Leslie more than a decade ago, and it was the best pizza experience of my life.)

Yet leaving Midland ended up being the best thing that could've happened to me in high school. I left everything I'd ever known. I left my friends, family, faith community, and the kingdom of popularity I'd built there. But as I look back, I was headed down the wrong road. Unbeknownst to me, I desperately needed the rubber to meet a totally different road—and Austin was that road.

We moved in right around Christmas day. I had no friends, nothing to do, and the basketball gym was closed over the holidays. *What kind of a hell was this?* I thought to myself. The road I was on in Midland was filled with families trying to keep up with the Joneses— whoever those people were. I was obsessed with being perfect, being the best at everything, getting straight As, getting a full-ride scholarship to Tech, and becoming the best female basketball player in the history of the world.

As I sat there, alone and lonely in this new house in this new city, I somehow found my mom's old guitar, which was barely functional and missing a string. I picked it up and started to play. In a world that had stopped making sense, this guitar seemed to make sense. It was as if I'd finally heard something that I'd subconsciously always longed to hear. Within a few months, I'd taught myself how to strum and play basic chords—I even wrote my first song. I kept playing and singing and writing songs, and that became my new road. I'd been forced to leave Midland, and now I'm thankful for that.

One of my favorite authors, Henri Nouwen, beautifully describes the joy and pain involved in leaving:

> Every time we make the decision to love someone, we open ourselves to great suffering, because those we most love cause us not only great joy but also great pain. The greatest pain comes from leaving. When the child leaves home, when the husband or wife leaves for a long period of time or for good, when the beloved friend departs to another country or dies . . . the pain of the leaving can tear us apart. Still, if we want to avoid the suffering of leaving, we will never experience the joy of loving. And love is stronger than fear, life stronger than death, hope stronger than despair. We have to trust that the risk of loving is always worth taking.[2]

LAYERS OF LEAVING

I wouldn't be where I am today if we didn't leave Midland for Austin. Instead of going to Texas Tech and playing basketball, I went to Texas A&M and played music. Instead of becoming a basketball coach and marrying my high school sweetheart, I became a full-time singer/songwriter recording artist and married a chick. Hell, now I've married two chicks so . . . you just never really know, do you? (To clarify, I was married to one lady, then we divorced, and years later I married a second lady, Brynn.)

I thought leaving Midland and moving to Austin was hard until I realized what true pain and horror can come from leaving. I experienced first-hand the gift of leaving when I found myself kicked out of evangelical Christianity in 2009. As I previously wrote about my painful coming out experience, leaving the closet was both the hardest and best decision I've ever made. I was terrified of what might happen when I actually got up the nerve to leave everything I'd ever known in regard to my faith.

Forced Out of the Closet

I'm going to tell on myself here. I didn't really come out of the closet or leave the evangelical machine. At least, I didn't get to do it *on my own terms*. I was forced out, and it turns out that's exactly what I needed. My then-partner's mom outed me to pretty much everyone within weeks of me coming out to her. We chose to come out to Jenny's parents first because they were the liberal, pot-smoking hippies who raised Jenny to love, welcome, and accept everyone. We figured if it didn't go well with telling my parents, at least we'd have somewhere to go for the holidays that year.

Much to our surprise, Jenny's parents were not supportive. That's putting it lightly. Her mom then took it upon herself to share a story that was not hers to share. She shared it with my friends and family and sought out organizations and churches with whom I'd led worship. In fact, she even went so far as to Google my dad's law firm, find his office number, and called him while he was at work to tell him that his daughter was gay.

This might sound crazy, but I'm now thankful that she outed me because I'm honestly not sure I could've left on my own. I was too scared, too wrapped up in my identity as "Lindsey Kane," and way too involved in the entire experience. These were my people. This was my community. I'd led these folks in worship, prayed with them, cried with them, and celebrated with them. I sang at their weddings and their funerals. I knew I needed to get out, but I had no clue *how* to go about doing that.

Thankfully (and I've done enough therapy to be at a point where I can genuinely express gratitude for this), I am eternally grateful *to this day* for HOW I was outed. It left me no choice but to leave and move on to what God had for me, which was so unimaginably better. I had to leave the evangelical Christian community in order to find a true community that had unconditional love and no hidden agenda. I had to leave the God of my youthful understanding behind in order to connect with my true Higher Power, whom I call God/Source/Love. Leaving the evangelical Christian community is what enabled me to pursue my life's higher purpose. I didn't realize until many years after coming out how constrained my life was by the fundamentalist-dark-side of evangelical Christianity.

God cannot be bound by any certain religion, denomination, or faith construct. Though I absolutely and unashamedly left the "church," I never for a second left my relationship with God. I left a false construct that I didn't even realize was the opposite of what I knew in my heart. Sunday school teachers would emphasize the exclusivity of the gospel. They said that everyone who didn't accept Jesus as their personal Lord and Savior would spend eternity in hell. That sure wasn't the God I had come to know, love, and trust. The Jesus I knew and know deeply to this day was altogether loving and **made room at the table for anyone and everyone.**

I was also taught (either overtly or covertly) that homosexuality was an abomination, drinking leads to alcoholism and drug use, and pre-marital sex would get me pregnant and scar me for life with an STD, maybe two. My faith was fear-based. Fear-based faith will always crush the light. But not forever. One of my favorite scriptures in the Bible says this: "Where the Spirit of the Lord is, there is FREEDOM."[3] 2 Corinthians 3:17 (that's SECOND Corinthians, not TWO Corinthians, in case you're wondering).

As I continued to walk in the way of authenticity, pursuing my genuine self and pursuing a much more real relationship with God, I found more and more freedom. Staying in the closet is what sucked all the oxygen out of the room of my soul. That season of leaving the closet and thus the church was filled with newfound moments of deep, full breaths of freedom. I didn't leave the church for the woman I'd fallen in love with. I didn't leave ministry for a gay "lifestyle." I didn't leave God, period.

I LEFT FOR ME.

I chose me. I chose love. I chose a deeper relationship with God than I'd ever known. I chose authenticity, and I chose faith. It brings me deep pain when I hear of LGBTQ+ people who feel they must choose between their sexual orientation or gender identity and their faith. You may need to hear this today, so I'm going to say it: you don't have to choose between your faith and your sexuality or gender identity. It's not a mutually exclusive either/or proposition.

GOD IS ALL ABOUT THE BOTH/AND.

You can hold on to your faith and also be *fully* yourself. Take a deep breath and read that again. You don't have to choose between the two. I know you may think you do, but you don't. From the moment I stepped out of that dark closet and into the light of all that God had planned for me, I found a deeper relationship with my Higher Power than I ever thought possible. I knew deep in my bones that God loves me *unconditionally*. God created me exactly as I am, and I was created *to create*. I couldn't even fathom living a legacy because I was so obsessed with leaving one. It's in the leaving that I found my way. Leaving the lie I'd been living for far too long is what fueled the very life I was created to live—the abundant life, the ten-out-of-ten life that is above and beyond anything I could've ever asked, thought, dreamed of, or imagined.

But it wasn't easy. In fact, those were incredibly dark times with many dark nights of the soul. I'd lost countless friends and family relationships. My albums were pulled from Christian bookstores. I was threatened by the entire legal team of one of the largest Christian organizations in the country (whose name I can't include here for legal reasons). My best friend looked me in the eyes and accused me of "spitting on the cross of Christ." I was cyberbullied and even received a few death threats. I lost those closest to me, but not once did I want to turn back. I knew I was doing the right thing, despite how excruciatingly painful it was. And still is sometimes, even today.

It's Not About the Destination

Leaving caused loneliness. I desperately feared loneliness. As American psychologist Matina Horner puts it, "To 'feel less alone' is, without doubt, an ultimate quest of all life, yet perhaps never before has loneliness been so widespread as it is today."[4] Yet, I found God in those lonely moments. I found me. I found the intersection of faith and sexuality which gave me the strength to reconcile the two. I hurt a lot of people when I left ministry, the church, and my closet. But sisters, I assure you, I was hurting myself way more by staying.

What good am I if I gain the whole world but lose my soul? There's a reason I became more and more physically sick, depressed, and anxious as I crawled deeper into the closet to hide my sexuality from ever getting out and ruining my ever-growing Christian music career.

> I realized that there's a big difference between
> deciding to leave and knowing where to go.
> **—ROBYN SCHNEIDER**[5]

Sometimes we leave and we won't know where to go. We won't know where we'll end up, but the destination isn't actually *that* important. What's essential is taking those first few steps. The game changer is when you take steps one, two, and three *immediately* after you do the leaving.

THE WANDERING ELEPHANTS

I love elephants, always have and always will. When I think of one of the world's most majestic creatures, I think of elephants. In fact, when I was in Kenya back in 2014, I saw droves of elephants in their natural habitat. One came so close to me, I could've reached out with at least one, maybe two, selfie sticks and scratched its cute little (HUMONGOUS) head. Elephants have mastered the art of leaving and wandering without having the confidence of where they're going or where they'll end up. According to a fascinating NPR segment I heard one morning while driving to work, a group of 15 wild elephants found their way into a Chinese city after wandering for over 300 miles on a journey that took a year.

"Along the way, they have traversed forests, forded streams, tromped through villages and towns, broken into farms and raided crop fields. One young elephant was even reported to have become drunk after snarfing down a stash of fermented grain used to make liquor."[6]

Though the segment title reads "Elephants Wandered Hundreds of Miles into a Chinese City. Nobody Knows Why," the article is clear about the *why*. The biggest reason experts think these large mammals left the comfort of their nature reserve has to do with a search for resources. The segment goes on to say that elephants keep moving to avoid risks and danger and to find food and water. They move for social reasons and to find mates.

But the part of the article that jumped out at me the most had to do with a few experts presenting the option of simply taking the group of elephants back to where they came from. Elephant expert Joshua Plotnik had a brilliant response to this: "If you move them back but you haven't dealt with the reason they left in the first place, they may just leave again . . . In fact, I'd be pretty confident they would."

How many of us can relate to this? How many times have you or someone you've known attempted to leave and then leave and then leave again, except their sole focus is on *what* they're leaving behind, not necessarily why they're leaving and where they're leaving TO?

Unless you and I get curious about *why* someone has left a situation, or more importantly why *we* have left or are considering leaving a situation, we'll just keep repeating the same patterns.

I have a friend who jumps from job to job to job. She can't find happiness in her current job, so she keeps chasing the next job over there where the grass is sure to be greener. Yet, with each job change, she ends up in the same place mentally, emotionally, spiritually, and psychologically. As the old saying goes, wherever you go, there *you* are—meaning we can't escape ourselves. We can move and live in countless different places and move to a variety of different job roles, but guess whom we take with us always? Ourselves.

There's a temptation to leave when your needs are no longer being met. I get that. But before you start your 300-mile journey, make sure you know why you're leaving and what you hope to accomplish. How will this time be different? What can *you* do to play more of an active role in blooming where you're planted instead of constantly searching for that next flowerpot? If you get married and divorced, but then refuse to work on yourself to grow and learn and become a better version of yourself post-divorce, you'll most likely end up running into another marriage that might also end in divorce. If we stay stagnant and keep doing what we've always done, thinking with the same mindset that got us where we are (yet where we don't want to be), we'll stay stuck. We will stay in captivity.

Having the *choice* to leave is empowering. That, in a sense, is the gift, not merely a means for escaping.

WHAT DO YOU NEED TO LEAVE?
WHO DO YOU NEED TO LEAVE?
WHY DO YOU NEED TO LEAVE?
DO YOU ACTUALLY NEED TO LEAVE?

If you don't know, that's okay. You'll know when the time is right—if that time ever comes. And sometimes, the leaving process will begin before you're even aware of it. In fact, something may already be set in motion that just might give you the small ounce of strength you need to let go—something that you're completely unaware of. As Ray Bradbury writes: "Learning to let go should be learned before learning to get."[7]

Don't leave out of fear. Don't just bail and leave out of cowardice. Don't leave because you're hell-bent on getting something different. If you're going to leave, do so with intention and purpose.

LEAVING AN ABUSIVE SITUATION

If you're reading this and you're currently in an abusive relationship, get the hell out as soon as you can. Easier said than done, obviously. Of course, you're scared; you may be scared for your life. Please don't go it alone. I know it's not that simple. It's not a clear-cut, black-and-white scenario when it comes to leaving an abusive relationship or friendship. Reach out to someone you trust, and start making a safety plan if you haven't already. A nugget of wisdom I heard in the rooms of Al-Anon once: "You don't have to like the situation you're in. But you do need to like yourself in the situation."

It's not easy. In fact, in some cases, it's a matter of life and death. And it won't happen overnight. I believe there's an essential distinction that must be made between the leaving I'm writing about in this chapter, and the leaving associated with abuse. If you're going to a church right now and you're being told that divorce is not an option, even in cases where abuse is involved, or that you're somehow *less-than* if you get divorced . . . please leave that church. Forever. Never look back.

Look, I know what you might be thinking: *Is this chick really going to attempt to try and convince me that there's a gift in an abusive situation?* No. I am *not* going to say that at all. Will you find gifts when you get out of the abusive situation and get to the other side? Maybe. But only time will tell. Leave that for later. First, right now, in this moment, instead of even attempting to find a gift in an abusive situation, **get out**. Find a way to take care of yourself in the situation and work toward getting out of it as soon as possible.

If you keep telling yourself it's going to get better, despite seeing zero improvement from whoever is abusing you, you will prolong the inevitable and exacerbate the suffering. And for God's sake, PLEASE don't blame yourself. No matter how much of a professional gaslighter your abuser may be, never take that blame upon yourself. What would you tell your best friend, sister, or daughter if she was in the exact same situation you are in now? What advice would you give her?[8]

Write it down. Then read and ingest your own words.

A quote commonly attributed to Henry David Thoreau says, "Don't go where the path may lead, but go where there is no path and leave a trail."[9] And always remember to search for guilt and shame, as they are hell-bent on keeping you in your suffering.

LEAVING 101

Always be mindful and aware of potential gifts that may be found along the *leaving path* you're on. When you take those first few terrifying steps toward wherever you're headed once you make the decision to leave that relationship, organization, etc., it may not feel liberating at first—or who knows, maybe it will. Either way, it's not going to go according to plan.

I expected my coming out journey to look a certain way. I had it all planned out to minimize the impact of the pain I knew would come from leaving the closet and, thus, my career. What happened in reality was horrific—initially. I'm so incredibly grateful I didn't quit before I found the gift or turn around and go back into the closet because shit got real hard there for a while.

Your leaving journey won't happen as you're expecting it to happen. By the same token, the gifts resulting from leaving will also most likely come in a way that you are least expecting. Leave FOR something better. Many of us know what we want to leave *from*, but how many of us truly know what we want to leave *TO*? You don't have to have all the answers or see the full picture before taking that first step.

There was an old Bible song I learned as a kid about God's words being a "lamp unto my feet and a light unto my path." I can't remember exactly where or when I first heard this next concept, but it stuck with me and bears repeating here: God's Spirit and the words that flow to us from that love are a lamp. Back in the good ol' biblical times, folks used oil lamps. These lamps were helpful, sure, but they only gave off a tiny bit of light—not even enough to light up a room. The lamp won't show you the whole path, just as love's messages to our hearts give juuuuuust enough light for whatever step comes next on the leaving path. One foot in front of the other, one single and solitary step at a time.

As you keep in lockstep with spirit, you will eventually end up in the right place. That doesn't mean the journey will be a nice, neat, straight line, but you'll get from point A to point B somehow, some way. You can be sure of one thing on this unknown path: you'll never be able to see the whole path. You'll have a lamp unto your feet, the ones directly under you. How often do we get caught up obsessing over other people's journeys and their feet? How often do we let the comparison trap keep us from hopping on our own road to see what we are made of? I know it's hard. We all want a flashlight to point the way!

But that's not where faith is built. Our faith is strengthened in the step-by-step process. We have enough light for the next step but not the whole path or staircase. I don't know about you, but if I had a flashlight to show me the full path and where I would end up, I'd probably never start the journey. This is why I just keep on walking in the direction of my vision and dream for my life. One step at a time, one day at a time, and one choice at a time.

Instead of complaining about the lack of the full flashlight wisdom, strive to be grateful that you have a path and know the next step thanks to your good ol' oil lamp. All you and I really need is enough light for the next step on that dark road. There's no Holy Spirit bypass, and there are no shortcuts to make leaving easier. The hardest part is when you and I finally make a choice to take the *first* step of leaving whatever it is we feel called to leave.

We can and must take that first step, even if we don't know where we're going. We know regardless of where that might be, we will be held in that moment and in all the moments before and after, by *love*.

> Remember that the minute you take your first step
> into the life of your dreams, the first to greet you
> there will be fear. Nod. Keep walking.
> **—BRIANNA WIEST**[10]

Break It Down for Me

- Stay laser focused on the journey, not the destination. Taking the first step always makes it easier to take subsequent steps.

- Leaving will tear us apart. Yet, we can't avoid the suffering of it. If we try avoidance, then we will also inadvertently avoid the joy of loving and truly living.

- Sometimes we need to leave our preconceived notions and comfortable beliefs behind in order to find a deeper, truer version of faith or spirituality.

- If you return to whatever or whomever you've left (or something similar) but haven't dealt with the reason you left in the first place, you will most likely end up leaving again and going right back to where you started.

SAGE THAT SHIT

Chapter 11

THE GIFT OF LOSS

"If you rid a woman of her head and limbs you can't really expect her to do anything other than roll around."
—Fleabag, *Fleabag* (S2, E4)

"It's funny to think about the things in your life
that can make you cry just knowing that they
existed, can then become the same thing that makes
you cry knowing that they're now gone."
—Ted Lasso, *Ted Lasso* (S2, E1)

Recently, I heard a story on NPR about a gigantic tree. "The city of Vancouver, Washington, is mourning the loss of one of its oldest and most beloved residents. Fondly referred to as a matriarch, she was born in 1826 and is survived by an untold number of descendants . . . it began with a love story."[1]

Long ago, after a young British lieutenant ate an apple for dessert at his going away party, his lover took the apple core and begged him—should he find himself thinking of her—to plant the seeds from it as soon as he arrived at his new wilderness home. He did as she asked. Years flew by, and an apple tree flourished with bright green apples. This tree became the head honcho mama of the entire apple industry in the state of Washington. Eventually, some assholes started chopping these prolific apple orchards down. Once the axeholes (see what I did there) came for head honcho mama apple matriarch, the community said NOPE and fought for the old tree. Much later in its life, a crack finally appeared in its trunk, and it eventually died. The community celebrated the tree's life with The Old Apple Tree Festival (which takes place annually to this day).

At the first festival, attendees received and planted tiny old cuttings from the original tree, thus allowing for its spirit to live on in the countless trees that grew out of those cuttings planted by complete strangers. Her loss was very realistically the world's gain. As NPR host Lulu Garcia-Navarro so eloquently puts it, "So, while gone, she is not forgotten. The Old Apple Tree will continue to live on in the hearts and in the stomachs of the people of Vancouver."[2] Her end started with a crack and became the beginning of a whole new slew of apple trees that would bloom and provide juicy fruit to many. The crack may have finally taken the Vancouver tree down, but the crack led to a death which ultimately led to new life.

THE GREAT CRACKING OF 2009

As you know, I was outed before I was ready to come out of the closet on my own. As news spread about me being gay, I went from touring 200+ dates a year in front of thousands of people to cleaning breadcrumbs off the carpet of a seafood restaurant where I started waiting tables to earn money. In the span of three weeks, I was unemployed, undone, and injured deeply. I lost friends and family members. In one month, I can honestly say my life blew up. The explosion led to new life, but it would be years before I would truly witness that new life.

As I look back on those dark days, I see my life as the seed exploding. I see treasures and gifts that came as a direct result of the intense pressure I was under for quite a long time. Coming out, and everything that grew from that experience, blew up my life in a way I so badly needed. I needed to have my self-reliant, egocentric construct blown to pieces. I'd built my own kingdom, and I had no identity apart from who I was as Lindsey Kane, worship leader and Christian recording artist. I would not be where I am today without the Great Explosion of 2009.

Without the seed of my life exploding, I may not have ever come out. I would've never met my then-partner who would become my wife. We may never have adopted our girls. I wouldn't have found my way into the world of finance.

> Any spirituality of joy is also a spirituality of tragedy . . .
> it is the struggle itself that defines us.
> **—ERNEST KURTZ and KATHERINE KETCHAM**[3]

This is why my Al-Anon mentor says she can no longer distinguish between a tragedy and a miracle. I absolutely knew 2009 was the year of loss and tragedy. I didn't see it as a miracle then. It would be many years later before I started to see the gifts that would come out of the loss. I now see how much new life came out of that cracking. If the death of my ministry and career was like the death of the old tree, then the new life I've experienced since then reminds me of the new orchards that flourished as The Old Apple Tree Festival attendees went on to plant the clippings they received from the old, dead tree.

LOSS IS AN ENDING (AND A BEGINNING)

Whatever loss you've experienced isn't the end. It's not the final word, and loss doesn't get the final say. The loss is an explosion into a new beginning. The time between the two (loss versus new beginning) might be excruciatingly long. You may never feel like you're moving along the spectrum of loss into appreciating the life that comes from it. And that's okay. Even if you don't feel it, I assure you it's happening.

Life comes with its fair share of loss and explosion. It won't define our *entire* lives, but we will not get through life unscathed and free from loss. I think it's impossible.

I don't think God causes cracks in trees or exploding seeds. Scientifically, it appears that the seeds explode under great pressure, and the purpose for the explosion is built into the seed's DNA. The shattering of the seed is happening FOR the seed and FOR the future. When our lives are shattered, even beyond recognition, it's all happening FOR us, not to us.

I know it doesn't *feel* that way when you're in the thick of the loss. That's completely normal. Feel alllll of those feelings. Don't skip any one of them. Eventually, there will come a time when you'll see the fruits associated with the loss. As you know, the end doesn't justify the means here. However, **the "end" can redeem the means.**

Sometimes, the end result of experiencing new life can only be found in the loss, pressure, and explosions. Has a loss blown up your world completely? If you're over the age of ten or so, with a beating heart, chances are the answer is yes. Maybe you have many yeses in relation to that question. You don't necessarily have to feel something for it to be true. Just because the seed doesn't know it's about to explode and bring forth new life, doesn't mean it's not going to happen. The seed has little control over when and where its explosion takes place. The pressure builds, the contraction and expansion process occurs, and eventually, the seed blows up. (Go search this on YouTube. It's quite fascinating.)

Sometimes, the reason we're afraid is that we feel like we're going to lose everything.

There is no life without loss. Loss comes in many different forms. When you hear the word "loss," you may be like me and think of death, tragedy, loss of dreams, a job, etc. But what about the loss that comes from getting married? Yep, you read that correctly. There is loss associated with even the most joyful of moments, even when people get married. Loss of being single, loss of independence (in a way), loss of being able to do whatever the hell you want whenever the hell you want to do it . . . There is loss in both marriage and divorce, in birth and death. Even in the celebration of a new birth, there is loss. Loss of having time to yourself unless you sneak away to the bathroom. Loss of sleep. Loss of independence. Loss of the ability to really go anywhere for a while without having to create a well-thought-out childcare action plan to ensure your baby stays safe.

Sending your kids to college is exciting, but that's definitely a loss. Retiring after a successful career can be exciting, but there's also loss involved there—of identity or the career itself. We can find an element of loss in the best of times and in the worst of times. Loss, simply put, is an unavoidable part of life. But it's not ALL of life. It might feel like it clouds every corner of your life right now, depending on the nature of the loss and the length of time since it occurred. We must remember, however, that loss doesn't get the final say in how our lives turn out.

My life was upended in 2009 when I "lost" everything. It forever changed the course of my life, and today, I can honestly say I'm grateful for everything that happened. I'm thankful it happened the way it did. It's okay if you're not at a place where you can say this about your loss. You may *never* be able to say something even remotely close to that, and that is also completely fine.

Truth is, we all have something to "come out" of, whether it's a closet or a zombie stupor resulting from not fully participating in our lives. Maybe you're testing the waters of polyamory with your spouse, and you are already freaking out about having to come out to your parents about your non-traditional lifestyle. Or maybe you need to come out of a situation or job, similar to what we talk about in the chapter about leaving.

There is a coming out process when it comes to loss, especially when it's someone you loved. You must come out of the shock, emerging from the fog of non-stop grief. The loss may continue to serve as the underlying soundtrack of your life, but it's not all there is. It can feel that way, but in reality, this event isn't the end-all-be-all of life, but it can be the entry point into finding new life and a new way to move through and experience life in all its forms. Coming out in any sense can be the path to freedom.

THE JOY OF ADOPTION

Just as loss can lead to good, so can sorrow lead to joy. For example, if I were to draw out for you every joyful moment in my life up to this point, I could tie every single one of those moments to a corresponding moment of sorrow. I know that sounds dark. But let me explain . . .

After my coming out process and the subsequent healing journey that took place, a couple of years later, my then-wife Jenny and I started toying very casually with the idea of building a family. The problem was that I didn't really want kids. Jenny definitely did, but she was patient with me. I told her I'd think and pray about it (though I'm pretty sure I didn't really mean that because, like I said, I didn't want kids).

In my case, God has to speak to me through dreams because during the day, my mind is so jumbled and inundated with thoughts that when I finally go to sleep, God is like *YES! Finally! I can get her to listen and meditate.*

One night, I had a very lucid dream where I was laying a little baby girl in a pink blanket on a bed. I was filled with so much love, gushing over her, and then Jenny and my parents came in to look at this wonderful baby girl. I woke up bawling.

The next night I had another dream about babies. This time I had a baby girl wrapped in a pink blanket, in a car seat, and I set her down on the curb to close the car door—a simple daily thing that all new moms do. And again, I looked at her sitting in that car seat, and I was in love—crazy in love—with this little girl. I woke up crying and said to Jenny, "Let's start a family! Let's do the adoption thing now. I'm ready!"

So, we did. It was a fairly painless process, which I've found out is rare in the area of adoption. It also didn't take as long as we thought. We assumed no birth mom would ever choose us because we were a Christian lesbian couple living in Texas. But lo and behold, after home studies and classes, reading books, and talking to countless people in the adoption triad, the call came.

The day the adoption agency called me with the best news I

could've ever asked for was one of the best, most memorable days of my life. The social worker called me at my office and said "Lindsey, I'm thrilled to let you know that a birth mother has chosen you based on your profile, and she'd like to connect with you by phone. They're due in September."

I said with a shaky voice, "They're?"

And she said, "Yep, she's having TWINS!"

I hung up on her. That's true. I freaked out and hung up on her right after quickly yelling, "I'm freaking out!! Please call Jenny!" Despite my initial reaction (that I'm not proud of), I was SO stinkin' excited to finally get "the call." In the adoption world, the call is everything. It's when you learn the news that a birth mother has chosen you as her top candidates for the adoption plan she's created.

We connected with our birth mom later that night, and the conversation could not have gone better. We clicked instantaneously. I'll never forget how tender the moment was when she explained why she was choosing adoption. She shared with us that she knew she couldn't give the girls the life she wanted them to have and all the love she knew they deserved. She chose us to be the girls' forever family. To this day, we continue to enjoy a beautiful open adoption experience. As someone who started the journey into open adoption full of fear and misconceptions (thanks to all those Lifetime movies that convince you that birth moms are evil and only want to steal their baby back), I've come a long way. I couldn't imagine our journey unfolding any other way.

But here's the thing about adoption: adoptive parents' greatest joy can be the birth parents' greatest loss.

We had the good fortune of being in the room when they were born, and we got to watch them come out. I almost fainted, and all I kept thinking was, *Are they supposed to look like shar-pei puppies?*

As I stood with Jenny in the hospital hallway that day, I was feeling all eighty-eight keys of emotions, like a tsunami. Meanwhile, in the room nearby, our birth mother was in the midst of the profound signing process with the adoption agency social worker. In that room that day, our birth mother was signing her name to the documents that would legally seal this adoption. With the stroke of a pen, she was cementing her commitment to the selfless choice to do what she felt was the most loving act she could perform for those babies.

As we waited in the hallway, the statistic we'd come to fear so well wasn't far from my mind: one in four birth mothers change their mind and choose to parent instead of going forward with their adoption plan. One in four. We waited and waited, and the fear slowly crept in. Who am I kidding? It was always there. After what seemed like an eternity, the social worker emerged from the room and walked toward us. She said in a somber yet joyful tone, "She has completed the paperwork, and it's your turn."

I burst into tears. UGLY crying like the world has never seen. They weren't tears of joy. How could I feel sorrow in this moment which should've been one of the happiest moments of my life? We were going to be mommies! So, why the hell was I weeping uncontrollably from the core of my being?

At that moment I was completely overcome with Sorrow. The sorrow that existed in me that day deserves a capital S. Of course, I was over the moon excited and thankful and joyful. But y'all, I could physically feel the loss around me. I'm an empath, so that's my life. When I know or sense that people I love and care about are breaking, I can feel it physically in my body. I could feel pain in my heart and all over my chest. Even though it'd only been a month (yes, we had one month to go from "we're having a baby probably soon, at some point, maybe in two to three years, who knows" to "okay, we're bringing twin newborns home in four weeks"), my love for our birth mom had blossomed into one of the most beautiful loves I've ever had the privilege of experiencing.

Sorrow swirled around me and got all up in my insides. The tears wouldn't stop flowing. My heart broke because, in that moment, I felt a tiny piece of the brokenness and gut-wrenching pain she must have been feeling right then. Her greatest loss was my greatest joy. How could I be joyful when the catalyst for my joy is suffering with pain and sorrow? No one wakes up in the morning and says, "I think I'll get pregnant today and have a baby and then place them for adoption."

Quick aside, I have qualms with the phrases "put up for adoption" and "she gave her baby up." I can only speak for our specific situation, but our birth mom didn't "give up" those babies. She didn't "put them up" for adoption. I invite you to research the origins of the phrase "put up," and you'll be thankful I'm sharing this advice with you. Pro tip: use language like "she *placed* her child for adoption."

Since the girls were born, we've made it our mission to carry this narrative around forever in our hearts as we impart the truth into their hearts: "Your birth mom loved you SO MUCH that she chose me and Mommy to be your forever family. She loved you so much, before you were even born, that she made an adoption plan. She was mature enough to realize that she couldn't give you the life and love she so badly wanted you both to have. So, she made the selfless decision to be a part of our story and make our dreams come true. We so badly wanted to be mommies, and thanks to your birth mother, our dreams have come true. We are eternally grateful for her, and we love her so much. Few people know that kind of love." To this day the girls have a picture of her hanging on the wall in their bedroom.

LOSS IS ALSO GAIN

In every transition we experience in our lives, there will be a hint of loss—or a heap of it. Think of the birth of a baby. What could be more joyful than that! But for every transition, there is also a component of loss. As a mom, I can so relate to this. There is loss in becoming a mother. Let's stop pretending there's not.

Take marriage, for example. It's a beautiful, joyful union between two people who want to commit their lives to each other so they can grow old together (and bother each other for decades) and experience a love that knows no bounds. But if you look hard enough, you'll find loss is experienced simultaneously with this beautiful new gain. What is lost when someone gets married? It depends on the person.

For me, it was personal independence. A loss of doing whatever the hell I wanted to without any regard for another human being.

The loss of my own space, my closet—this is especially true when two ladies get married. Lord, the amount of closet space that lesbians need. Our poor son. He will have no closet space.

The sooner we adjust our expectations and reframe our thinking when it comes to grief, sorrow, and loss, the sooner we can start fully participating in our lives that were meant to be lived to the fullest.

I disagree with various components in the Bible, but one thing I am confident of is the verse about "when you suffer . . ." You won't find the word "if" in there. Life is beautiful. And it's tragic. And it's messy and scary and sacred. Life is all these things and more. If there are eighty-eight keys on the piano of our emotions, there are millions of keys in the multi-stacked organ that is life. Our work is in reframing our thinking and reconceptualizing how we see the world, our lives, and ourselves.

I remember seeing a bumper sticker when I was little: "Shit happens then you die." Here's the thing—there's some truth in it, but not the whole truth. Shit does happen. It's hard to escape, even if you tried. And trust me, I've tried. For over three decades, I've tried to build my life upon a foundation that was constructed to be foolproof when it comes to heartache, sorrow, and shit happening. But that's not reality. There has to be a balance, otherwise, our little blue sphere would pop off its axis and shoot somewhere far into the galaxy.

Shit does indeed happen. Good shit and bad shit. The good shit is REALLY good. And the hard shit totally sucks. And the shit might keep happening—but it will not kill us. I know it feels like it's going to, but it's not. You've survived up to this point. You've made it this far, and so have I. If this plane went down right now as I type this, I'd know that I lived a full life. I want to live more of this full life, and a part of that is learning to accept the reality of the joy–sorrow chaff. Learn from it, don't dwell in it, and move through it. Emotions are simply energy in motion. If your emotions and feelings aren't moving, you're going to find yourself in a whole lot of trouble. Stop prolonging the inevitable. Find a way to fully participate in your life. All facets of your life.

I'm not a big fan of sermons, but there's one I've loved since the moment I heard it. The speaker says in a rich Irish accent, "There are no good or bad days. No, there are only days of grace. Sometimes the grace of God allows you to enjoy what is happening and some days the grace of God allows you to endure what is happening. But either way, there are no bad days. Only days of grace."[4]

Days of grace. May we live each one of those days to the fullest, in spite of and in honor of all of life's losses.

Break It Down for Me

- Life and loss are inextricably linked. Experiencing loss is a painful end, which can lead to a healing beginning. Loss doesn't get the last word. Love does.

- Shit happens, both good and bad. It will keep happening, but it's not happening TO us. All of it can be redeemed, and life can be renewed. You've survived this far.

- There are no good or bad days. There are only days of grace. Sometimes grace allows you to *enjoy* what is happening, and other times grace allows you to *endure* what is happening.

- Reframing our relationship with loss will unearth the gift of opportunity to learn, grow, and appreciate the present moment.

YOU
NEED
A
BISCUIT

PART THREE

"Just as in the second part of a verse, bad poets seek a
thought to fit their rhyme, so in the second half of their lives
people tend to become more anxious about finding actions,
positions, relationships that fit those of their earlier lives,
so that everything harmonizes quite well on the surface:
but their lives are no longer ruled by a strong thought, and
instead, in its place, comes the intention of finding a rhyme."

—Friedrich Nietzsche, *Human, All Too Human*[1]

BUT

WHAT'S YOUR DOG'S NAME?

Chapter 12

THE GIFT OF POWERLESSNESS

"Who knows what will befall us tomorrow, John?
You could be hit by a Mack truck or bopped on
the head by a tiny piece of space debris."
—Moira Rose, *Schitt's Creek* (S6, E1)

"I find that worry is just undernourished enthusiasm."
—Moira Rose, *Schitt's Creek* (S6, E13)

We live in a world and culture obsessed with *power*. Power plays. Power moves. Power couples. Power trips. Power hungry. Power dynamic. Power grab. Power cords. My wife's personal favorite: power naps. The wealthiest of people eventually get bored with wealth because they've amassed so much that it almost doesn't matter anymore. That's when they turn to power. Most humans, like it or not and whether we know it or not, are obsessed with having power and control. This is problematic because it's mostly an illusion. Even when we think we have control over something, we don't. Even if we feel as though we have all the power in a specific situation, we likely don't.

Some of us put power on a pedestal, and the obsession for greater and greater power grabs is costing us. We will call this The Power

Paradox. In a *Psychology Today* article, the author writes about five facts that prove why having power *sucks*.[1] (Their words, not mine.)

1. Power makes us selfish, increases our sense of entitlement, and results in selfish and self-centered leaders.

2. Power makes us insensitive to other people's emotions—research proves that more power leads to less empathy.

3. Power makes us overconfident in our talents and abilities. We tend to think more highly of ourselves when we're in charge, which negatively impacts decision-making.

4. People don't like when others have power. This creates a power imbalance between the dominant individual and the individual who will typically respond to that power imbalance with insecurity, a temptation to become small, and feelings of being intimidated. How well do you learn from someone or listen to someone who is exerting power over you in a way that makes you feel small? Probably not much because your fear is louder than your ability to learn and hear from the intimidating person whom you perceive as more powerful than you.

5. Having power means that there are always people out there who want to take it away from you. When you have absolute power that corrupts absolutely (as the famous quote goes) then you will eventually be despised for it. Having power also leads to paranoia and obsession.

All this to say, **pursuing power is as pointless as it is purposeless.**

HOW POWERLESSNESS = FABULOUSNESS

The exact opposite is also true. Pursuing a life of *powerlessness* is the key that will unlock the ultimate power (the good kind) in your life. Ironically enough, it's in our powerlessness that we find true power and hope. Letting go of what we can't control and taking full responsibility for what we DO have control over makes life worth living and much more enjoyable. In response to the *Psychology Today* article, I give you my top five reasons why powerlessness is fabulous and way too underrated:

1. Powerlessness—and the acceptance of its essential role in our lives—is directly proportionate to our level of peace and serenity. Most of us experience anxiety and disappointment because we think we have more control over our lives than we actually do. We have expectations of grandiose power over not only our own lives but also the lives and experiences of others. We are all guilty of this. How many times have you thought this: *If everyone would just do what I wanted them to do, I'd be happy! Why can't these people just follow my advice?* It can be very frustrating. If I've heard this once, I've heard it a thousand times: **expectations lead to future resentments.** Alternatively, getting to a place of acceptance as it relates to our powerlessness will bring forth endless freedom. As I said, this is The Power Paradox. In letting go of power and control, we end up gaining more of it. As we look in the mirror and practice rigorous self-honesty pertaining to our life's unmanageability, we grow by leaps and bounds. Know powerlessness, know peace. No powerlessness (and acceptance thereof), no peace.

2. Understanding our powerlessness leads to a palpable sense of relief. There's something refreshing about not having to be in control of everything all the time. When I am reminded of my powerlessness and my lack of control over others, I am filled with a deep sense of relief. That relief is my lifeline because I've always struggled with thinking I had the burden of the whole world on my shoulders.

3. Powerlessness leads us into the arms of an all-loving Higher Power greater than ourselves. A quote commonly attributed to Corrie Ten Boom says: "When we are powerless to do a

thing, it is a great joy that we can come and step inside the ability of Jesus."[2]

If it's not Jesus for you, take all the license you need to replace "Jesus" with whatever you call your Higher Power. Too often we get bogged down with semantics, what people *call* their Higher Power. Zoom out a bit; don't get lost in the weeds. Powerlessness is pointless if it doesn't point us to a Power greater than ourselves—the God/Higher Power/Spirit/Universe of *our own understanding*.

Throughout my life, I see evidence of God's ability to step up and step in when my life is drowning in unmanageability. You and I are completely powerless over most everything in life except one thing: ourselves. All we have control over is the way we *respond* to various situations or people. Trying to control people, places, and things is as futile as trying to control the weather in Texas, trying to calm a toddler having a meltdown in the middle of Target because her "socks hurt," or attempting to control a hyperactive goldendoodle who is hell-bent on making your life miserable every moment of every day (Hi, Ellie!).

4. Powerlessness increases our ability to be present with ourselves and others—thus, leading to an increase in compassion and empathy. One of my all-time favorite authors Henri Nouwen eloquently writes:

> When we honestly ask ourselves which person in our lives means the most to us, we often find that it is those who, instead of giving advice, solutions, or cures, have chosen rather to share our pain and touch our wounds with a warm and tender hand. The friend who can be silent with us in a moment of despair or confusion, who can stay with us in an hour of grief and bereavement, who can tolerate not knowing, not curing, not healing and face with us the reality of our powerlessness, that is a friend who cares.
>
> **—HENRI J. M. NOUWEN**[3]

5. And finally, understanding our powerlessness serves as the much-needed catalyst we require in order to make a real, sustainable change in our lives. We move from leaning on a fabricated form of power to living our lives from a place of surrender, letting go of what and whom we cannot control. The first step of change is to admit we are powerless to make the desired change. There's a damn good reason that the *very first step* in the 12-step program of AA/Al-Anon starts with: "We admitted we were powerless . . . that our lives have become unmanageable." Have you ever tried to use willpower to change something over and over again, yet continually come up empty and disappointed? Were you filled with defeat, guilt, and shame, which then leads to the perpetuation of the exact pattern or addiction you're trying to change? I've experienced this throughout my life. I try to do everything in my own power, white-knuckling every aspect of my life in hopes of forcing a solution and changing an undesired behavior. I fail every single time. Even if I succeed initially, I end up failing.

In my various travels across the world, I've had the privilege of meeting and getting to know the most powerless of people. Yet, these folks who (on the surface) seem to have zero power or influence, have all the peace and joy. They are able to focus all their energy on their own lives and how they respond to whatever life throws at them. I've spent ample time with the poorest of the poor, saddest of the sad, and people drowning in total despondency and isolation. Yet, it is these very people who have shown me how to live a life of surrender and acceptance. This doesn't mean you and I are expected to surrender and accept unacceptable behavior. Absolutely not. That's where boundaries come in. What it *does* mean is that the magic of accepting our lack of control over everything outside of ourselves brings with it more magic that leads to greater fulfillment in our lives.

NO POWERLESSNESS, NO FREEDOM (KNOW POWERLESSNESS, KNOW FREEDOM)

We carry all the power we need inside ourselves already. The power isn't outside of you, over there, or whenever you get that next job, promotion, or new relationship. The power we so desperately need and long for is found in the acceptance of our powerlessness to effect change in our lives without the help of a Power greater than ourselves. This all may sound foreign or contradictory to you, and that's okay. Be open and curious. Be willing to be willing. Get curious about the power dynamics that exist not only within yourself but also between you and others.

I would argue there is no freedom without powerlessness, and freedom is a gift. Let me be clear with a point of clarification. When I use the term "powerless," I do not mean "giving up" or "giving in" as if to put hopelessness on a pedestal. When I use this term, I use it in the most powerful sense of the word. What would our lives look like if we lived as if we deeply believed that true freedom is found in the letting go of that which we are most terrified of losing?

Are you scared of losing control? Then let go of it. Are you scared of not having power in a specific situation? Then accept your powerlessness and ask for help. Search inward because that's where your true power lies. I have fantastic news for you, because you are officially off the hook! Yup, that's right. Take the burdens off and throw them down. You are not responsible for other people. You're not responsible for their feelings. And you can't really do much of anything to create change in your life except by changing the one person you do have some control over—yourself.

Dr. Wayne Dyer quotes Max Planck: "If you change the way you look at things, the things you look at change."[4] Instead of obsessing over changing others, situations, or things outside our control, let's shift our paradigm of thinking and focus on how we can change ourselves and the way we look at things in our lives. This alone will have a major impact on the lives of others, in addition to us. Change begets change, and it all begins with acknowledging our own powerlessness in the face of life's unavoidable unmanageability.

Still not buying it?

DROWNING IN A TEASPOON OF WATER

Let me tell you a story. When my son was little, he was terrified of water and swimming. He would get in deep enough to cover his ankles, maybe. It took many swim lessons before he felt comfortable becoming one with the water. When he was about four years old, we were at the pool. As was his custom, he opted for the kiddie pool. It was extremely shallow, and no other kids were in it at the time. On this one hot summer day, Atticus was playing around and having fun with his floatie toys when all of a sudden, he slipped and started panicking.

From across the pool, I could see him flailing about and making a splashing scene. I ran over to him to check on what might have happened. Did he get stung by a bee? Did he get urine-infested pool water in his mouth? No. He simply slipped. But in his moment of panic, he forgot something very important: all he had to do was stand. In his hysteria, he lost sight of how deep the kiddie pool was. He forgot that just a few seconds ago he was confidently standing up in the kiddie pool. He was trying to regain control and power so he didn't drown, but he was doing so ineffectively. I was finally able to help him calm down and told him firmly and loudly to stand. "Atticus, STAND UP! That's all you have to do. You're not drowning. It's not deep. Just stand up on your two legs, and all will be well."

We talked about the situation later that day when I was putting him down for a nap. He shared how he felt silly for making such a big deal and splashing in reaction to slipping in the kiddie pool. In hindsight, he realized he was safe and didn't need to panic. In fact, in his effort to "fix" the slip, he created more problems for himself.

I wonder how often you and I drown in a teaspoon of water. I'm guilty of this, for sure. In my panicked state (usually brought on by failed expectations), I start trying to control the situation and change the narrative from whatever reality I happen to be in. I make a mountain out of a molehill and overcomplicate everything. I've struggled and wasted so much energy striving, when really all I needed to do was stand up. My perception tells me that this water is deep and I'm drowning. Surely, I'm going to die soon. That's the fight-flight-freeze response kicking in. But when I'm able to pause and breathe, I get a clearer head and realize that I'm okay. I'm safe right here and right now, and all I need to do is stand up.

This act of "standing up" will look different for everyone in every situation, but it always starts with awareness. What is happening? Where do I feel this in my body? Am I okay? Is this a perceived fear because I heard a noise in the dark or a legit fear that I need to attend to so I don't get eaten by a tiger (you know, with all those tigers hiding in the dark in your home)? But what do we do when we can't stand up in the kiddie pool? What do we do when we're so flooded and overwhelmed that all we can seem to find the energy for is to continue flailing about and splashing water all over the place? What then?

That's—yet again—when the power of powerlessness kicks into high gear.

When the twins were less than a year old, I hadn't slept more than one or two consecutive hours a night, for the most part. We couldn't get them on the same schedule, and they were on completely different cadences for sleep, waking up, crying, needing to be changed and fed, etc. Those were beautiful days and also dark days because sleep deprivation while trying to keep preemie twin babies alive is no small task.

At the height of my sleep deprivation, stress, and complete overwhelm, I remember this one night in particular. It had been a rough day for my then-wife Jenny and me. I'd had a long day at work, and Jenny had a hard day tending to the girls. You know those days—when it rains, it pours. It felt like we were having to dig deep into the corners of our souls to find the energy to do their bath time and bedtime routine later that evening. We were figuratively army crawling from moment to moment as if trying to find our way out of a war zone. If we could only get to bedtime, then we could collapse, regroup, and possibly make dinner for ourselves.

Somehow, we did it. The babies ate, had their baths, and miraculously went to sleep without a hitch. We did it, and no one died. For about three and a half minutes, the house was quiet. JUST as the sense of relief was starting to enter my periphery, I heard a screeching cry. A cry that would wake a bear up in the middle of hibernation. And y'all, I had JUST POURED MYSELF A GLASS OF WINE.

I'm still not certain why this particular evening was different from all the others, but something was indeed different. Normally, I would stop whatever I was doing and go tend to whichever baby happened to be crying. I would jump into mom mode almost subconsciously and figure out whether said baby needed food, to be changed, cuddled, etc. But on that night, I didn't.

What happened immediately after I heard that spine-tingling cry was a first. I completely shut down, couldn't move, and had the first and biggest panic attack of my life. As I look back on that moment, I now know what was going on. But at the time, I was clueless. I now know that I was overwhelmed, over-tired, sleep deprived, stressed out, and losing my mind little by little each day. My job was exhausting, and I hadn't been taking care of myself at all. I was running on empty—hell, below empty. Running on the fumes that are left after the other fumes are gone.

I had built up that moment of rest so much during those three and a half minutes of quiet after we'd gotten the babies down, that hearing the cry sent me into outer space. I froze. But Jenny went to check on the babies, and one of them needed a diaper change. I couldn't move and was so overwhelmed with emotions that I began sobbing uncontrollably. I wasn't crying because I wouldn't get to rest that night. I wasn't losing my shit because I didn't get to keep drinking my wine. No . . . I was sobbing because I'd been drowning for the better part of a year, with no sleep and very little self-care. I was sobbing because I just couldn't take it anymore.

Something inside me broke in that moment. I felt completely paralyzed by anxiety and helplessness. I don't remember a time when I felt more powerless. I couldn't stand up from the couch I was sitting on. My heart started racing. I'd never experienced something like that before. Sure, in the past, I've had moments of anxiety and panicky situations, but I'd never felt what I felt that night.

Unbeknownst to me, I was having a major panic attack that left me temporarily paralyzed. It got so bad that Jenny was about to call 911. I was shaking, bawling, and heaving. Sounds were coming out of me that I hadn't heard before. I was in bad shape. I tried walking so I could go to bed, but I couldn't. After Jenny changed the diaper, she tried valiantly to walk me to the bedroom. After a while, I finally made it and laid there flat on my back. I was writhing in pain. The more I panicked, the worse it got. I became flooded with anxiety about the anxiety attack I was having. Nothing I did worked. Whatever I was doing to try and survive this was only making matters worse. I looked down at my hands as they tingled and saw they were cramped up and deformed. My head was spinning, my heart was beating out of my chest, and I thought surely I was going to die of a heart attack that night.

JUST . . . BREATHE (AND AGAIN AND AGAIN)

It was only when I thought Jenny was left with no other choice but to call 911 that I finally shook myself out of the panic stupor *enough* to do one simple yet challenging thing: breathe. I realized in that moment that although I couldn't move my body or straighten out my fingers, I could breathe. Although I couldn't focus on anything other than the intense anxiety attack I was having, I was at least able to focus on the act of breathing.

At the height of my panic attack paralysis, I took the first step of inhaling one deep breath. Then another. Then another. And over the course of an hour, I started to slowly come out of it. My heart rate finally started slowing down. My fingers eventually straightened out. And after another hour had passed, I was able to sit up and eventually stand up.

I sure as hell didn't see a gift at that moment. I felt completely powerless in a way I'd never experienced before. No matter how badly I wanted to move, I couldn't. It wasn't a willpower issue or a positive-vibes-only issue or the power of positive thinking issue. It was a case of total and complete panic that I couldn't do anything about. Except breathe.

Even if you haven't had a full-blown panic attack that has left you temporarily paralyzed, I'm sure you've experienced something where you felt like all you could do was breathe. While lying paralyzed and motionless on the bed in the midst of the panic attack, I realized I was spending too much energy trying to fight it. I was my son, Atticus, and my bed was the kiddie pool. But I couldn't just stand up. It wasn't that easy. So, I did what I could do: breathe. I've never felt as physically powerless as I did in that moment. It was only when I stopped fighting, ceased striving, and gave up on trying to make it all just go away, that I was able to begin calming down. I gave in to whatever was happening in my body, mind, and soul. I had no other choice but to let it run its course. My only job in those terrifying moments was to breathe deeply and intentionally. And then, once I'd caught my breath and my body and emotions started to reach a more stable state of regulation, it hit me. There was no denying it any longer. I was having some serious challenges in the area of anxiety.

Before that panic attack, I would've probably described myself as being an anxious person, but I never did anything about it. I tried meds once in college, and it made me feel weird, like I was crawling out of my skin, so I stopped. Instead of simply trying a new medicine that might be better suited for me, I just stopped taking it. But I couldn't deny it any longer: I needed help. That panic attack caused me to reach out for a lifeline.

THE DAY I GOT HELP

I don't remember how I ended up getting her name, but the very next day, I called a psychiatrist and booked an appointment. I've been working with her ever since, and her role in my life cannot be overstated. Dr. Warmann scooped me up, truly saw me and listened to me, and began helping me. We found a medicine that worked well with my body and mind. I started therapy (which I'd stopped for a short time). I slowly started putting one foot in front of the other and addressing this head-on. I was diagnosed with Generalized Anxiety Disorder, and things started making much more sense.

I'd inadvertently ignored the signs of anxiety for so long that it took something *this dramatic* to wake me up to the reality of this thorn in my side. Will it always be? Not sure. But for now, I'm incredibly thankful that I set down my pride and ego and took a step in the right direction, which for me involved therapy and medicine. And lots and lots of queso. Does queso fix everything? No. But it can make life suck a lot less when I'm dipping that chip into that cheese.

The day I finally admitted I was powerless over the anxiety that had plagued me most of my life was the day I finally surrendered and let go of what I thought my life was supposed to look like. Growing up, no one really talked about anxiety or mental disorders in general. We were all raised to put on a happy face and smile. I didn't know I could still be my awesome whole self and also struggle with anxiety. The two aren't mutually exclusive.

We humans are complicated creatures who live in a world full of gray areas and both/and . . . real life isn't so black-and-white or either/or as we once thought. There are people just like you and me walking around with mild to severe mental health issues. No one is going to come and save you, riding in valiantly on a white horse. No one is coming to your rescue, so we have to be advocates in our own health journey.

If you are riddled with anxiety or depression, or maybe for you it's OCD or bipolar disorder, get curious about it. What do you notice? Have you tried to fix it or stuff it down? Are you waiting for it to get better miraculously? Are you waiting on some person or that next wonder pill to cure you? I'm afraid there's no easy button for mental health. The onus is on us to take back the power we've given away over and over again, trying so desperately to hide our true struggles. We need to normalize mental health conversations so our closest friends and family can begin to come out of the shadows.

Has your life become unmanageable? If so, step one is coming to a place where you can honestly say, without hesitation: "I am powerless over _____ and my life has become unmanageable." Here's the best part. The very next step after we admit that we're powerless goes like this: come to believe that a Power greater than ourselves can restore us to sanity.

Sign me up for that!

TELL SELF-WILL TO SUCK IT

Can we embrace our powerlessness without being swallowed up by it and debilitated by it? Yes. If we get right-sized with ourselves and spirit, we will find the true meaning of powerlessness and, thus, the magic of power (i.e., the power of love that exists in each one of us, begging us to let it fill us up so full that we overflow onto everyone around us).

There's a reason life gets to be too much. There's a reason that our lives become increasingly unmanageable. We've been going about it all wrong. For most of our lives, we've tried to do this experiment called life in our own power. If this, then that. If we can just do it right, be strong enough, pretty enough, smart enough, and whatever enough, maybe we'll find sanity again. But that would be a fool's errand. Like trying to hold water in your hands. The more you try to hold on to something, the more it will quite naturally elude you.

Ego isn't the answer here. Pride isn't it either. The answer is in the surrendering of our self-will and our obsession with doing everything ourselves in our own limited and finite power. Oh, how my life completely changed when I came to realize that only a Power greater than myself can restore me to sanity. Isn't that what we all long for? Sanity, peace, and some semblance of calm? All those qualities are already in you. It's not that you have to go find them. The work is in finding what all is covering up those qualities—the baggage, unresolved trauma, childhood wounds, and the damage we so desperately try to run away from. As we begin to peel back those layers of guilt, shame, trauma, pain, etc. with the help of Love Intelligence (one of my favorite names for my HP) we will catch a glimpse of the peace that surpasses all human understanding.

If insanity is doing the same thing over and over again but expecting a different result, then how about we try something different? It can't hurt, right? Anything is better than continuing to run on the hamster wheel of insanity. I've heard it said that if nothing changes, nothing changes; if you keep going down the road you're on, you'll get to where you're going. I have a feeling Captain Obvious said that, but in reality, it's not that obvious. It's hard and takes time and a lot of pain. I tend to change and grow at the speed of pain, and that typically ends up being the only way I can get out of the insanity and be restored to a life of peace and serenity.

We must move from helplessness and victimhood to powerlessness and victory. It is time to embrace life in its entirety: wounds, scars, and all.

Break It Down for Me

- Pursuing power is as pointless as it is purposeless.
- Powerlessness (and the acceptance of its essential role in our lives) is directly proportionate to our level of peace and serenity.
- The power we so desperately need and long for is found in the acceptance of our powerlessness to effect change in our lives without the help of a Power greater than ourselves.
- There is a Power greater than ourselves who can (and desperately wants to) restore us to sanity.

JUST DO IT LATER

Chapter 13

THE GIFT OF HEARTBREAK

"Talk to the heartbroken ones. They will teach
you what is real, how to live alone, how to
finish, and how to start all over again."

—**Sahil Verma, "Talk to the Heartbroken Ones"**

David Rose: "Uh, it wasn't that bad."
Moira Rose: "That's the heartbreaking part.
You were so blissfully unaware."

—*Schitt's Creek* (S4, E10)

If we look at the end of heartbreak, we typically see total
devastation. That perception causes us to lose sight of the beginning,
the seed. We've already covered a lot of ground when it comes to seeds
exploding, but allow me to share one more seed-related concept with
you. Cynthia Occelli writes, "For a seed to achieve its greatest expression, it must come completely undone. The shell cracks, its insides
come out and everything changes. To someone who doesn't understand growth, it would look like complete destruction."[1]

I've been that person who didn't understand growth. So to me, it
absolutely looked like complete destruction, the end of the story, that

moment of "it is finished." Period. No sequel. No hope. Just the end. If you've ever had your heart broken, and I mean REALLY broken, you know what this feels like. You know the experience of feeling like your insides are being torn apart—so much so that you feel it physically. It's not just emotional or mental or physiological. It's physical, and the depth of the pain is so overwhelming that you aren't quite sure how you'll put one foot in front of the other. Why is heartbreak so painful to humans? Why haven't we evolved and figured out a way to skip the phase where getting our hearts broken makes us feel like we're going to physically die?

I've come to realize that heartbreak is an entirely different type of pain. Not only has someone else broken your heart, but you have broken your own heart. Let me explain. I have a friend whom I met in Al-Anon. We'll call her Sally (names have been changed so I don't have to chase "Sally" down and get her to sign a release form). Sally and I were commiserating in the bathroom one night at an Al-Anon retreat while brushing our teeth. We briefly talked about our past relationships and divorce, or in her case divorces. Sally finished rinsing out her mouth and had an ah-ha moment right in front of me. There's something magical about watching firsthand a huge bomb of awareness hit someone right between the eyes.

She set her toothbrush down, wiped her mouth, looked in the mirror, and said something I'll never forget: "Wait, I've been divorced three times and I'm on my fourth marriage, which isn't working out. My husbands have all been fairly similar, and they've all been alcoholics or addicts. I think I just realized something. I'm the common denominator. No wonder I keep repeating all these unwanted patterns because I'm only just now realizing it and working on myself so I can grow. Oh my gosh. I've always thought it was all him, whoever the him happened to be. But it's not all him. It's me, very much me, too."

She seemed stunned. I was so impressed by her realization that I couldn't help but bury her in my arms with a huge bear hug. If Al-Anon taught me one thing, it's that in every situation, no matter how minuscule or major, I will grow the most when I can look at my role in whatever happened.

This realization completely changed the way I approached the aftermath of my divorce. But, last I checked, *two people* are involved in a marriage, legally speaking.

<<<record player screeching noise>>>

Before I go on, I need to add a very important point of clarification. If you've been divorced, are going through a divorce, or are considering divorce, please hear me when I write this. I'm not saying that there are two parties at fault in *every* divorce. I understand full well that there are marriages where one person truly is the sole culprit, especially when it comes to abuse. I'm not referring to those marriages, which are more of the exception rather than the rule. Lots of marriages (41 percent of first marriages, according to Wilkinson & Finkbeiner, 2020)[2] end in divorce. But the majority of those marriages end because of the actions and choices of two people.

If there was a who-screwed-up-the-most balance sheet in marriage, I'm sure one spouse would have more transgressions in their column than the column of their ex-spouse. But still, the good ol' saying holds true with the majority of marriages and divorces in our society today: it really takes two to tango.

What's most interesting to me are the statistics for second and third marriages. According to Wilkinson & Finkbeiner, 2020, an estimated 60 percent of second marriages end in divorce, and a whopping 73 percent of third marriages. WHOA. Read that again and take it in. Why do you think that is? Maybe it's because the longer we live, the more comfortable we get with the way we move through life. Maybe, just maybe, over time our patterns become that much more set in stone. This makes it that much harder for us to gain the awareness during the second or third marriage that we might be participating in the problems that occur in our relationships.

A breakup is the shake-up you need to redirect your life.

—AMY CHAN[3]

I'm in my second marriage currently, and I would very much like for this one to be my last. As I move through life with Brynn, I can see why these statistics are what they are. If I hadn't really leaned in to the part I played in the saga of my first marriage coming to an end, I wouldn't have identified those parts of me that need work. I would have missed so much awareness about myself if I'd never looked in the mirror and asked: What role did I play in the events that led to heartache and divorce? How can I learn from this heartbreak and become a better me? What baggage needs to be unpacked and what core wounds need to come up to be healed before I go and enter another relationship or marriage?

The problem is, most of us prefer to play the blame game and shine a spotlight on our ex-partner instead of picking up a mirror and getting rigorously honest with ourselves. It's super easy to ignore our own issues when we have a clear answer for why a divorce happened in the first place. Maybe for you it was infidelity, an inability to work out differences, lack of communication, money issues, intimacy challenges, incompatibility, distance, or the notion of "falling out of love." There are countless reasons people get divorced or split up, but I think it all boils down to a common theme: one or both people get to a breaking point where they can no longer endure, deal with, and cope with their spouse. This is precisely where I would speculate that we start (or continue) to break our own hearts.

SELF-INFLICTED HEART-BREAKING

When you and I stay in situations that are ultimately not meant for us to continue, be it a marriage, relationship, friendship, job, etc., we break our own hearts. Haven't you experienced this? Think of a friendship or relationship that ended long after it should have. You know you should've gotten out earlier, but you didn't. Looking back, you chose to stay for longer than you now feel you needed to.

When we stay in situations that are harming us repeatedly, we are harming ourselves. We are actively participating in the process of heartbreak. We become angry and resentful at ourselves for not speaking up sooner, and we project that anger and resentment onto the other person. It's much easier to hate someone else than it is to admit self-hatred. We've bought in to the fallacy that blaming others will save us from shame. The opposite is actually true. The more we hurl blame on others and refuse to practice rigorous self-honesty, the more shame we invite into our lives. Each time you and I give away our power and deny our own needs, we break our own hearts.

This is why heartbreak compounds in a way few other types of pain do. We endure a myriad of feelings and emotions. It cuts deeper than deep. Experiencing a broken heart is debilitating in every sense of the word. What's interesting is that every chapter in this book could easily be related to heartbreak. Pain, whether that pain results from loss, humiliation, fear, and every other title of this book, can be traced back to a broken heart. It's tied to everything, and there is a clear through line to all painful experiences in our lives. Just because a heartbreak isn't romantic in nature, doesn't mean it's any less painful. Sometimes the loss of a friend can be just as excruciating as the loss of a partner. It's just different, but no less painful. Love is messy, and so is the loss of love. Getting your heart broken can leave you feeling like a failure.

I certainly felt like a complete and utter failure when I came to terms with my divorce. I felt like I'd failed our daughters, ourselves, our families, and even our birth mom to whom we'd promised to be together forever so we could keep the twins in a strong, stable family. I hate breaking promises. I felt like a failure because we broke our vows that we took very seriously before God—even before gay marriage was legal in the country. That crushed me.

One of my favorite books is *Grace Walk* by Steve McVey. I don't agree with everything in the book now that I've de- and reconstructed my faith, but there are so many nuggets of wisdom in the book that jump out at me to this day and played a special role in my healing during my divorce. Steve writes: "Through the sense of failure I experienced, God was bringing me to the end of self-sufficiency . . . and allowed circumstances to develop in such a way that He brought us to the end of our resources. He kept on until all we had left was Him."[4]

While I agree with most of this theory, I must point out a few areas where I vehemently disagree. While I don't believe God causes or causes-by-allowing bad stuff to happen in our lives, I do believe God (insert whatever name you use for your Higher Power here) redeems and reutilizes all of it for our good. As I said earlier, sometimes shit just happens. The sooner we can get to the end of self-sufficiency and reach out for help, the better off our lives, relationships, and experiences will be. Surrendering to spirit's sufficiency changes everything. The problem is, we tend to go through life as if we believe we can do everything on our own, as if we've got this and we don't need anyone or anything to help us.

How's that working out for you? It didn't work out very well for me.

When I dropped the rope I had tied around my neck (metaphorically) and reached up and out for my Higher Power's help—Her rope—I experienced my first taste of freedom. But I had to come to the very end of myself and my means for surviving in order to get there.

Getting our hearts broken has a mystical way of helping us get to the end of ourselves, to hit rock bottom. Few things break us like heartbreak, and I believe this is by design. We need to have our hearts broken from time to time to shake us and wake us up out of our unconscious stupor.

STAY ON YOUR OWN LADDER

When my kids were tiny, they would demand, "*THELF DO IT!*" I'd try to help with buckling seat belts, assist with putting on socks and shoes, try and grab something from a tall shelf, yet I was met with a very loud and confident "THELF DO IT!" This typically ended up in disaster because tiny kids are terrible at being self-sufficient. They need ALL the help. Lord have mercy, even to this day, my kids refuse to ask for help because they're convinced they can do anything on their own.

Finally, when they realize they've completely run out of options, they ask for help reluctantly.

There's a balance between *that* and resisting the temptation to save our kids from potential hurt by helping them too much. Sometimes we have to let our kids—and others we love who are adults—crash and burn so they can have the dignity to fail and fail forward with purpose in order to learn.

Once in an Al-Anon meeting, I heard someone talk about two ladders. Imagine you're on one ladder, the metaphorical ladder of your life. Your loved one (kid, spouse, best friend, etc.) is on their own ladder next to you. Instead of keeping your eyes affixed to your ladder and your journey, you're fixated on the other ladder. You study, analyze, and plan so that when you start seeing the person next to you falling off their ladder, you'll have plenty of time to jump off your ladder and move to the bottom of their ladder. Imagine lying down under their ladder, so that when they fall, you absorb their impact. You soften the blow. You do so with the best of intentions, but it ends up hurting that person much more than helping them. Because we softened their blow, the other person has no concept of the potential consequences of their actions or choices. They simply get up (off you, since they fell on you), dust themselves off, and get back on the ladder to continue repeating the patterns which led them up and eventually down their ladder in the first place.

What would happen if instead we remained committed to our own ladders, our own lives and journeys? This isn't selfish or self-centered. It's the exact opposite. Focusing on what *we* can do to become higher and higher versions of ourselves is the very best way we can love the person on the ladder next to us.

Waving the BS Flag on "God Helps Those Who Help Themselves"

I want to debunk this bullshit belief that I've heard many Christians say but isn't rooted in biblical truth at all. You've heard it, I'm sure: God helps those who help themselves. Cringe. We're all God's kids.

Can you imagine helping your kids on the one condition that they help themselves? This doesn't hold any weight in reality. Imagine letting your kid drown because you see that there's a floatie right beside them, but since they're not trying to reach out for the floatie, you don't think they're doing a good job of "helping themselves"—so, I guess your kid is SOL.

Personally, I've been that drowning kid many times. And sure, I bet the floatie IS right next to me, but I can't see it. Sometimes we all are helpless and need a hand UP, not a handout. We need a Power greater than ourselves to reach out and lift us up.

So much of the heartache we encounter is due to the fact that we are looking outside of ourselves to get our needs met. We think that next job or that next relationship or that next _____ will save us or at least relieve the pain momentarily. There is a spiritual element here that cannot be overstated or overlooked. If I've said it once, I've said it 1000 times (another Al-Anonism): **whatever you came here looking *for*, you came here *with*.**

You've got it. It's already inside you. But it's not *just you*, it's the spirit inside you who drives you, gets you out of bed each morning, and gives your life profound meaning. This is NOT a religious statement. I genuinely believe each of us was made to create with the help and partnership of the Creative Spirit of all things. Moment-by-moment presence with spirit is where the gift lies.

THE DIVINE DANCE

Be present with yourself. Present with your broken heart. Present with the broken pieces scattered all around you as you painfully watch the picture of what you thought, dreamed, and hoped your life would be turn into rubble and dust. Spirit can take the wheel all day long, and even take the night driving shift. But you and I still have to sit all the way down, buckle up, and more importantly BUCK UP, and nurture a culture within our day-to-day lives where we are experiencing conscious contact with the Divine inside each and every one of us. You and I were created to play an integral role in the cocreation of our own lives.

We must never lose sight of how this crazy experiment called life is much like a divine dance. Sometimes it's the tango, and you have a thorny rose in your mouth jabbing into your gums. Other times, it's a slow dance set to a magical love ballad from the '80s. Other times, it's a conga line, fun and jovial. Yet other times, it's a full-out hip-hop dance choreographed to a recent Cardi B hit that makes the world's most iconic dancers jealous. (In this last scenario, you and I are good at hip-hop dancing.)

It's not the type of dance that matters. It's the fact that you're on the dance floor *participating*.

In order to survive and thrive in spite of and because of heartbreak, we must acquire a different level, a deeper level of consciousness and awareness to break through those old, worn patterns that no longer serve us. Even if you aren't yet willing, are you able to get to a place where you're *willing to be willing*?

I want to live in a world where we are each spending our lives *in love*—receiving spirit's unconditional love, loving *ourselves*, and thereby loving all others equally and fully. This sounds like an impossible and way-too-tall order. But I have to believe it's possible. Reaching new levels of consciousness and awareness about love will help heal not only us but the whole world. Love spurs us on to evolve from our false realities and tired narratives. Love gives us the courage we need to stop punishing ourselves and breaking our own hearts. Love pushes our butts out of the chair so we can start standing up for ourselves, embracing our power/Power, and honoring ourselves. Love provides the ink so we can begin to rewrite the records and reverse course by changing the very dynamics in our brains. It all starts with the brain and mind, not the heart.

The author of the Book of Romans puts it this way in chapter 12, verse 2: "Be transformed by the renewing of your mind."[5] That's it. If you want transformation or renewal in a specific area, it starts with the mind. This isn't a uniquely biblical concept. It's backed by a mountain of scientific data and research. So much of the misery we experience and perpetuate in our lives comes down to one thing: *thinking errors*. One writer puts it this way:

> Thinking errors are patterns of thinking (often automatic) that are twisted, distorted, or false. Usually we resort to thinking errors when we want to avoid or escape painful feelings, or we want to avoid responsibility and accountability for mistakes.[6]

The writer goes on to say that these thinking errors can be the result of a lack of experience, wisdom, or maturity or could stem from a disruption in development. In order to have positive relationships and even function, it's important to recognize and eliminate these thinking errors.

THE FUN KIND OF EXERCISE: THINKING ERRORS

I want to take you through an exercise. You can either write your thoughts down or think of them in your head. Bring to mind a memory of when your heart got broken. If you're currently experiencing heartbreak, maybe you don't want to choose your existing example because it's too close and too painful. In that case, maybe choose a heartbreak from the past. Ask yourself these questions and resist the urge to make the answers sound "good" or polished:

1. What happened in this situation that resulted in heartbreak?
2. How did you handle it while it was happening and after it happened?
3. What thinking errors came up for you during this time? (e.g., blame, shifting focus away from the core issue, denial, escaping, making assumptions, believing somehow that the rules don't apply to you, selfish and self-centered thinking, etc.)
4. How were you and the situation affected by your *thoughts*?

You and I each have a set of thinking errors that we are most susceptible to falling into and giving life to. So, each time a situation presents itself (even if it's entirely different from a past situation), we tend to grab those go-to errors for the next situation. This is typically what drives people to get married, divorced, married again because maybe this time will be different, divorced, and then married again because maybe this time or this person will be different . . . Throughout this cycle, what we *really* need to let drive us is gut-level, rigorous self-honesty.

During and after my divorce, I reached this point. I was more than fed up with myself and my unwanted patterns. My divorce was excruciatingly painful, and I wouldn't wish it on anyone. But much quicker than anticipated, I started noticing the gifts and finding hidden treasures underneath all the heartache. I embarked on a terrifying journey of loving myself—all parts of myself—even those parts that I worked tirelessly to hide from anyone and everyone (including my own spirit and God's Spirit). It was in my brokenness that I found myself.

Just like I had to lose God to find my true God during my faith deconstruction, I had to lose myself and my marriage to find out who I really am and who I am destined to be. I stopped looking over there, out there, and to that person, situation, award, position, etc. I dove in with both feet to become acquainted with myself for possibly the first time. I learned to love myself and accept God's love. I started rebuilding, rewriting my story, and reimaging what my life could be like. Truths about my past, present, and the future I dreamed of revealed themselves to me. It all started with my mind, the thoughts I entertained and allowed to percolate throughout my brain, and all those tiny little broken parts of my heart.

Gregory Bateson writes, "We create the world that we perceive, not because there is no reality outside our heads, but because we select and edit the reality we see to conform to our beliefs about what sort of world we live in . . . Sometimes the dissonance between reality and false beliefs reaches a point when it becomes impossible to avoid the awareness that the world no longer makes sense. Only then is it possible for the mind to consider radically different ideas and perceptions."[7]

I would add that sometimes getting our insides torn out and our hearts busted up into a bruised, unrecognizable cluster of pain serves as the catalyst for reaching that point. If there's no learning without pain, then I would argue there's no growth without heartache. I hate it. I wish it wasn't this way, because it hurts so much sometimes that we're not sure how we'll achieve our next breath. Our chests hurt, our bodies cave in, we lose our sense of self, and our worlds completely turn upside down and then some.

The wise spiritual teacher Rumi poses this essential question: "Try not to resist the changes that come your way. Instead, let life live through you. And do not worry that your life is turning upside down. How do you know that the side you are used to is better than the one to come?"[8]

| **MIND. BLOWN.** |

GIVING LOVE YET *ANOTHER* CHANCE

There have been more times than I can count when I swore I'd never let myself love again. I soon came to find out that I might as well ask myself not to breathe. Loving, for me, is as natural as breathing. I love love. I love loving others. I love feeling loved and giving love. Yet, after my divorce, I remember crying to my best friend while saying the following words which I believed to the very core of my being: "Love is cruel."

That was my perception. And my perception was my reality. I couldn't imagine a world where I'd ever consider letting myself love again. I *knew* I was never going to get married again, that was for damn sure. I figured I'd just hang out with friends and family (nothing wrong with that) and live a full life along with my eighty-five rescue dogs and whatever other animals I ended up finding and forcing to live with me. I'd ride off into the sunset with my independence, my heart healed, and free of pain.

This may be possible and the most appropriate path for some, but not me. I know me. I was created to be in relationships with others. I am most alive when I'm loving and being loved fiercely by another. Instead of resisting the changes I knew were coming (and needed to come) my way, I let go. I practiced surrender on a daily basis because that's not just a one-time thing. I worked on forgiving others, and most importantly, forgiving myself. I knew my life was turning upside down, and the second I stopped trying to fight it was the second I found some semblance of peace.

And I let it flow. Instead of jumping out of the whirlpool I felt trapped in, I gained a new perspective and realized I was actually floating in a lazy river. I didn't have to fight or tread water. I stopped fighting and started floating. I lay back into the flow of the spirit and let whatever happened happen. I repositioned all my energy to loving myself and creating a life I could be proud of.

HEARTBREAK HURTS (HEALING HURTS, ALSO)

My ex and I divorced when the girls were very young, so most of my energy was spent pouring into *me* during the times I didn't have the girls, and then pouring into the girls when I did have them all to myself.

Initially, I beat myself up because I thought I was robbing my girls of something I was convinced they needed in order to survive and thrive in life: for their moms to stay married. Now, looking back, I'm able to accept myself, knowing that both Jenny and I did everything we could to try and make it work. We both eventually had to choose ourselves because the girls needed healthy, whole moms. I wasn't robbing my girls of anything. I was giving them the best gift I could possibly give them—the best version of their mama, loving them wholly and completely from a full reservoir of love.

I will never forget those special moments when it was just me and my girls in our space. I gave them my all, as I strive to do to this day. Though I'm definitely a work in progress, I can honestly say that when

I'm with my girls, I am fully present most days. I work hard every day to ensure they're getting the very best version of me—even if that version is just "okay," because that's okay, too. The more I honor myself and love myself, the more capacity I have to love and honor my kids.

My healing process wasn't just a one-time thing that occurred at a set place for a set number of days, months, or years. It was all over the place—just like life. Each day was different; some days I'd be filled with rage, other days, peace and joy. I'd go from crying to yelling at the sky to laying down out of sheer exhaustion. Why is it that sometimes the very process of healing can cause more pain than the original wound? How does that work? I'm honestly not sure, but I know that's what I experienced. There's the initial pain that causes the wound, and that stings like a mothereffer. But then there's the thing that comes after the thing. I assume this happens because having your heart broken is traumatic. As Bessel van der Kolk writes, "Trauma comes back as a Reaction, not a Memory."[9]

Maybe that's why the healing process is sometimes more painful than the original situation that caused the broken heart in the first place. Every time we recall the memory, we are re-reacting to it and creating re-traumatization. This reminds me of a story a friend recently told me about his sister who was suffering from third-degree burns. She shared with him how intense the initial burn pain was but also how surprised she was to learn that the treatment for the burns was even more painful than the injury itself. The very treatment that is required for her healing is the thing causing her more and more pain. It is necessary pain, no matter the level of torture. It doesn't seem fair, but since when has anything really seemed fair these days? I think it's the same with heartbreak. There are different degrees of heartbreak, first-degree, second-degree, and third-degree. The healing process will depend on the degree to which your heart was broken.

Love is *not* cruel, as I previously thought in my emo days. Loving someone and having that love ripped from you is hurtful and excruciatingly painful, but it cannot be cruel. Love, by its very nature, is incapable of cruelty. **Love is for us, in us, and all around us.** The byproduct of romantic love with another human can and typically will result in heartache because relationships involve humans, and humans aren't perfect. We will always hurt the ones we love and be hurt by them, whether intentionally or unintentionally. That doesn't mean we should just throw in the towel on the whole concept of love. It certainly feels that way at times, and that's okay, too. You don't have to fix it or change whatever you're feeling in response to heartbreak. Just be present with it. Learn from it. Let it move through you. Learn to live the *other side* of the upside-down life you've got in front of you.

During times of heartbreak, it's important to prioritize and double down on self-care. I recently read a Healthline article about how heartbreak affects our health: "Though we may not know exactly why heartbreak affects our physical bodies the way it does, the effects are many and can be debilitating . . . Treating the effects of heartbreak while allowing the person to mourn the loss of a relationship can be a tricky balance."[10]

This is especially challenging when you are forced to continue interacting with the person whose loss you're trying to grieve. The friend I wrote about earlier continues to fail at getting out of her toxic relationship because she's addicted to him. She can't cut things off because she would rather stay in the toxicity than experience the pain of letting him go. Staying connected to him, whether in person or via social media, simply delays the inevitable while compounding the heartache.

The article goes on to quote licensed therapist Courtney Nesbitt: "Unfortunately, the only remedy for heartbreak and emotional pain is time . . . Unless there are children involved, the best option is to refrain from contact with the person; that includes on social media."[11]

LETTING GO FOR DUMMIES (LIKE ME)

Back in the day, I used to stalk my exes on social media like it was an Olympic event, so I know that Nesbitt quote might have stung for a few of you. But she's right. How are we supposed to successfully grieve and move through the pain someone has caused us if we continue to be around them and remain tied to them? It's virtually impossible. It's hard to get to a place of openness and willingness to find your next person if your wagon is still hitched to the old one.

We know from research that heartbreak changes the physiological makeup of our brains. Our brains are essentially rewired by pain. This can either be a good thing or a bad thing depending on how the rewiring process unfolds.

So, how the hell are we supposed to heal and move on from someone with whom our lives are inextricably linked? This is also where I found a great deal of wisdom and hidden gifts: co-parenting with my ex-wife. I am happy to report that despite our ups and downs, we co-parent beautifully when it comes to our girls. It's not perfect, and we fail many times, but for the most part, we are able to set aside our disagreements and differences of opinion for the sake of putting our best foot forward. This didn't happen overnight, though. It has been a continual work in progress—the work of letting go. I needed to be reminded of the power of letting go so much that I got a tattoo of the words "let go" on my left wrist facing toward me so I can read it whenever I'm starting to go off the deep end.

LOVE AT FIRST SWIPE

In 2018, I felt a shift. After a solo date night with a bottle of wine, I got a wild hair to join a lesbian dating app called HER. Within hours I saw her. A gorgeous woman wearing a Stetson hat whose smile pierced my very existence. We connected, started messaging immediately, and set up our first date within hours of texting. It was my birthday, and she wanted to take me on a date. The moment I saw her—that was it. She was it for me and still is. I NEVER believed in love at first sight until we met.

This was a woman I wanted to get to know deeply, whom I wanted to pursue, court, and find a way to spend more time with. This was someone I could see myself spending the rest of my life with, despite all the past pain and heartache, despite all the past failed relationships and trauma. I didn't care. I didn't care about anything really, other than being around her. Our date was pure magic. At one point, I felt the entire world around me disappear.

We've been together ever since. We dated for about a year before she and her son, Atticus, moved in with me and the girls. Brynn asked me to marry her in August of 2019, at Austin Pride. Then, I asked her to marry me at the International Balloon Fiesta in New Mexico in October that same year. I had it all planned out perfectly. I was going to propose in the air, at sunrise, in a private hot air balloon. Weather had other plans. All flights were grounded, so I proposed when we got out of the basket. A local news crew ended up capturing the entire experience.

THE CLASSIC COVID PIVOT

We planned our dream wedding, which was supposed to take place on April 10th, 2020, at the historic, iconic Hotel Ella in downtown Austin. Covid shut Austin down toward the end of March and derailed all our wedding plans. Heartbreak isn't unique to romantic relationships, and this most certainly isn't a chapter just about divorce. Heartbreak can happen at any time, anywhere, for any reason. When I read the Austin Mayor's orders limiting the number of people who could be in a group due to Covid and declaring the eventual total shutdown of the city, our hearts and our kids' hearts broke.

It took a while to work through the death of our dream wedding. But eventually, we were able to pick ourselves up off the floor and start dreaming of a new, different, yet equally special wedding. Initially, we'd assumed that our rescheduled wedding would be six to twelve months out. Then, on April 9th (the day before our would-be Good Friday wedding—because nothing says "He Is Risen" like a good ol' fashioned lesbian wedding!), I got a call from my dad that he had been diagnosed with Covid. My heart sank and fell out of my body. At that time, we didn't know if Covid was going to kill everyone or just a few people. We were still spraying down our groceries and rationing toilet paper and hand sanitizer as if there would *never* be any more production of toilet paper or hand sanitizer ever again until the end of times.

As soon as my dad and I ended that paralyzing phone call, I knew we couldn't wait on this wedding. I didn't have a clue what this virus would do to my dad or my mom, for that matter. And I didn't want to find out. I did know, however, that I would never forgive myself if we postponed the wedding and Covid ended up robbing my parents from attending. The fact that my parents *were* planning on attending our wedding was HUGE. They had a very hard time when I initially came out. They struggled and wrestled, but they have loved me and shown up for me in major ways. I knew I had to do whatever it took to ensure my parents could attend our wedding.

We had a badass wedding planner who mastered the art of thinking outside the box. She called a few days after I found out that my dad had Covid with a brilliant idea: "What if y'all got married at a drive-in movie theater where everyone could come and stay in their cars with their quarantine pods to ensure the safety of all guests?"

Brynn and I looked at each other (while Cassie, our wedding planner, was on speaker) as if to say, "SOUNDS INSANE, WE'RE SO IN!"

We started brainstorming and dreaming of this crazy drive-in movie theater wedding idea. On Saturday morning (April 11th, the morning after our Plan A wedding date), instead of being on a flight to Mexico for our picture-perfect honeymoon, we made a cup of coffee and sat on the couch to watch cartoons with our kids. Within minutes of what should've been a typical Saturday morning, out of nowhere, Brynn lunged off the couch in excitement . . . "Oh my God! There's a drive-in movie theater that is still open in Buda, Texas!" Thrilled by the possibility of making the greatest wedding pivot in history, we immediately started to take action.

After a phone call with the owners of Doc's Drive-In Movie Theatre, it was all hands on deck. We began planning a polar opposite wedding to our original vision and had seventeen days to get everything ready. We chose our new wedding date because everything fell into place. Plus, that was the only date that worked for my dear friend and officiant Jen Hatmaker, who was in the middle of launching her umpteenth *NYT* best seller. We never thought we'd be getting married on a Tuesday during a global pandemic at a drive-in movie theater in Buda, Texas. But everything about it fit us. April 28th became our new wedding date.

In seventeen days filled with scrambling to coordinate details and make this completely out-of-the-box ceremony happen, we did the damn thing. Instead of a magical ceremony under a beautiful oak tree facing a 1920s historic mansion, we stood in a gravel-paved parking lot off of a farm road surrounded by ninety cars. Instead of a bougie cocktail hour with the perfect blend of music, food, drinks, and fun, we enjoyed popcorn, mini corn dogs, and soda with our kids and who-ever else actually attended our wedding—we had no idea, since we couldn't really see inside anyone's cars.

We traded our heels for cowboy boots (let's face it, no woman—even the femme-est of femme lesbians—can gracefully walk in a gravel lot with heels on) and because we didn't have time to get our dresses hemmed, they dragged in the dirt. We swapped an unforgetta-ble dance-party reception for a movie (*Airplane!*) that played for our guests after our ceremony and switched our Tulum honeymoon for a two-day staycation in an airstream trailer.

All of it felt right.

The ceremony was live-streamed on various social media plat-forms so that our distant friends and family—those who couldn't fly to attend the wedding because no one was flying at that time—could join in the experience. The ceremony audio was ported into everyone's car just like a typical drive-in movie theater. The video feed enabled our entire ceremony to be seen on the two giant big screens that typ-ically show movies. Word spread about the wedding, and I got a call the day before that *The New York Times* would be in attendance to do a story about our out-of-the-box idea that was still entirely Covid safe. We ended up having about ninety cars attend. We asked people to dress up in their PJs and decorate their cars. There were cars with rainbows, draped with streamers, one truck had a tent pitched in the truck bed—there were cars everywhere. Each time someone felt like clapping or screaming, they honked.

Then, out of nowhere, our wedding went viral and has since been featured in the *NYT*, *People* magazine, tons of other news outlets, online blogs worldwide, and *The Today Show*.[13] Our wedding going viral wasn't an indication of how great Brynn and I are. Our wedding went viral because that's how powerful love is. People could not get enough of the story because we are all crying out for the same thing: to experience love. To witness love, to feel love, and give it. Simply put, we are all created to BE loved and to BE love.

FROM HEARTBREAK TO HEALING, FROM SORROW TO JOY

The story of how everything unfolded still boggles my mind, even though it's been a while since it happened. I wouldn't trade a thing. I wouldn't change one moment or make a different choice. I'm only able to say this now because of the work I've done to heal and grow, but I certainly couldn't say this way back during the middle of the heartbreak of divorce and the painful process that followed. I'd go through it all again just to make sure I ended up right where I am.

Every *ounce* of my life's pain, loss, trauma, tragedy, heartbreak, fear, humiliation, anger, addiction, rejection, waiting, leaving, powerlessness, emptiness, and conflict up to this point has somehow mystically and mysteriously culminated in the life I'm living today. Throughout my journey, shit has happened—*and yet*—I've still not found gifts in all of it. And I've made peace with that. **Maybe that is the gift, making peace with the fact that NOT everything happens for a reason.** Sometimes shit just happens because we live in a broken world full of broken people who are trying to figure out what the hell is going on and how we're supposed to do this thing called life.

I'm only forty years old. I have a good sixty more years left in me. I know that my life will be full of beauty, joy, happiness, and all the goodness in life. I also know there is more pain to come, more loss I'll experience, and more fear I'll have to contend with. It's all a part of the deal. My acceptance of life being filled with stuff that hurts and stuff that makes me happy is where my power, magic, and strength lie.

We will keep encountering life on life's terms and all it brings with it: the good, the bad, the ugly. Old wounds will continually come up to be healed. This will keep happening until we heal from whatever or whomever we need to heal from. We *are* forever changed, we *will* forever change, and we *will be* forever changed.

Break It Down for Me

- In every situation, no matter how minuscule or major, painful or purposeful, we will grow the most when we can look—with rigorous honesty and self-awareness—at our role in whatever happened.

- Heartbreak may be the very shake-up we need, the crucial catalyst that leads to a completely new direction for our lives.

- The sooner we can get to the end of self-sufficiency and reach out for help, the better off our lives, relationships, and experiences will be. Surrendering to spirit's sufficiency changes everything.

- Reframing the way we perceive heartbreak can move us from perpetual victim to peace-filled visionary, seeing life with new eyes.

Chapter 14

THE GIFT OF EMPTINESS

"The last time I felt this emotionally encumbered,
  I was playing Lady Macbeth on a Crystal Skies
  cruise ship during Shakespeare at Sea Week!"
  —**Moira Rose**, *Schitt's Creek* (S4, E1)

"If airplane safety videos have taught me anything,
  David, it's that a mother puts her own mask on first."
  —**Moira Rose**, *Schitt's Creek* (S3, E9)

I wasn't on a mountaintop. I wasn't meditating in the fields of Tibet.
I wasn't attending a revival. No one was praying for me. There was
absolutely nothing magical, and I wasn't doing anything "spiritual" . . .
when God broke in. Truth is, I was on my couch having a date with
my favorite sweatpants, a glass of wine, and Netflix. It was the movie
Aloha, starring my Kinsey Scale mover, Bradley Cooper. (BTW, the
Kinsey Scale, also known as the Heterosexual–Homosexual Rating
Scale, is a continuum used to describe a person's sexual orientation. It
was created by sex researcher Alfred Kinsey and his colleagues in the
late 1940s and early 1950s as a way to categorize individuals' sexual
behaviors, desires, and fantasies.)

THE NIGHT BRADLEY COOPER CHANGED ME

I'd always heard that God uses the ordinary to do the most extraordinary. Riding in on a donkey, anointing a Shepherd boy to be King . . . but a cheesy romantic movie with my main man-crush? And yet, there I was in an ordinary, everyday-life kind of way when God broke in. When God broke *me* and broke through. Something in that movie pierced me deeply, and I was suddenly a champagne bottle whose cork had just been busted off after being shaken for hours.

All the feels came pouring out. Before I knew what was happening, I was on the floor, weeping uncontrollably. Not about the movie, but about the move of God that was happening in and around me. Over the course of what I would later realize had been three hours, I had released so much.

Toward the beginning of the breakdown, my eyes saw "23" on the TV screen clock. Though not an avid Bible reader anymore (due to its recent use in the past years as a bludgeoning tool), I found myself thinking of Psalm 23. The Lord is my Shepherd; I SHALL NOT WANT.

I shall not want.

I shall not want.

I couldn't go any further. Those words became a *pre-op* of sorts (as in preoperative). Slowly and with loving precision, I felt God begin to remove every layer of stuff I'd filled myself with. I saw a picture of a CRATER in my mind's eye.

What happened next physically felt like surgery. As if every molecule of counterfeit filling was being surgically yet gently removed. It was excruciating. I was being dug out. The enormous crater was being emptied. It was disappearing or going anywhere. From weeping to flat-out ugly crying, the crater was showing itself. A dark, empty void. It was painful. There was nothing. Pure unadulterated nothingness, as if an atomic bomb had been dropped in the middle of my chest. But it had always been there, and day by day I did my best at filling it. But not this time. I could see, sense, and feel the bottom of the crater.

And that's when love ravished me. In that empty moment, I felt the iridescent light and all-consuming love of God break in. I felt the light of love touch the bottom of the newly emptied crater. And slowly, the light and love kept filling the dark, empty space. I have never felt so loved. So powerfully, unconditionally, and unshakably loved. I was drowning in light. This light did not make the crater obsolete. The crater went nowhere. But for the first time, it was filled and overflowing with complete "I shall not want" light, plus love; the "God-shaped hole, plus there's a void only God can fill" cliches . . .

Well, I'm taking it back with a slight edit. "Void/God-shaped hole" is far too sweet. The light and love of spirit *broke in*. It emptied me *completely* to fill me up with rivers of living water. I've never been the same since that night.

YOUR EMOTIONAL CAR IS ABOUT TO BE A STAR ON *OPERATION REPO*

When I first got into the banking profession, I didn't have a clue about debt. I didn't know how debt worked, and I certainly didn't understand interest rates. In fact, when Becky recruited me to work for her at Wells Fargo, I confessed to her right out of the gate that I didn't even own a credit card. I had to have lunch with my dad before my initial interview for the job and ask him how interest worked. What is a home equity loan and why do all these credit card companies want to give away free t-shirts to college students who sign up for these cards? I was clueless.

And then I got into banking, learned the ropes, and after over a decade of experience and knowledge, I would consider myself a debt expert. I know more about debt, amortization tables, interest rates, and a slew of other super boring jargon than I ever cared to know. This knowledge is power because it allows me to help a bunch of clients. But I'm still surprised that the debt-confused waitress is now the director of wealth management at one of the leading firms in Austin.

Here's the thing about debt (and no, this isn't ultimately a chapter about *financial* debt but *emotional* debt, so keep reading): typically, you get into debt slowly over a period of time. In some cases, people get into debt right away because of something major that happened unexpectedly. I had a client who went from owning his own mansion free and clear, having zero debt, and beaucoup cash lying around to a destitute, debt-ridden individual in a matter of months. The only reason? His wife got cancer, and they didn't have health insurance. This is one way to enter the quicksand of debt.

Another way is the way of the majority of people in our country. We don't just wake up one day and hope to be drowning in debt by the time we're thirty. It happens slowly over a long period of time. First, it starts with the credit card you got because of the attractive perks. Then you moved to the 0 percent interest card that you had every intention of paying off in the time frame disclosed . . . but the debt builds up because you put more on the card or you sign up for other credit cards. Then you've got the car payment, the mortgage, student loans, Rooms To Go, and maybe even those pesky medical payments. Either way, it sometimes takes years for people to find themselves drowning in debt.

Here's the dirty little secret about credit card debt. The interest accrues daily, and each time you make your payment, it typically goes to the interest charge and not to the principal balance. What that means for us—imagine trying to chop down a tree that keeps growing each day, and all you have is one of those plastic sporks from KFC. You aren't going to have a lot of luck getting that tree chopped down. Unless you pay off the balance each month, you'll start being charged interest and possibly some fees. It can get out of hand really quickly, especially if you're only making the required minimum payments.

Why does this matter? Debt sucks. Guess what sucks more . . . EMOTIONAL debt. Yes, that's a thing.

RAISING THE EMOTIONAL DEBT CEILING

I was talking to my best friend Julia, and I have to *credit* her (pun intended) for this mind-blowing illustration.

Here's the picture Julia painted for me that day on the phone, which I know we all can relate to:

When each of us was born, we were given an emotional bank account. A thousand variables play into the balance of this account. You know this. Look back on your life or even more closely on your day yesterday. Certain activities, conversations, tasks, and people tanked your account balance. Other activities, conversations, tasks, and people deposited into your account, bringing your balance up. But somewhere along the way, we women had to start using an emotional credit card. Our emotional bank account had been zeroed out and gone into the negative. After years of racking up overdraft fees, we've had to turn to credit. So, we put more and more of our emotional energy on credit cards. We have to apply for more and more cards because we keep maxing each out.

In finance, we encourage people to keep their credit utilization below 50 percent on all trade lines. Translated: if you have a $50,000 limit on your Amex, keep the balance below $25,000 at all times. Even better, keep it below 20 percent. Most people find this extremely difficult. We tend to max out credit lines, and we opt for asking the credit card company to increase our credit limit versus doing the work to pay down the balance.

We've been doing this from an emotional perspective for far too long. As women, we are raised to give and give and pour out constantly for the benefit of others. We empty our bank accounts, incur overdraft fees, and turn to credit. We max out all the credit cards and attempt to take advantage of the 0 percent interest game, thinking maybe if I roll this debt onto a new card, I can pay it off in eighteen months while I have 0 percent interest. But guess what? Which card will you use when you need to pay for that new AC unit? Research shows you'll opt for the 0 percent credit card. By the time the eighteen months are up, you haven't paid off the balance. In fact, you've added to it. So before that 24 percent interest kicks in, you start hunting for a new 0 percent credit card to transfer that balance to.

OUR EMOTIONAL CREDIT CARDS ARE MAXED OUT

Emotionally speaking, I've most definitely done this. Once emotional credit card A is maxed out, I'll look for a 0 percent option. Maybe that's yoga, exercising, journaling more, going to therapy, eating my feelings, taking on a new hobby, or taking a stab at what your weird aunt calls "crafternoons."

While I'm sure most of these options are beneficial, it doesn't ultimately get to the root of the issue. You're simply swapping debt and usually adding to the original debt. The tree keeps growing, and there you are with your plastic spork wondering how the hell you got here. It's similar to dieting. Yo-yo dieting produces results. Let me clarify: yo-yo dieting produces *negative* results. Typically, you'll lose weight at first and then gain all the weight back once your diet is over and you start eating normally again. PLUS INTEREST. Lord knows I've tried every diet on the planet. And guess what? I've ALWAYS gained the weight back plus interest.

It's no different with our emotional bucket and our energy bank account. I'm fairly certain we've all done this. We encounter a season of ridiculous busyness. We find ourselves empty and overwhelmed, so we prune our schedule and cut back. We find some peace; we create space. And then, we subconsciously fill that space because that's what we do. And the yo-yo continues to rise and fall.

We're Conditioned to Be Human Doings Instead of Human Beings

We are in debt. Emotional debt, energy debt, everything debt. Why? Because we have been conditioned to be human doings. Do this, do that. Don't do this, don't do that. Oh, they're doing that? Well then, you certainly have to do it too. Oh, they're NOT doing that? Well then, you can't do that. We are pressured to do more and more and more. But guess what (and hopefully this isn't new information to you): you were created to BE a HUMAN BEing. The act and art of

BEing. Nothing more, nothing less—just be. You are a human. You are a divine being created for limitless living.

Are we though? I would argue no. We are most definitely limited, and we are not soldiers. Some of you are actual, literal soldiers and we thank you for your service. (Several of my closest friends are veterans.) But that's not the type of soldier I'm referring to. I'm describing soldier as a verb: soldier as in "I wasn't enjoying trying to fit into my Spanx on my wedding day, but I soldiered on." I'm all about soldiering on, but not at the expense of your entire life and joy. I am pro-perseverance, but not if it involves setting yourself on fire to keep everyone else warm.

Most of us have spent our lives emptying all the accounts, burdening ourselves with debt, and now the jig is up. The repo company is coming; the mortgage company is going to foreclose on your house; you're about to be kicked out on the street. You're considering filing for Chapter 11 bankruptcy. What other choice do you have? You can either try and dig yourself out, or you can file.

If you're going to move from your bank account to putting deficits on credit, then you need something like this for your emotional debt. What would it look like to decrease your credit utilization? You can't calculate that number until you know your limit. But how on earth do you find out your limit? The emotion fairy isn't going to mail you a disclosure informing you of your credit limit per emotional trade line or credit card. So, how do you know? You can't. That's the point.

EMOTIONAL BANKRUPTCY

I'm fully aware this notion of emotional bankruptcy is not new. Even though I first heard of it from Julia, I've since become aware that this is not a unique concept. Regardless of whether you're just now learning of this phenomenon or you've heard about this many times in the past, it still matters. This is a matter of life and death; I truly believe that. This either resonates with you or it doesn't.

Have you experienced emotional bankruptcy? Chances are, if you're over the age of ten and have a pulse, the answer is yes.

Are you open to accepting the reality that your emotional bank account has zeroed out and you've got overdraft fees? Are you drowning in debt and you just got kicked out on the streets? Where are you on the continuum? Maybe your bank account is overflowing and you're flush with cash. Why is that? Figure that out and do more of that.

Awareness is the first step in the 3 A's—awareness, acceptance, and action. You can't skip steps, so where can you start? Become aware. Ask God to help you become more aware. Is it time to take a long, hard look in the mirror and have a hard conversation with yourself? Are you ready to stop the runaway train and take the first crucial steps to replenish your emotional account?

How is this bankruptcy messing with your life?

Where are you on the cycle of emotional depletion?

What purpose is it currently serving in your life? Spoiler alert: there's a reason you've been doing life like this over and over again . . . How is it serving you? Dig deep.

Why should you address these issues and potential icebergs?

Are you in denial? Or are you super-focused on this problem and feeding it with counterproductive energy? Whatever you focus on expands, as scientists have been telling us for quite some time. Your mind is the most powerful tool you're most likely not using.

Are boundaries the answer? I know, no one likes *that* B word.

I recently read a *Forbes* article that said, "We all have a limited amount of energy we're trying to manage each day, and a host of new challenges to tackle while we're at it. We do not set boundaries because we fundamentally dislike someone or don't have enough time for them, but because we have to prioritize our own health and well-being before we can effectively take care of anything else."[1]

Maybe we've been doing this whole boundary-setting thing wrong. If you're setting boundaries, ask yourself why? What is your motive for doing so? Are you honoring your boundaries by refusing to accept when others don't honor them?

What causes your emotions to be spent? Time to do an inventory.

TAKE OFF THE SELF-PITY SPECTACLES

Do you see yourself as a victim without power? Or are you an empowered woman refusing to stay in your victim prison? You can't see the world from an empowered perspective if you've got your victim goggles on. The inverse is also true. Check your perceptions and perspectives.

Have you heard the story about the couple who kept watching their new neighbor hang up her laundry on an old-school clothesline? They kept dogging on this woman because all her clothes looked so disgusting. They were dumbfounded by how dirty her laundry was, even though she just washed it. After about four weeks of gossip and judgment, their monthly window cleaner came. The same day, the couple thought their neighbor finally learned how to do laundry because her clothes were sparkling white and vibrantly clean, bursting with color.

How many times do we do this in our lives?

You feel like the walls are closing in. You're in debt simply because you've been operating in a world that praises human doings and not human beings. It's not just been one small thing that's woken you up to this newfound reality, this new awareness; it's been the proverbial "death by a thousand cuts." There are a million little things, countless tiny steps that have gotten you where you are today. A key component in all this is taking responsibility for where you are. There's no one else to blame. Sure, you can think of dozens of people and reasons why you are where you are, but until you take responsibility for where you are right here right now, you won't get past this. **It all starts with forgiving yourself.**

Spiritual guru Paul Selig puts it plainly: "You must forgive yourself, for not knowing any better than you did at the time that you make something so. If you can do this much, you can release yourself from a magnitude of contention that you have created against the self. If you decide, right now, that every choice that you have ever made was born in awareness that you held at the moment that choice was made, you can be understanding of the way that you operated and when. If you knew now what you knew then, you may well have done differently, but you cannot."[2]

A path exists where we can take responsibility for our lives and choices without beating ourselves up about them. Self-acceptance is the antithesis of and antidote for self-loathing.

THE VOID VALUE

If we simply stop at emptiness and don't finish the story, we will never truly have hope. As we're learning throughout this entire book, we have to sit with all that life throws at us, while honoring our feelings. And somehow, we have to toe the fine line of not being consumed by the emptiness to the point of no return.

This is where I find the value of the void, the gift of the empty spaces that exist throughout our lives. I like to think of it this way: emptiness is simply defined as the "state of containing nothing." Might seem obvious, but to most, it's not obvious at all. It's time to finish our story by finding the right *stuff* to fill the void.

Break It Down for Me

- We all have voids of emptiness inside us that we tirelessly try to fill in unhelpful, unsustainable ways. The work is in the excavation of the void, undoing the packed layers of our various vices to give room for light to break in.
- There will come a time in our lives—once our emotional bank account is empty and we've maxed out all the emotional credit cards—when there is nowhere else to turn but inward.
- You were created to create. You are not a human DOing. You are a human BEing, so BE. Be love. Be light. Be unapologetically YOU.

- Boundaries exist for *us* and must be established for our own protection. Setting limits helps us establish healthy relationships with others, and most importantly ourselves. **Boundaries are the new Bodyguard.**

I RUN A TIGHT

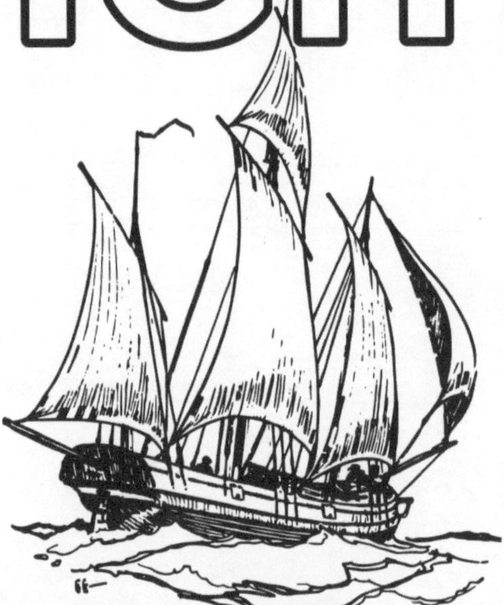

SHIPWRECK

THE GIFT OF CONFLICT

"I may have been wrong. You may have been not wrong."
—Moira Rose, *Schitt's Creek* (S6, E5)

"I want you to know, I value each of your
opinions, even when you're wrong."
—Ted Lasso, *Ted Lasso* (S1, E8)

In all transparency, I am *not* looking forward to writing this chapter. I hate conflict. I will go to great lengths to avoid it, similar to the lengths I went to a few years back when I saw my OBGYN at Pottery Barn.

As I look back on my personal experience with Covid, I realize it isn't entirely unique. These past few years have been riddled with pain, suffering, conflict, loss, fighting, arguing, isolating, and digging our heels into the polar opposite realities in which we live. In my forty years of living, I cannot remember a time in my life or in the history of our country when people have been so incredibly polarized. Humans today split hairs and fight over the tiniest of things.

It's hard for me to write about the GIFT of conflict, because as I sit here right now, typing furiously away on my laptop while listening to and watching the rain pour down powerfully, I don't see any gift in our current environment of conflict. When I first saw all the heart-wrenching news showing the droves of devastated Ukrainian people and the death and destruction they've suffered at the hands of Russia, I see ZERO GIFTS in that conflict. In fact, I can't even use the term "conflict" to describe what's going on there. Better to use the terms atrocity, war, devastation, destruction, and evil. Sometimes, you can look as hard as you possibly can at a conflict, and you won't see a gift. You may never see a gift. Because—if I've said it once, I've said it a thousand times—NOT everything happens for a reason.

Watching the dramatic rise of conflict and polarization in our families, communities, and countries has stolen more joy than I care to admit. Sometimes all the infighting paralyzes me, and I'm at a complete loss for words. These days, people will find anything to fight about. Did you know that there's a serious scientific argument amongst many people pertaining to this question: *Is water wet?*

IT'S NOT *OUT* THERE (IT'S *IN* US)

Conflict has always been and will always be a part of life and a part of any relationship or friendship. You and I know this full well. But here's what I think we may have been missing. The conflict isn't uniquely *out there* . . . it's within us. Stay with me here. We're going to start at the very beginning and we're going to let all this begin with ourselves.

Take today, for example. I'm having a very intense conflict with someone I love very much. It makes me feel blah, confused, upset, overwhelmed, anxious, and fearful. I cry a little, and then I'm filled with rage. I want to argue my points, and I get trapped into a cycle of thinking, *If I could just say it this way or make this person understand XYZ, then I'll be happy and this pain will pass.* Remember, I HATE conflict. But I'm learning to embrace it—slowly. Hopefully someday, I'll actually learn to appreciate it.

But for today, I'm definitely not living with a mindset of appreciation or gratitude. Sometimes the conflict and tension swallow me up, and it's because it's not simply outside of me but very much inside me as well. Let me explain . . .

We all have light and dark energies inside of us. Religious and political beliefs aside, no matter how you feel about light and dark, both exist all around us and inside each one of us.

You know this as the yin-yang symbol that we used to wear on necklaces in middle school. According to the religious tradition of Taoism/Daoism (and good ol' Wikipedia), yin and yang is a "Chinese philosophical concept that describes interconnected opposite forces." It goes on to say that "yin and yang can be thought of as complementary (rather than opposing) forces that interact to form a dynamic system in which the whole is greater than the assembled parts . . . everything has both yin and yang aspects (for instance, shadow cannot exist without light)."[1] These terms, "yin" and "yang," refer to Chinese characters that mean "dark side" for yin and "white side" for yang.

For most of my life, I've tried to fight the dark side, the not-so-pretty parts of me, the corners of my heart and soul I'd rather keep out of view. However, as I unpack in this chapter, my life changed the moment I realized that I very much NEED the dark and light energies, and I need them to collide in order to create something new. We wouldn't have water unless a little-known element named molecular hydrogen reacted with oxygen back in the day. Did you know that when H_2 and O_2 are combined and allowed to react together, their molecules could actually combine to form either water OR hydrogen peroxide? It's true. Because science.

Just because two different components combine to form something new, doesn't mean that it can only form one new thing. It's the same with the light and dark coexisting within each and every one of us. Maybe you don't believe you have both dark and light inside you. I encourage you to sit in traffic and let someone cut you off and then analyze your reaction. Or what about when your loved one does something that pushes all of your buttons and finds new buttons you didn't even know you had? You'll find your dark side. Then, the choice becomes how intensely you're going to love your dark side, or as Dr. Phil Stutz refers to it, our "shadow self." If you haven't yet watched the Netflix documentary *Stutz*, please do so as soon as you put this book down.[2]

FAQs: Frequently Avoided Questions

Before we move on, let's gain more awareness about the power of polar opposites, which will lay the foundation for the gift of conflict. Ask yourself the following questions and reflect on your answers:

- Where can you sense dark and light within you and where do you feel it?
- Are these energies constantly fighting each other and colliding like bumper cars?
- How does that constant collision of polar opposites cause you to feel?
- Can you feel the tension between your internal yin and yang?

WE'RE BOTH DARK AND LIGHT

When working with my mentor and spiritual guru Jon (whom I've written about numerous times throughout this book), he led me through an exercise that was life changing. Instead of stressing and hyper-focusing on all the chaos and conflict in the world, I went inward. I started to focus on the chaos that lived within me. I became more and more aware of how these opposing forces were impacting my mood, mindset, and spirit. I slowly began to realize that the magic is found when we work toward bringing these polarizing energies into alignment.

I can feel both light and dark without being consumed by either. Instead, I become aware of my feelings, and I ask my Higher Power to bring these opposite energies into harmony. If I'm feeling extra woo-woo, I'll ask the light and dark to harmonize with one another. Why not try it? Especially if you find that what you've been doing isn't working like you want and need it to. We're all tormented internally by these opposing forces. They have many names: the imposter, the dark side, the dark passenger, the angel on one shoulder and devil on the other.

When I start to feel conflict and tension within me, I simply ask spirit to help me be fully present with the opposing energies I'm experiencing. There is power in being present, and even more power in asking for harmony versus what I used to do, which was a constant failed attempt to ignore the darkness and hope it would simply go away at some point. I believe in a cosmic balance where light and dark—good and evil—will always exist. Not in some fictional *Harry Potter* kind of way, but in a very real this-is-how-I-see-the-world way. Where we get tripped up is when we hyper focus on the dark over the light. Then we start to get off balance. Or . . . when we focus on the light and positive thinking over the dark. That can also knock us off balance. We humans are complex beings with both yin and yang energies within us. It's not so much about destroying the side of that coin we hate, but rather acknowledging and accepting that we have both sides of the coin within us, and both matter and serve a purpose.

Before reading this, you may have been completely unaware of the need for this collision, for the importance of the work to harmonize opposing energies instead of continuing to let them repel each other like me and mayonnaise. When you and I refuse to accept the dark along with the light, we push the dark deep into the shadows, and that's when it comes out sideways and usually worse than if we'd simply accepted that both light and dark are a part of our story (and thus, a part of our world).

Think about nature and the universe. Some planets and galaxies have more light or dark energies. Hell, we wouldn't even be here sucking up oxygen on this planet unless polarity existed. We need the polarity within us, but only if we can find a way to bring them into harmony to create something new, something balanced.

Here's what I think: I believe the reason we have conflict in our lives and bodies is that we are not allowing the forces of opposing energies to collide and create something entirely different and whole. I need to give my brain permission for this collision to happen and to let go. Sometimes I have to tell my brain, "Hey brain, this is all happening to help you, so you can relax, which is what I know you want and need. Enough is enough. Let this happen so we can let it go." No matter the nature of the conflict, whether internal or external, there is a treasure found in the tension between these polar opposite forces. Say what you will about Covid, but I believe the pandemic forced us to evolve. It pushed us into a space where we had to start dealing with stuff and feeling things.

One day, when Jon and I were discussing this topic of light and dark and the balance of everything, he saw a vision. He explained to me that he got a very clear picture of my heart shooting out radiations which were adorned with both light and dark lines. He described the vision as feeling dense, not separate. It was a grounded energy that was born out of me, finally allowing the darkness I'd been fighting against my entire life to crash into my heart. I became aware of the force as a result of his vision, and it was one of the most powerful things I've ever experienced.

NO LIGHT WITHOUT DARK

I've spent my whole life obsessing over putting my best foot forward and only showing people the parts I deemed as "good." Then, I worked tirelessly on beating back and cutting out anything I judged as the opposite of good. Now, I realize all I was doing was cutting off a very real piece of myself. I can't fully enjoy all the light my soul and spirit have to offer if I'm not aware and completely open-eyed to all parts of me, darkness included. Once we truly meet our shadow selves and approach with unconditional love, everything changes.

Since Jon shared that vision with me toward the end of 2020, I've not been the same. Even though some times are more challenging than others, I genuinely try to live a life where I'm not hiding one part of myself. I figured if I could do it with coming out and being gay, then I could also do it with the parts of me I don't necessarily like. Instead of shielding everyone from my dark, sad, and gloomy days, I'm trying to be more real about it.

People would describe me as a bubbly, upbeat, and optimistic person. But that's because that's all I've ever shown to the world. There's so much freedom in letting other sides out, too, when you feel safe and comfortable. This is the value of vulnerability. When we're ready and feel safe, we can finally stop hiding those parts of us that we've been so judgmental of. Just last week, I was talking with Jon, and he said, "If darkness is the absence of light, then fear is the absence of love." We have to stop fearing our dark side and start loving it.

Guess what happened when I started to be more real with people instead of hiding the parts of myself I didn't think they'd like? I started connecting with people in a way I'd not connected before. Why is that? Think about it this way: If you and I have dinner every Tuesday night and I'm always chipper, always happy, always positive, and exuding confidence and light, you will most likely only see me in that light. (Pun intended, as all mine are.) BUT . . . what if I was always real with you at dinner, no matter what I was going through? What if I shared the good, the bad, AND the ugly with you? Wouldn't that make you more comfortable to be *your* full authentic self? Once I stopped trying to perform for everyone and be whomever I thought they wanted and needed me to be, I started being more relatable to others.

The problem with conflict, especially when it comes to politics, is that the people who see themselves in the light can't see the dark or the people they perceive to be in the dark. They may see them in theory, but they view them only as villains in the us-versus-them shitshow. Then, on the polar opposite side of the spectrum, you have people who think *they're* in the light and thus, they cannot have anything to do with "those people" "over there" in the perceived darkness. The reality is, we are all light and dark and *in* light and dark. The sooner we find a way to synchronize these opposing energies within us, the sooner we'll start witnessing the harmonization of polarity in our families, relationships, and communities.

The following lines, frequently attributed to Albert Camus, give us greater insight into the power of the push-and-pull within each of us: "In the midst of hate, I found there was, within me, an invincible love. In the midst of tears, I found there was, within me, an invincible smile.

In the midst of chaos, I found there was, within me, an invincible calm. I realized, through it all, that in the midst of winter, I found there was, within me, an invincible summer. And that makes me happy. For it says that no matter how hard the world pushes against me, within me, there's something stronger—something better, pushing right back."[3]

None of what Camus describes would be found if he didn't look *within himself*. That's the key. Go inside to grow, and you, too, will find an abundance "within me." All of this comes together to produce balance. A worthy goal is to become more balanced in all areas of our lives.

I am TERRIBLE at this and would put "tendency to go to extremes" on my business cards if I could. I have very little balance in my life, but I'm definitely better than I used to be. Now, when I become aware of a conflict within me or outside of me, I pause. I feel the overwhelm and fear it causes. I realize that the conflict is overwhelming, which makes me want to retreat into one corner where I'm sure to be met with anxiety and a feeling of being trapped. Then, I pause and breathe some more and realize there's nothing I need to run away from because this opposing energy, this feeling of conflict, is there to help me be more balanced. This is precisely where we find the gift of both/and. It's where we start to see through the deception of either/or.

MY DEAR OLD POP HEARING TWO VOICES

No story reflects the power of harmony to me better than an experience I had with my grandad, whom I called Pop. Shortly before Pop passed away at age ninety-nine (!), I went to visit him in the hospital. Pop was the kind of man you wanted to be around. No matter his age, he could outsmart anyone in the room. He made me laugh, question things, and look at the world differently. He practiced law until he retired at the young age of ninety-two. He would run circles around the younger attorneys who attempted to go toe-to-toe with him in the courtroom.

Pop always called me Lindy—so much so that into my adult years,

I wasn't sure if he actually knew my name was Lindsey. He would often still call my dad Mike, even though my dad's name is Mark. Pop was a stinker and we all loved him for it. He enjoyed getting under people's skin and would lick his food before he left the table so that no one would dare eat from his plate. He was one of the most generous people I've ever met and helped all of his grandchildren get to college without being saddled with tons of debt.

Pop wasn't much of a feeler, and I don't ever remember him getting emotional. He was rough around the edges, and I only ever remember him drinking clear liquids. And 99 percent of the time, it wasn't water.

I remember when I was young, I went over to his house after church where we would spend countless hours swimming. I started to tell him about the Bible story I learned: Jonah and the whale. At that time, I believed the Bible was literal, but Pop very much did not. He wasn't huge on God or anything religious or spiritual in nature. Pop was passionate about law. And he could argue his way out of a jail cell, if given the chance.

In response to me telling Pop about the fabulous Bible story I'd learned, he shot me down. I was all of maybe eight years old with a faith the size of the continent of Africa, but Pop wasn't having any of it. He made it clear that there was no way in hell (his words, not mine) that a whale could swallow a human and that the person would be okay. Pop always made good points, and he'd frequently challenge my belief systems (which I am very grateful for upon looking back).

Growing up, I thought it was my responsibility to tell Pop about Jesus so he could be saved. I would try and "share the gospel" with Pop, and he'd look at me with those beady brown eyes, almost as if to say without saying, "Bless her little heart." He wasn't having any of it. I would share miracles with him that happened to me personally, and he wasn't buying it. If he couldn't prove it with science and law, it wasn't worth a damn. I wish I would've had more of his thought process inside me when I was growing up in church, but unfortunately, I pretty much believed everything I was taught.

When Pop started to get very sick, he spent quite a bit of time in the hospital. I'd been to visit him many times, but I'd never gone with the intention of singing to him. For whatever reason, the last hospital stay he had before he passed away was the time I felt compelled to bring my guitar and sing for Pop while he lay still in his hospital bed. I walked in and his face lit up. He loved my music even though it was very religious in nature back then. He couldn't really even hear anything, so maybe that's why he loved it—because he couldn't hear the lyrics about God or faith. I spent some time talking to him and laughing with him as he shamelessly flirted with every single nurse on the floor.

I remember a middle-aged nurse (maybe fifty years old) was helping him the day I visited. She was cute and I said to Pop, "She's a cutie! Why don't you ask her out?"

And he quickly retorted, "HALE NO, she's way too old for me." He was ninety-eight years old at the time. For this and so many other reasons, I loved my Pop.

That day in the hospital, I begin playing the guitar and singing. I sang random songs that I knew he might know and then some original songs. Toward the end of our time together, I started singing my favorite hymn: "How Great Thou Art."[4] He wouldn't take his eyes off me. It was the most intense focus of attention I'd ever seen in my grandad. He also didn't interrupt or say anything to try and deflect from the seriousness of the moment. He stayed completely present and locked in to the song. At one point, his eyes got really big and he seemed amazed. I mean, don't get me wrong, I'm an okay singer, but I'm not THAT good.

After I stopped playing the guitar and singing, Pop kept saying with an awe I'd never seen in him before, "Lindy! How'd you do that? How'd you do that thing with your voice?" I had no idea what he was talking about. Was it my fabulous vibrato or my smooth tone and timbre? Was it the one high note I hit just right with my chest voice or the low note I attempted and didn't do so well with? I was clueless. But he pressed on and kept asking me what I was doing with my voice and more importantly, how was I doing it? It was as if he'd finally met a puzzle he couldn't crack.

I asked Pop to explain what he meant and what he heard. Here's what he said:

"Lindy, you are here by yourself, but I heard two voices. I heard you singing, but then there was another voice harmonizing along with you, but it was your voice. I just don't know how you're doing that with your voice, but it's amazing! Keep singing!"

I'm no music expert, but I know what harmony means. Harmony is the combination of one or more sounds of a different pitch. If you sing an A note and I sing a C note within the same chord family, we would be harmonizing. Except that day at the hospital, I was alone. I didn't have anyone with me singing harmony. (I don't bring my backup singers or backup dancers to my hospital gigs.) I also can't split my voice into two different pitches simultaneously like some people can. Whatever Pop heard must have been supernatural, that's the only way I can explain it. There wasn't a nurse standing outside harmonizing with me. There was no logical explanation, and that drove Pop nuts because he's accustomed to explaining everything with evidence.

I still don't know exactly what he heard that day in the hospital, but what I do know is that it filled his spirit with peace and joy. He lit up and could not get over whatever it was he was certain I was doing with my voice. Pop experienced harmony where there shouldn't have been any. I didn't hear it. I only heard my voice. But Pop, in those dark moments where he lay sick in his hospital bed, experienced light and hope in the form of two separate notes harmonizing to form something new.

Fast-forward to a short time after the hospital visit, Pop went into hospice care. Within a few days, he went from being the life-of-the-party stinker to preparing to say goodbye to this world he'd left an undeniable and indelible mark upon. My mom was with him (Pop was her dad) before he died and as he breathed his last breath. To make him comfortable, she put one of my albums into the CD player. After Pop finally passed, my mom shared with me that Pop went into the arms of God while listening to my music. And guess what song he listened to at the very end? You guessed it—"How Great Thou Art."

There is great power in learning to harmonize the separate but equal parts of you, in bringing opposing energies into alignment. As you become more aligned internally, you will naturally become more aligned with others. That doesn't mean you have to agree with them, but you will at least get to a place where you don't constantly want to punch them in the throat because they disagree with you on so many things.

Understanding that conflict and dissonance are crucial (*and very much needed* in order to move us into a place of greater harmony within ourselves and others) will change the way you look at and experience almost everything. There is no harmony without dissonance, just as there is no light without darkness.

And when we do agree with someone, it's okay to go overboard. I'm reminded of a favorite scene from the TV show *Parks and Rec*, guest starring (the real) Michelle Obama.

Michelle to Leslie (Amy Poehler): "We need passionate people like you in our national parks . . . Are you nodding because you agree with me?"

Leslie: "I agree with you on all things. Throughout history, until the end of time, forever."[5]

CONFLICT IS THE NEW CATALYST

Instead of wasting energy fighting against the conflict inside us and around us, we would benefit from noticing and becoming more aware of what makes up the conflict and how it impacts us. We can't find any gifts in conflict until we realize that certain conflict is there to help us, not further divide us. There is no growth without conflict and dissonance.

As I write several times throughout this book, never waste a trigger. When something or someone causes you to start spinning out, pause and get curious about what's going on inside you. Never waste a conflict by using it as an opportunity to hurl your weapon of choice at *those* people over *there*. You and I can hold on to our beliefs without having to pound them into someone else's head. Let's start with allowing our own internal opposing forces to collide, harmonize, and create something new. What if we all did this and started approaching others this way? I bet there'd be a whole lot less drama and infighting with our spouses, friends, families, communities, and in other relationships.

Conflict sucks. Dealing with it also sucks. But I can promise you, if we look at conflict with new eyes and a different perspective, we will find that it's there to help us. There are gifts that can be found even in the darkest of places—like a global pandemic where our country was increasingly divided based on beliefs about Covid, science, community, and individual freedom.

I believe we can turn our conflict into a catalyst for change, our tension into a new tie of love that could bind us. What you and I have endured, especially in the past few years, has brought so many things to light that have been hiding in the shadows for decades. Our happiness and sense of security cannot be dependent on factors outside ourselves—who is president, which laws get passed that seek to destroy us and the fabric of our nation, who we're doing life with and how to react when their views are polar opposites to ours, how our boss treats us, what our partner is doing that's pissing us off, etc. There are gifts waiting for us if we can take the time to look past the bullshit and noise. The voice of the spirit longs to harmonize with our voice to create something new—a voice for the voiceless and a voice that speaks truth to power.

May we allow ourselves to be open-minded to a universe that is delicately but intentionally held together in a cosmic dance of dissonance and harmony. Once we experience that balance *within* us, we will have a much easier time finding balance *outside* of us. Imagine a life where, instead of worrying about everyone else and what they believe and how they behave, you focus on living the best possible life that you and you alone were created to experience.

Turn worry and WTF moments into realizations of "Wow, I *can* change the world by changing my one, tiny little place in this world . . . myself."

Break It Down for Me

- The more we are hell-bent on avoiding conflict within and around us, the more we will attract conflict into our experiences.

- There is power in learning to harmonize the polar opposites that exist inside all of us. The tension found in the push and pull is the very key to unlocking the potential for peace. When polarizing forces collide, something new is created.

- Two things can be true at the same time and exist in the same space. Sometimes I get goosebumps in a super-hot bath. I'm both freezing *and* burning up. Both are valid.[6]

- Open your mind to a universe held together in a cosmic dance of dissonance and harmony. Experiencing that balance within us will enable us to find balance outside of us.

Chapter 16

THE GIFT OF PAIN

"It took me forever to conceptualize that core wounds are sacred allies."

—Monika Carless, "The 2 Emotional Wounds that Cut the Deepest"

"Oh, I'd kill for a good coma right now!"

—Moira Rose, *Schitt's Creek* (S1, E13)

"As I often tell my students, the two most important phrases in therapy, as in yoga, are 'Notice that' and 'What happens next?' Once you start approaching your body with curiosity rather than with fear, everything shifts."

—Bessel van der Kolk, *The Body Keeps the Score*

Though this is the last chapter you're reading, it is the very first chapter I started writing. In fact, my original working title for the book was *The Gift of Pain*. In the following pages, you'll learn about my arduous journey from giving up and giving in to pain to embracing the pain that would become the basic foundation for everything you've read thus far. If it wasn't for my twenty-plus-year battle with chronic pain and my subsequent work with my mentor Jon who inspired so much of what you'll find in these pages, I may have *never* written this book—this book that became my medicine and the catalyst for my own healing.

I've experienced a long list of symptoms that have plagued me and have impacted every area of my life. For the majority of my adult life, I have felt physical pain *somewhere* in my body. I didn't start experiencing any relief until I started getting curious about *why* this chronic pain never seemed to go away. No breaks. Not even very many small moments of reprieve. And it's not just the pain. It's the debilitating fatigue, exhaustion, tiredness, and overall lack of energy. In this chapter, I share with you how my perception of pain changed and how relief followed—but only after I learned whatever lesson (or in my case countless lessons) the Pain was trying to teach me. Capital "P" Pain, who has become my life's greatest *and most annoying* teacher.

Contrary to what I used to believe for the majority of my life and most likely contrary to what you believe as you read this, **pain isn't always there to harm us.** Pain is the loudest and sometimes quietest tool the universe uses as a wake-up call of epic proportions. The wake-up call pulls us out of mindless living and serves as the catalyst to increase our awareness about something. If you were to put pain under a metaphorical microscope, you would see a vast harvest of hidden truths buried deep within both emotional pain and physical pain. I now live a life that isn't wholly dictated by pain, though it's still very much a daily struggle and journey. I want to invite you and all your past, current, and future pain (regardless of the specific nature of it) along on that journey with me. Let's go . . .

We'll start with a challenge. I would give myself a solid B for my ability to deal with life in a healthy way. But what about pain? I find that much harder to grade. I'll go with a C+ and a B. Why two grades? Because I'm grading *emotional* and *physical* pain.

While I understand for the most part how to manage physical pain (e.g., ice an injured shoulder, take ibuprofen, complain to my entire family every chance I get), I fall short of understanding how to manage emotional pain, despite reaching out for the emotional equivalent of ice and meds. There's no product I can go pick up at CVS for emotional pain. What about you? What grades would you give yourself in these same areas? Why do humans find it so difficult to manage pain when it is a universal language, an experience that connects us all?

PAIN: THE PROBLEM *AND* THE SOLUTION

You know all that pain and baggage from your past? It has a purpose. And the pain you deal with every day? It also has a purpose. You may hate this next sentence but try to remain open-minded. **The solution is in the pain.** The healing we so desperately long for can only be found by looking *deeper* into the pain. Why is it there? What is pain trying to teach us? It's happening FOR us, not TO us (even though our feelings and perceptions would have us very much believe that all the pain is definitely happening TO us). I admit, that's absolutely how it *feels*. But as my mentor Jon says, feelings *aren't facts*. Speaking of Jon, he was my last resort. I'd tried every possible option to find relief from pain for over two decades, yet nothing helped. A dear friend of mine connected me with Jon, whom I was initially quite leery of. How would this complete stranger help me with my pain? The answer to that question still boggles my mind to this day.

As we all know by now, *shit happens*. It will keep happening. That's one of the few predictable elements of life. And yet, a world exists inside each of us that enables us (if we're willing to be brave and do the work) to see all that pain and baggage with new eyes. I have good news. It's possible to shift our perspective and paradigm as we reframe our thinking around the topic of pain that *on the surface* threatens to destroy our lives. Life is going to hurl rotten lemons at us. That's what life does, in between all the glorious and beautiful times.

It's not about making lemonade out of hard, gross, rotten lemons. It's about holding those rotten lemons and getting gut-level honest about what it all means and what you're going to do now with your increased level of awareness. **You're not a victim.**

Again, I know it can *feel* that way. And there are serious situations where you very well may be a victim. That's not what I'm referring to in this chapter. What I convey throughout the next few pages is that you and I are in control of *way more* than we realize. I desperately want you to understand that this whole "everything happens for a reason" thing isn't what you always thought it was, have been taught it was, or what you've always been led to believe. Shit happens, and not all shit happens for a reason.

Thankfully, there's a hidden treasure in *most* of the shit, a sort of magic to life where Spirit/Source/Higher Power/etc. has the power and desire to create beauty from ashes. The secret: Don't waste the pain. Don't judge the pain. Don't numb the pain. Don't waste a pain trigger. It *all* has a purpose even though the trauma wasn't planned, and you most certainly didn't deserve any of the trauma that you've experienced.

Pain isn't a fuck-you conspiracy masterminded by some evil deity who sits idly by, waiting to punish its subjects. Pain isn't the universe's way of *punishing* you. I've found that pain is a useful tool in protecting me from future pain, from living a life full of pain and helplessness. If the proof is in the pudding, then the paradigm shift that could save your life is in the pain.

The most horrific of moments and experiences *can* serve a purpose. Hear me very clearly: the end *does not* justify the means. But the way you think about and perceive these "means" can absolutely alter and forever change the ending. You and I have the power to rewrite the chapters of our story related to pain and suffering.

My prayer and hope is that after you finish this book and close it, you'll never be able to unsee what you've seen in these pages. The intention behind me writing this book and you reading it is that we will both have new eyes with which to navigate this insanely unpredictable and messy world.

MY BODY FEELS EIGHTY YEARS OLD

My body feels absolutely wrecked with pain this morning as I write this chapter. It's my old friend, this great teacher named pain with whom I've had a long-standing love–hate relationship.

I feel a new pain today in my pec muscle (read: boob area). It's like someone is stabbing me right on top of where my heart lives. I've conditioned myself through lots of practice to shift my awareness from being angry with the pain to getting curious about it. This is what it sounds like: What is the pain I'm feeling? Where do I feel it in my body? Is this tied to a certain emotion? What else seems to be connected to the pain? Then I ask myself, what do I have control over in this moment that I could actually change right now? I got the answer almost instantaneously—I'm experiencing a physical manifestation of a broken heart in this moment.

My nervous system and amygdala are going haywire. Haven't we all felt this in our bodies? Try something the next time you become aware of this: Get curious. Ask questions. Think of all the crazy stuff your brain is doing at that moment.

VOILÀ! AMYGDALA!

The amygdala is the brain's extremely powerful self-protecting mechanism that helps us survive by mobilizing the brain with the body to unite and fight against a perceived threat or enemy. Unfortunately, it hasn't evolved.

Since the first human brains, the amygdala has produced a habit loop of sensing a threat, responding to it, and kicking the nervous system into fight, flight, or freeze mode, which gives us the power and strength to fight and survive. There's a bear chasing you, RUN!

Despite the general daily absence of lions, tigers, and bears (oh my) in our modern era, the amygdala has been working overtime on overdrive. When we sense any type of threat, no matter how big or small or true or false, the amygdala goes into action and stays in that cycle of action. It's overly sensitive now to endless false alarms because it's auto-matically and subconsciously trying to mitigate the risk and minimize the threat. When the amygdala's Spidey-sense goes off, it completely shuts down the rational part of the brain to prepare me to leap into action. It's there to help me, keep me safe, and keep me alive—but in our current lives, it's *doing it too well.*

When the brain's alarm bells start ringing wildly, our brain focuses on negative thoughts and shifts to a memory that is filled with pain and trauma from a completely separate experience *in the past.* It could be the smallest thing. But a trigger is a trigger, no matter how big or small. Someone much wiser than me once said, "If it's *hysterical,* it's *historical.*" There are unintended consequences of the amygdala's actions that are making it very difficult for you and me to thrive in our day-to-day lives due to nervous system burnout.

Burnout can lead to depression, anxiety, and a whole bunch of stress, which makes it almost impossible for our brains to stay rational and distinguish between actual threats and *perceived* threats. As our brains continue to lose the ability to properly address this automatic activation, the cycle is perpetuated.

The work is in becoming more aware of what these false alarms look and *feel* like so we can regain equilibrium and peace more quickly once a false activation has taken place. Our nervous systems are tired from running on overdrive for decades. The work is also in identifying triggers and finding a way to have a more balanced, healthy response to life.

We must direct our hyper-vigilance in a new way, by stopping and pausing anytime we get triggered or feel pain. The amygdala is power-less when it's hijacked because all it can do is *react* and respond based on a previously laid foundation built with bricks of stored patterns. These hijacks suck up all the energy in the room and cause a constant release of adrenaline and other hormones that are slowly killing us with each false alarm.

Joseph E. LeDoux was convinced of the possibility that you and I can learn to control the amygdala's hair-trigger role in our emotional outbursts. "Once your emotional system learns something, it seems you never let it go. What therapy does is teach you how to control it—it teaches your neocortex how to inhibit your amygdala. The propensity to act is suppressed, while your basic emotion about it remains in a subdued form."[1]

The term "amygdala hijack" was coined by Daniel Goleman in his book *Emotional Intelligence: Why It Can Matter More Than IQ*. He writes: "The best way to prevent an amygdala hijack is to understand what things trigger the reaction so you can avoid them. Alternatively, you can use practices like mindfulness to help you better control your body's responses when you feel the reaction."[2]

Triggers Make the Worst Roommates

I used to metaphorically gag when I heard the terms "mindfulness" or "meditation." But y'all, it really is the best weapon we have against these hijackers. Look, if the best way to prevent these hijacks is to avoid triggers, we're doomed. I don't know if you're anything like me, but most of my triggers are unavoidable. My triggers tend to live in the same house as me and occupy the same spaces I occupy.

My triggers tend to arise at work with people I can't just avoid or stop working with. Triggers are everywhere, and that's not going to change. To piggyback on the advice to never waste a trigger, I would also encourage you to explore the use of these two "M" words for dealing with triggers when you can't avoid them.

The magic of the mindfulness–meditation marriage can be found in presence. Nothing brings us back to the present moment, to the NOW, more than the practice of centering and being fully aware. This is such a foreign concept to most of us, though. If every human meditated once a day, can you imagine what the world would be like, and more importantly what it *wouldn't* be like?

Think of how much empathy we gain when we are in a state of mindfulness. The acknowledgment of one's *pain* and the acceptance of one's *presence* unlock *empathy*. Meditation and mindfulness conspire together to bring us back to the present moment and keep us in the NOW.

Though I was told Eckhart Tolle was never to be trusted back in my evangelical Christian days, I'm a huge fan of his teachings now . . . specifically his teachings about NOW. He says, "Most humans are never fully present in the now, because unconsciously they believe that the next moment must be more important than this one. But then you miss your whole life, which is never not now. And that's a revelation for some people: to realize that your life is only ever now."[3]

A proper understanding of the power of the NOW is one thing, but *empathy* is another piece of magic we have access to if we can commit to becoming more empathetic. When we put ourselves in someone else's shoes, we get a sense of their pain. I've found that as I become more and more mindful of the pain and struggles of others, it helps me acknowledge and begin to heal my own pain. Empathy unlocks a certain level of "we're in this together" that cannot be overstated. It seems that so many of us lately have abandoned empathy. We know we can't possibly walk in someone else's shoes, so we abandon the task altogether. If I can't put myself in your shoes or imagine what your life might be like, it's much easier for me to push you away to the "other" table. Like Brené Brown so eloquently says, "People are hard to hate close-up. Move in. We have to listen to understand in the same way we want to be understood."[4]

Some—or in my case, *almost all*—of our internal pain, whether physical or emotional, could be attributed to internalized hate (either of self or others), trapped trauma, harboring resentment and unforgiveness, or unresolved conflict. When I lean into my inner child who needs healing and when I become more aware of the still small voice inside of me that has been silenced for so long, I am able to get curious about what might be causing the pain.

A few years back, I was having major pain radiating throughout both of my legs. After a vein surgery that was supposed to help, the pain persisted. I was referred to an orthopedic surgeon to rule out a possible culprit: my back. I ended up getting an MRI of my back and here's what the doctor said when I came in for my appointment to review the results: "Lindsey, you have one of the most perfect backs I've seen in my twenty-five years of practice. There is nothing structurally wrong with you. You have a back that I typically see in a twenty-year-old. I'm not saying your pain isn't real, your pain is absolutely real. But there is nothing structurally wrong with your back that is causing you pain."

I was happy to hear that something in my body was considered perfect (hello, recovering perfectionists), but I was not happy to hear that *yet again*, the test results are NORMAL! To date, there is no physical or structural explanation for my chronic pain. No rare disease. No crazy gene mutation. No explanation.

THE ONLY TIME I'M CONSIDERED "NORMAL"

Throughout my chronic pain journey, I've lost count of how many times a doctor has informed me that the results were normal, this X-ray looks great, or this MRI is clear. Don't get me wrong—I am incredibly grateful that these tests have all been favorable and that I am apparently in good health. But what's hard is that I have no explanation, and I still mostly don't have the answers I've so desperately been looking for.

In the past few years, I've realized one of the purposes behind my pain is to give me the superpower of joining other people in their pain. Because I know what it feels like to suffer constantly and enjoy very little relief, I can much easier sit beside someone who is struggling with their own pain journey. I won't ever truly know how they feel or what they feel, nor will I ever tell them, "I know how you feel," because I don't—our situations are just as unique as our fingerprints. But my pain has birthed a deeper level of empathy, which has enabled me to help others and be present with them.

When I read the following quote by Brené Brown, it stopped me in my tracks. I try to read it regularly: "My mom taught us never to look away from people's pain. The lesson was simple: Don't look away. Don't look down. Don't pretend not to see hurt. Look people in the eye. Even when their pain is overwhelming. And when you are in pain, find the people who can look you in the eye. We need to know we are not alone, especially when we are hurting. This lesson is one of the greatest gifts of my life."[5]

If you can find no other gift in your pain, I hope you can at least find *that gift*.

You may be experiencing intense pain even now as you read these words. You're not ready to even go to the place where you're open to considering that there might be a gift or hidden treasure buried deep within your suffering. And guess what? That's completely OKAY. You get to do this at your pace. No one can rush you, and you don't have to rush yourself.

There's a season for staying in the pain and being fully present with it, and there's a season to get curious about what the pain is there to teach you. You don't have to do both, especially not right now. **Your time will come.** And then more pain will come. And then peace and healing will come. Lather, rinse, repeat. Bad things don't happen to good people or bad people. *Things just happen . . .* to people. Sometimes bad things happen to good people, and sometimes good things happen to bad people. It's not really about that anymore. It's time we shifted our focus to *how we feel* when any "things" happen and how we are going to respond. That's where the growth is.

OWN YOUR ROLE

One of the hardest things for me to admit to myself was when I finally accepted the fact that I play a role in perpetuating my pain. It's so much easier to distance myself from my pain when I'm able to blame it on everyone else outside of myself and blame whatever is over *there*. When I started gently looking into the role I play in my own pain, that's when I really started to transition from unconscious incompetence to conscious awareness—and even acceptance.

The more I looked into the role I played in my divorce, the more I realized *why* my marriage ended. I am still awestruck at the personal level of growth I experienced after getting gut-level honest about the parts I played in what led to the end of a marriage I thought would last for a lifetime. Looking back (please note that it's important to look back without any judgment, self-loathing, or shame), I've come to realize that I've subconsciously been trying to hurt myself. I've erroneously thought that if I can hurt myself, then no one else can hurt me.

I'm afraid most of us do this without even realizing it. We don't allow ourselves to be loved because we're afraid of it. We stay in pain because we're not sure who we would be without the pain. Sometimes it seems easier to self-sabotage than go through life having to deal with messy relationships and friendships. If I'm not *feeling* the love or connection or peace, then I'm obsessively chasing after it like a butterfly that has zero intentions of being caught. But then, once I do feel the love, I tend to sabotage it.

It all boils down to hurt and our tendency to do whatever we can to avoid feeling pain. This is where we miss the mark in a way that can derail our entire lives if we're not careful. Avoiding pain might be what we're *doing*, but it's that very avoidance that leads to an exponential growth of the pain that we are *experiencing*.

Whiskey, the Crate Demolisher

What better way to drive this point home than with a dog metaphor? One time, I tried to leave my dog Whiskey in a crate. He'd been pooping on the carpet whenever we'd leave, and he'd find a way to get into the trash can, eat some gross shit, and then pee on the trash he just ate. So, we got a giant crate, made it comfortable with all his favorite toys and blankets, and left for the day. Unbeknownst to us (since he was a rescue), he'd apparently *never* been in a crate.

Brynn and I got home after running some errands and there was Whiskey, very much not in his crate, wagging his tail and smiling. Off to the right was his kennel on the opposite side of the room from where we left it. It was completely destroyed. This was a heavy duty, hardcore kennel made of steel. But it might as well have been made of string. The door was completely broken off and separated from the kennel. The lovies and blankets were strewn about. He hadn't pooped or messed with the trash because he was too busy planning his prison break. The crate was so mangled, it looked as if a giant had found the crate and shoved it down his giant kitchen disposal.

The Crate of Pain

We can create a tidy, secure kennel for our pain. We can even lure the pain into the crate with a treat. We can leave for the day and come back, in hopes of ignoring the pain and walking right past the intact kennel. But this isn't how it works. Our unresolved pain and trauma will do whatever it has to do to come out and rise to the surface so it can be dealt with. It will tear down every wall, knock down every obstacle, and destroy every container we try to shove it in, until the pain is seen, addressed, heard, and moved through.

The more we *resist* our pain, the stronger it becomes. The more we *resent* our pain, the more resilient it becomes. If it doesn't come out naturally in a healthy manner, it will surely come out sideways. To clarify, sometimes yes, of course, pain is medical, and there may very well be something structurally wrong. Seek professional help from a medical expert, because I know nothing about any of that.

What I'm specifically speaking to here is the generalized pain you and I experience daily in various forms—the pain that has grown from a tiny seed of past broken dreams to a forest of brokenness. How long have we been resisting the pain that has culminated over a lifetime of upset dreams, unmet expectations, and loss?

Some of us have found creative, sneaky ways to ignore, suppress, or quelch the pain. We've given in to a new trend that I've seen circulating all over the place: bypassing the pain with a "positive vibes only" mentality. Pain will make every effort to bust out of its crate, just like my dog did.

I read an article recently by Billy Manas that captures the human tendency of spiritual bypassing, which he defines as "that funny habit some people have of trying to pretend that negativity is a choice and doesn't have to exist if we don't allow it to."[6] He points out that "negativity is something that can't be swept under the rug by repeating positive affirmations."

Look, I'm all for positive affirmations and positive self-talk. That's crucial. Toxic positivity is not. If the blaring volume of positivity is drowning out the muted voice of pain trying to tell you what you're *really* feeling underneath it all, then we'll never be free.

There is no foolproof spiritual or mystical bypass that lets you off the hook from doing the work. There's no easy button. There's really only one surefire way to grow, and it requires a journey *through*. You know the old children's song "We're Going on a Bear Hunt"? It's constantly in my head, and somehow recently has been mashed up with "Elmo's World" and occasionally "Jingle Bells." (My brain is so weird.) This children's song drops some serious truth on our front doorstep.

WE CAN'T GO OVER IT
WE CAN'T GO UNDER IT
WE'RE JUST GONNA HAVE TO GO THROUGH IT
WE'RE GONNA HAVE TO GO THROUGH IT!

RUGS AREN'T FOR PAIN

For the majority of my forty years on this planet, I've worked hard at sweeping my pain under the rug. Actually, I've gone so far as to toss the rug altogether, take a sledgehammer to the floor planks, drill into the concrete foundation, dig a huge hole, and stuff the pain way down deep in the recesses of the earth. Now that I have more awareness about how pain is there to teach me, it has a purpose, and it can be my greatest teacher if I let it, I see everything much differently.

I now see how dangerous this under-the-rug approach can be. No matter how many positive quotes I tape on my mirror and how many inspirational TED talks I listen to, none of that will unearth the pain I've hidden deep, deep down. Those are tools and resources that will help, absolutely . . . but the bulk of responsibility to do the work will be ours alone. Each time we ignore, numb, or try and destroy our pain, we are participating actively in the hindrance of the growth we desperately need so we can finally learn to live a life of acceptance of that which we have no control over.

If you are a human with a heartbeat, you will experience pain not once, not twice, but MANY times in life. That is just as much a part of life as breathing. We all have a heavy, nasty old tire around our necks . . .

Wait, let me back up.

Tires Are the New Necklace

Did you hear about the elk who wandered the hills of Pine Junction, Colorado, with a car tire around his neck for TWO YEARS?[7] This is not the start of a joke. This is real life, folks. After all this tire-collar-roaming, wildlife officials were finally able to help him out. They caught the 600 lb. creature thanks to a tranquilizer and realized the only way to set him free of this tire was to cut off its 5-point antlers. The tire ended up weighing 35 lb. due to all the crap that was trapped in there. The only way to free this elk from the pain of the tire was to cut off something entirely different that was of crucial importance to it.

Side note: if you're asking yourself, *Why didn't they just cut the tire?* you are missing the point. However, since I asked that too upon first hearing about this, I will answer your question. According to the officers on the case, the only way to remove the encumbrance was to cut off the antlers since "they couldn't slice through the steel in the bead of the tire."

I think most of us are roaming around life with a tire around our necks. Some of our tires are 35 lb., others are 350 lb. They're filled with debris, crap, baggage, dirt, and who knows what else. Instead of exploring a different way to look at the debacle we're in, we give up. We try to cut the tire off, but we can't. We try to find someone else who can cut the tire off, but they fail. So, we give in to hopelessness and find ourselves living an encumbered life wrought with pain. Plus, people are starting to look at you real funny since you have a tire around your neck.

What if, instead of giving up, we got curious about a different way—and **there's always another way.** What if, instead of bitching about the tire and our inability to remove it, we considered an alternative? What would our version of antlers be in this metaphor? What can we shift our focus to so we can find a different way through a seemingly solution-less situation?

Maybe your "antlers" are obstacles that need to be cut off. Maybe your 5-point antlers are resentment, bitterness, fear, anxiety, and denial. Or maybe they are something entirely different for you. Either way, we must be brave enough to gain a deeper awareness of the nature of the tires around our necks, and the antlers that must be removed so we can be set free.

Break It Down for Me

- Pain is the universal language of the human experience. It does not discriminate, and no life is free from it. And yet, it can be our greatest teacher if we let it.

- Refrain from standing in judgment over the pain. Instead, get curious about it and don't stop getting curious until you've found the gift or learned the lesson. Hell, you might even write a book as a result of listening to your pain!

- Hypervigilance when it comes to threat assessment can lead to major problems, especially when the threat is perceived and not real. However, redirecting that same level of hypervigilance to regulating our nervous system by transforming our thoughts can lead to major breakthroughs.

- Never ever look away from other people's pain. Start the habit by never looking away from your own pain. Identify where you feel it in your body (whether emotional or physical pain) and look at the role you played, if any.

I PUT THE ass in SARCASSM

EPILOGUE

"I hope that someday when I am gone, someone,
somewhere, picks my soul up off of these pages
and thinks, 'I would have loved her.'"
—Nicole Lyons, *HUSH*

Elena Ferrante sums it up perfectly: "To read a book is to absorb, consciously or not, all the other books that influenced that book, as well as the books that influenced those books, and so on; to interpret even one paragraph on a page is to vector endlessly back in time."[1]

THE DUMBNESS OF NUMBNESS

In her book *The Gifts of Imperfection*, Brené Brown writes: "We cannot selectively numb emotions, when we numb the painful emotions, we also numb the positive emotions."[2] I wonder how long you and I have been numbing our emotions in lieu of getting curious about them. It's no wonder we fail to see the treasures buried deep within the vast array of emotions we experience daily as humans because we strive to do anything but fully feel them.

Numbing the feelings and emotions associated with fear, addiction, anger, humiliation, tragedy, rejection, unanswered prayers, waiting, trauma, leaving, loss, powerlessness, heartbreak, emptiness, conflict, and pain renders the gifts *invisible*. A classic numbing technique is to dilute ourselves and others with the concept that everything happens for a reason. This unhelpful and unsuccessful "spiritual bypass" will fail us every time. Accepting life on life's terms requires rigorous self-honesty and self-awareness about what's going on in and around us. Until we start seeing the world and its inevitable pain through new eyes, we will never truly find comfort (or be able to comfort others, for that matter).

Cosigning with the delusion that everything happens for a reason is a recipe for disaster in interpreting the shit that life throws our way. The phrase itself spews toxic positivity and is rooted in a desire to make sense of things that simply will never make sense. I do, however, believe that *certain* experiences, interactions, and circumstances are absolutely purposeful and happen for a specific reason. But everything? Not even close.

If you glean *nothing else* from this book except the next line, I'll consider that a win:

> **NOT EVERYTHING HAPPENS FOR A REASON, BUT SACRED GIFTS *MAY BE* FOUND IN EVERYTHING THAT HAPPENS—EVEN (AND ESPECIALLY) THE MOST PAINFUL THINGS.**

THE ENDING THAT WASN'T

After losing pretty much everything after coming out in 2009, I prayed a prayer that would forever change my life. The prayer I prayed occurred on the evening of Good Friday in April 2009. The answer that would save my life occurred *the very next day*. That is a seriously short wait time. My coming out journey was a mess of highs and lows, mountains and valleys, pain and joy, fear and doubt.

It was March 2009, and I was in Florida playing at an event that would become my last official "Lindsey Kane" gig. I thought it was *all over*. A definitive end to the life I'd always dreamed of. No more traveling. No more gigs. No more singing and sharing the hope and love and light of God with wounded, hurting, searching people.

I went from singing in front of thousands of people and touring about 200 days per year to being unemployed for the first time in my adult life. Over the course of three weeks, my entire career was decimated beyond recognition. Albums were pulled from stores and mailed back to me. Gigs were canceled left and right. Thousands of dollars in deposits were mailed back. It was the worst of times, and it was the . . . worst of times.

I flew back to Austin from Florida after playing my last gig. I must have been in a complete daze on the flight back because I barely remember how I got home. I wasn't just leaving Florida for Austin. I was leaving a career that I'd spent the majority of my life building. I was leaving an identity that I'd come to know as the real me. I was leaving a dream that became a reality and then quickly turned into a nightmare.

I landed in Austin on Thursday, April 9th, 2009. There was no reason to unpack my suitcase because I was flying to Tennessee the very next day to go visit my brother for Easter, where Mom and Dad would also be joining us.

As I laid my head down on my pillow that night in hopes of actually getting some sleep, I started weeping. Somehow, in that moment, it hit me. It was over. The life I thought I was going to live until my lungs gave out was over. Career path blocked. Dreams shattered. It felt like a death *because it was*. Weeping turned to sobbing and without thinking, I prayed a prayer silently in my heart that I still TO THIS DAY can't even believe I prayed.

I knew God was listening, but my faith was crumbling. How did I end up here after a life dedicated to serving Him? I knew I'd made the right decision, but I didn't understand why it all hurt *so damn much*. The prayer I prayed went something like this:

"God . . . help. I need a sign that **you love me**. That's it. I know I'm not usually one to pray for signs because usually I see signs of love everywhere. But tonight, I'm begging you for a sign. A simple sign to remind me that you do, in fact, love me."

I woke up the next morning. It was Friday, April 10th, 2009.

It also happened to be Good Friday, a religious holiday that our family and faith tradition celebrated.

On the flight to Tennessee, this bad/good Friday surprisingly turned into one of (*if not THE most*) life-changing days ever.

I normally fly Southwest because I'm a control freak and like to choose my own seat. But that day, I flew on a different airline that had the audacity to assign me a seat. Row 11, in the *very back*. It was one of those small, terrifying planes that should only be occupied by small rabbits or tiny woodland creatures.

Everyone on the plane had boarded, and I was the only lucky person with no one in the miniature seat beside me. And then, he walked in. This guy was one of the biggest dudes I'd ever seen. He was thick as an ox and wide as an NFL linebacker. What he lacked in height, he made up for in sheer *brick-house-ness*.

I just kept silently saying repeatedly to myself, "Nope. No. Seat's taken. Not a chance. Nuh-uh. Nope. Keep on walking, mister." But there was only *one* open seat on the plane's eleven rows that day—the tiny seat right next to me. I was in the window seat so I could stare outside while grieving the current state of my life. As soon as I saw this man's shoulders, I thought, *Oh dear God, here we go*. I knew I would soon be smashed up against that stupid window with no ability to even recline my seat! I kept my head down but could see him making his way toward me.

"Row eleven?" he asked.

"Um . . . yeah."

I must say, it was quite a sight to witness this gigantic man try to fit his behemoth body into the tiny airplane seat. But somehow, he did it. I instantly felt his width against my tense shoulders. I'm no small lady, so we were getting up close and personal real quick.

For some reason that morning, I'd picked up a new book that I'd just bought with the intention of reading it on the flight. I'm not normally a book reader on planes unless, of course, I'm forced to fake-look at the book's pages while trying to avoid human contact. The book was *The Shack*, by William P. Young,[3] and it turned out to be one of those once-in-a-lifetime kind of books that changes the course of your mindset forever. I'd tucked it neatly into the pocket in front of me.

While looking out the window at absolutely nothing, like one does when one has just lost almost everything, I heard my Row 11 compadre ask, "How you likin' that book?"

Before I could slam my hands over my mouth to ensure I did not answer the question nor entertain the conversation, a few random words tumbled uncontrollably out of my mouth. Despite not wanting to actually speak to this stranger, I answered the question.

"I love it so far, even though I'm only a few chapters in." These words managed to escape my mouth hole, despite my lack of consent. Immediately after I answered, I couldn't help but think of ways to escape the conversation.

Mr. Row 11 proceeded to ask, "Can I tell you something?" I reluctantly nodded *yes*, while internally shaking my head profusely back and forth NOPE. I didn't want *anyone* to tell me *anything* unless they were going to magically say something that would alleviate my pain even just for a moment. Looking back, I'm eternally grateful this stranger sat next to me and had the boldness to share something that was clearly weighing heavy on his heart.

The next words that came out of his mouth would stop my heartbeat right in its worn-out tracks. He warmly said, while peering through his tiny circular glasses directly into my sad eyes (and in the most non-creepy way), "*God loves you, and He thinks you're beautiful.*"

| **SILENCE. CRICKETS. TIME STOPPING.** |

"What did you just say?" I responded with mixed feelings of total disbelief and sheer intrigue. He went on to repeat the sentence with even more sincerity and authenticity. As he repeated the bizarre, seemingly out-of-the-blue statement, it hit me. I'd completely forgotten about the prayer I prayed just the night before, begging God for a sign that I was in fact loved by him.

After a few moments of silence, I asked him if he knew me. I wasn't that famous or anything, but I thought maybe this man was secretly a Lindsey Kane fan. Did he know what was going on in my life? Had he heard about the peril of my coming out experience? It was too fresh, and no one really knew anything, so I figured that couldn't be it. He answered, "No, ma'am. I'm just some guy named Randy who owns a bar in Kentucky."

I went on to ask him, "Hmm . . . okay, well then, are you some kind of angel?" This was the only explanation I could muster up in my finite brain. He *had* to be an angel, or psychic, or maybe a mind reader? How else could this complete stranger speak the words "God loves you" to me when hours earlier I'd begged God for a sign that he loved me?

His answer to my angel question was the most classic answer I could've imagined, and it still makes me cackle to this day.

"Do you know how big dem damn wings would have to be to fit me?"

I thought to myself, *Ooooooh, so you're a* funny *angel.*

Humor is the way to my soul, so I became more open to having a conversation with him. I had to see this play out. I couldn't deplane without understanding more about how Mr. Row 11 saw inside my soul that day. How did he know I needed to hear those exact words? How was I on this flight, in this row, next to this individual, on this day? How many different variables had to line up in perfect harmony to ensure our paths would cross?

I sat silently in full-on pensive mode as I marinated on the words he'd spoken straight from his spirit to mine. After a few more minutes, I introduced myself. I then proceeded to ask if he'd read the book I was holding. Not only had Mr. Row 11 "Randy" read it, but the book had dramatically changed his life, just as it was in the process of changing mine in real time. He shared a story with me about a major health nightmare he'd experienced.

Randy said, "Lindsey, when I came to after almost dying, I soon began to realize I would never be the same. As a result of what happened to my brain that day, I now have an *acute awareness* of people in pain." He went on to explain that this newfound ability to tap into others' pain was a gift, but also a curse, and maybe even more so the latter. Somehow, in some unexplainable way, Randy could feel and see what you and I and most other folks cannot.

I just listened. I wasn't in a talking mood, so I was happy to simply listen as he shared his story. He knew nothing of my situation nor my coming out and subsequent career end. Despite our fascinating conversation, I hadn't told him much at all about me. Yet, I would come to realize that he knew more about me than most anyone in the world did during that tragic time in my life.

Here are some more actual quotes from him, even though at this point in the conversation I still had not shared any personal information with him other than my name.

"Isn't it tragic when people use Scripture against you?"

This comment really came out of nowhere for me, but it also landed with a thud on my soul. The weeks leading up to my last gig in April had been filled with vitriolic hatred and verses from the Bible used by "Christians" to beat me down. We gays call these verses the "Clobber Passages." Bible-thumpers love plucking a few verses completely out of context to bludgeon LGBTQ+ folks into submission.

"Are you married?"

I said no.

He responded, "Well, I know that you don't *need* a man, do you? I can tell." The lesbian in me chuckled internally because little did he know how right he was about that one.

"You've suffered a great loss recently, haven't you?" Again, Mr. Row 11 Randy was winning at this odd game of in-flight Q&A. I nodded yes, to which he responded lovingly, "But you haven't lost *everything*. Not your family. You still have your family."

True. I thankfully still had *most* of my family. In fact, I was on that flight to go celebrate Easter with them. But I didn't say any of that to Randy. My coming out process was so fresh that I wasn't ready to talk about my story or any of the corresponding details with anyone. I'd been in the closet for twenty-six years, for God's sake!

The flow of our dialogue all but catapulted me into another dimension, one where love flows freely. By the end of the flight, I was convinced he had spiritual superpowers. I couldn't explain it, but I was in too much pain to try and explain it away, so I allowed myself to simply enjoy the conversation. It was evident that somehow, in some supernatural way, Randy was connected. Connected to himself, connected to his fellow man, connected to Spirit, Love Intelligence, God, Higher Power, <insert *preferred name for the One who cannot be placed in a human-constructed box—i.e., The Alpha and The Omega*>

The story could've ended there, since what happened on the flight that day had *already* resulted in the realization that my life would never be the same.

However, things didn't stop there. Just the opposite.

As we started our descent, I decided as a thank you to give him one of my CDs that I had in my carry-on. Still smashed up against the window, I looked out at the vast sea of clouds surrounding us. I felt safe and secure. I felt something I hadn't felt in a while . . . peace. I went from unconsciously gazing out the window into nothingness at the beginning of the flight to eagerly looking out my tiny window at a world that *just might not* be out to get me after all. Despite the ever-present pain that filled my soul and body, I felt a shred of hope.

How could I not? I'd uncharacteristically asked my Higher Power for a sign that he loved me, and the very next day a complete stranger in Row 11 looks me dead in the eyes and tells me exactly that. God loves me and thinks I'm beautiful. Even though I hadn't specifically prayed for the second half of that statement, I took it in and held those words close.

Randy and I began walking off the plane after exchanging some awkward "I know we just met but I feel like I've known you my whole life" farewell pleasantries. I was running a bit late for my connecting flight, so I was in a hurry to get off the plane. I walked toward the direction of the terminal, still dumbfounded by what took place on that flight. My logical, intellectual understanding of God's love started to *slowly but surely* make the marathon journey from my head to my heart.

In the distance I heard, "Lindsey, wait!" I turned around to see Randy approaching me. I stopped and waited for him to walk up. Whatever he had to say, I knew this was going to be worth potentially missing my connecting flight.

Randy explained that he had one more thing he needed to do. In his words, he felt "compelled" to share a gift with me. I felt like he'd *already* shared so much, but apparently, there was more. As we stood there in the intersection between terminals A and B, he asked me to hold out my hand and close my eyes. Reluctant but trusting, I extended my open hand to him and shut my lids.

I felt something small in my hands with zero clue as to what this could be. Right before Randy asked me to open my eyes, he said, "I've had this for a long time, and the Spirit made it clear to me just now that this belongs to you now. Like you, this object went through a great deal of pressure to become as beautiful as it is."

I opened my eyes, looked down at the tiny object and literally couldn't believe what I saw. What Randy placed in my hand that day was a brilliant, beautiful solitaire diamond ring.

I'd never seen anything like it. My mouth opened wide in total and complete awe. It took me a few seconds to realize what was happening. Then it all clicked. Just the night before in a moment of utter desperation, I'd begged God for a sign that He loved me. And here I was, *the very next day*, standing motionless in the middle of the Memphis airport with a diamond engagement ring in my hand. I couldn't think of a more perfect symbol of love. Before I could muster up any words to form a coherent sentence of gratitude, Randy had already started walking away toward his terminal.

As a dozen thoughts swirled around in my head, I became laser focused on one thing and one thing only—a realization that would plant a seed of love so deep in my heart that it would forever change the course of my life.

I'd just experienced a miraculous encounter that I'd never be able to explain, nor could I ever explain it away. Simply put, I had a *Divine Interaction* that could only be made possible by the intentional work of Love Intelligence. Somehow, some way, in a manner that I will never understand with my finite mind, the universal energy of love cared about me in such a personal, intimate way that a complete stranger gave me a diamond engagement ring exactly one day after I begged God for a sign that They loved me. This is the closest I've come to a real-life, modern-day miracle.

That day, Good Friday 2009, changed me forever.

I've worn the ring every day since. The only time I took it off was so that Brynn could design my engagement ring around the Row 11 diamond.

Fast-forward to the year 2011, yes . . . another 11. My phone rang and the call changed the way I saw myself, my music, and the gifts I was made to share. On the other end of the phone, I heard Randy's voice. He sounded subdued, which wasn't a word I'd ever use to describe Randy.

After exchanging obligatory small talk, Randy began sharing a story with me. I will paraphrase what he said on the phone that day:

"A few months back, I was going through a very hard time. I was really struggling with depression, and I didn't see a way out. I found my gun and put the barrel in my mouth. Right as I was considering whether or not to pull the trigger and end the suffering and pain forever, I heard your song in my head, heart, soul, and spirit. **'You'll Be Whole'** echoed all around me, specifically the lyrics about holding on. I took the gun out of my mouth and chose to live the life I knew I was created to live. And that's thanks to you and your music. You always tell me I saved your life with what I said on the plane that day and the gift I gave you. And now I can tell you that you saved my life with your gift."

I sat on the carpet next to my bed in complete silence. I couldn't move. I couldn't produce words to respond to my earthly angel. I just listened and was somehow finally able to thank him for calling me and sharing that with me. He carried such heavy burdens, and I got the sense that it was all too much for him sometimes. I can't imagine having the intuitive gift that he so clearly had and not being able to fully understand how to process and work through everything that comes with that.

I'm still awe-inspired with the full-circle nature of my relationship with Randy. I only saw him that one time, that one Good Friday in April of 2009. I never saw him again.

A few years back, Randy called me again. Despite not being sick or terminally ill, he proceeded to ask if I would sing at his funeral when he *does* pass away. Without hesitation, I answered "YES!" and begged him to not die yet. I wanted (hell, I *needed*) him to live a long life so he could continue spreading love and light to people like me who were lucky enough to cross paths with him. He was always so incredibly kind and thoughtful during our phone calls. Not a moment passed by without him asking about how I was doing or how my family was doing, and he always asked about the girls. His heart was just as big as his shoulders were that day on the tiny plane as he unintentionally smashed me against the airplane window.

I got another phone call in 2021, randomly and out of the blue during my work day. Someone named Moriah had called and left me a message on my office line. At first it didn't register, and then it clicked. I remembered Randy telling me all about his daughter, Moriah. I called her back instantly. We'd never spoken before, but somehow, I felt I'd known her my whole life. We hit it off right away and I knew some bad news was coming. She went on to tearfully share with me that Randy had died in a car accident. She went on to ask me if she could play one of my songs at his funeral.

I told her about the time Randy called me and asked me to sing at his funeral. My heart broke as I realized I couldn't *physically* be there due to family obligations, Covid, *and* the ice storm. I considered trying to make it work, but all flights would've surely been cancelled. It meant the world that she wanted to include my music in the ceremony honoring his life. Though I couldn't physically be there, I knew this would allow me to join the experience *in spirit*. I knew it was what Randy would've wanted. However, that didn't erase the pain I felt upon realizing I wouldn't be able to attend in person and share my story.

Turns out, I didn't have to physically be there to tell my story. Moriah took the podium at the church on the day of his funeral and began to share our story. I had no idea she had plans to do this, but I laid in my bed that day watching the funeral via Zoom. I never imagined in a million years that I'd be watching Randy's funeral from my bed via Zoom. Yet, there I was. And somehow, it was perfect and felt like it was all unfolding the way it was supposed to.

As I listened to Moriah share stories about Randy's life, and share specifically about my unique relationship with him, I saw people in the pews crying. Mind you, this all took place at a very conservative/old-school church in Kentucky. Moriah did not hesitate to talk about how much Randy loved me *and my wife*. She spoke with boldness about her father who loved *everyone* regardless of who they were or who they loved. I laughed. I wept. I was in total awe as I watched this all unfold. I miss Randy so much and think of him every time I look down at my now-wedding ring.

BONUS TRACK

I've spent most of my life unconsciously and subconsciously numbing my emotions after years of buying into the lie that everything in life happens for a reason. I've perfected the art of locking up the hard emotions, stuffing them all the way down, and leaving them there forever. The best way I can convey my emotions and my feelings *about* those emotions is to tell you about my kinked-up garden hose.

THE GARDEN HOSE

I am well aware I could buy a garden hose that never kinks up. I hear they make fancy ones now that claim to be free from tangles. Some hoses even fit in a nicely organized container. Call it the rebel in me, but I'm sticking with old faithful: the green, weathered, worn-out, kinked-up, and tangled poor excuse for a garden hose. I don't even bother anymore with finding a way to organize it and store it. Every time I try to wrap it around my arm in circles to put away for safe-keeping, old dirty water sprays all over me.

During the initial stages of lockdown, that hose was like a family pet. The spring Covid "break" turned into 101,032,041,320 days of "home" schooling, and life turned completely upside down. All our focus turned to trying to survive until summer, and I'll never forget the memories of spraying my three kids and taking them completely by surprise with the sheer force I could muster by placing my fat farmer thumb on the hose where the water comes out. We filled up water balloons and had Herculean water fights. You may see a kinked-up pile of hose-trash, but I see a pile of possibilities.

These Hose Ain't Loyal

Upon first purchasing said hose, it was perfectly functional, and no tangles could be found. Water flowed freely with no obstruction. This is how I believe our emotions and feelings start out when we're first emerging on the scene of life. One day, we're nestled safely and warmly in our mother's womb of placenta peace, and the next minute we are flung into a cold world where life just starts happening, and right away we are flooded with big feelings.

All I needed to prove this theory was to witness my twin daughters' births. They didn't come out of the chute happy and grateful. Hell no—they were screaming their tiny little wrinkly bald heads off all the way to the NICU. There was no stopping the flow of emotions or feelings in that moment, nor any of the subsequent moments/months/years. Can you imagine looking at a newborn who is crying profusely in the delivery room and telling the baby to bottle it up, suck it up, GET AHOLD OF YOURSELF, DAMNIT!

Of course not. The newborn baby's emotions are flowing naturally.

| **EMOTION = ENERGY IN MOTION.** |

Newborn babies become toddlers who become temporary assholes who become teens and then adults. Somewhere along the way, we subconsciously ingest messages that teach us a fabrication: some emotions (read: bad emotions) are never to be let out. We've been conditioned to see the emotion of happiness as good. However, sad, mad, or any other seemingly negative emotion is seen as bad. So, we turn the volume up on the "good" and press the mute button on the "bad," which causes our emotional garden hose to get all jangled up. Free-flowing, healthy emotional expression is cut off.

Emotions and feelings spring up from birth, and we enjoy the freedom of letting them out. It's how we signaled to the adult humans in our lives that we needed to be fed, held, nursed, changed, etc. And then, something shifts. The moment happens when we learn that some emotions are perceived as positive while others are perceived to be negative. Despite the reality that there are no good or bad emotions, we don't live like that is actual reality because the world bestows value on one emotion or feeling and puts a red X on another. So, how the hell are we supposed to keep up?

We can't—yet we desperately try.

Most of us have conditioned ourselves to become triage nurses when it comes to dealing with our emotions. Instead of trying to mindfully untangle our garden hose, we let it stay all kinked up and wonder why the water (an emotion or feeling) isn't flowing freely. We jump into our role as head charge nurse over the triage of feelings and immediately start evaluating the feeling, checking for vital signs, asking questions about what we're feeling, and inquiring about history, symptoms, and why that feeling is there visiting our emotional emergency room. Based on the way we perceive the information, we then develop our determination of which feelings go in the bad/hard column versus the good/easy column. Based on that data, we then develop the best course of action for moving forward.

GONNA POP SOME TAGS

My internal triage nurse has been working so hard, on overdrive, and in overtime for most of my life. She's always on and always stressed. She sees the emotions and feelings rushing into the sliding ER doors of my brain and gets to work. She knows exactly which emotions to assign red tags to—these are the feelings that need immediate treatment. She knows exactly which emotions to tag with a yellow color—these are the emotions that need to be observed. Maybe we'll triage those again later, but for now, let's just observe. Yellow tag emotions appear to be stable, so there's no reason to believe there's immediate danger. Next up, the green tags. As my triage nurse continues to operate at the highest capacity of color tagging, green tags are assigned to emotions that aren't life-threatening and could be considered the "walking wounded." Green tags receive care only after the reds and yellows.

Then, there are white tag emotions—these are feelings that may result in minor injuries, but no further treatment will be required. Last but not least, the black tags—these are reserved for the dead. Emotions and feelings that are too extensive and past the point of being able to survive get black tags.[1]

Once our internal triage nurse has performed her job duties, she proudly looks at her organization of colorful tags. Now she's ready to "deal with" or treat these emotions. It's automatic, and she doesn't even have to think twice about it. But we think obsessively about it, even when we're not aware of it. We develop judgments about each emotion and categorize every feeling as bad or good. Then, we respond and behave accordingly.

For most of my life, any non-green tagged emotions were completely ignored and buried deep. This technique did me a great disservice. We can't pick and choose which emotions we hide and which ones we feel and let loose. We can try but will fail every time. Look at the emotion wheel that follows and notice how many different emotions we can and most likely will experience during our lifetime.[2] The more time we spend judging and shaming ourselves for simply *having* certain emotions, the harder we'll have to search for the treasures buried deep within those exact emotions and feelings.

Each of us has an automatic filing system where we judge how each emotion should be dealt with. It was a helpful and necessary system during childhood, but the colorful tagging system isn't working anymore. Each emotion could have several different colored tags, depending on the situation and vantage point. Take sadness, for example. Depending on the day, the person, and the circumstance, a feeling of sadness could be tagged with a green, yellow, red, white, or black color.

My dear friend Jessica lost her sixteen-year-old son many years ago. He was her everything. Their relationship was profound and full of meaning, life, and beauty. I couldn't imagine anything more painful than what she's gone through. Over the years, she's said a bunch of brilliant things that have landed so deeply with me, but two stand out in particular:

1. The only certainty in life is uncertainty. So why continue to be surprised and paralyzed by it?

2. Some days you're gonna step in dog shit and ruin the bottom of one of your shoes. But at least you're up and walking and shit didn't get on your *other* shoe.

Shit is going to happen. It's inevitable. And it will bring with it a myriad of emotions and feelings that span the full spectrum. But sometimes, if we are aware and open, some really *good* shit can come out of the shittiest of times. Listen to people who have spent time in the darkness, lurking amongst the shadows of despair, pain, grief, and sheer hopelessness. You may find hope, light, peace, and gifts in their stories. These are the courageous ones. As my favorite TV star from my childhood (Mary Tyler Moore) puts it: "Pain nourishes courage. You can't be brave if you've only had wonderful things happen to you."[3]

Jessica is one of the bravest people I've ever known. She knows pain. She emits courage. When she speaks, I listen. Every time I step in dog shit, I think of her. (She doesn't love when I tell her that.) But the more life I have under my belt, the more I know she's right. We can count on uncertainty. We can bet it all on the unexpected happening. There will always be people, situations, and things happening entirely out of our control. It doesn't mean the world is going to spin off its axis.

When our white-knuckling fists turn to open palms, freedom follows. Our obsession with thinking we can control everything and everyone around us is an illusion that's killing us. We only have control over ourselves and the way we respond to life and all its unknowns. The unknown is sometimes all that *is* known. I've heard it said that we're not scared of the unknown. We're scared of the LOSS of the *known*.

Finally, after decades of punishing myself for being unable to control *perceived* bad emotions, and a lifetime full of fearing the unknown and dreading uncertainty, I'm letting myself feel the whole wheel as I approach life with open hands. I don't have to triage anymore or tag my emotions with colors. There are no good or bad emotions. There are only energies in motion. My feet will stay grounded no matter how difficult life may be. And on my darkest days when I don't *feel* grounded at all, my very acknowledgment of that feeling—and my increased awareness around that emotion—is what does the grounding for me. I am grounded every time I allow myself to fully feel my feelings.

May we all find a way to live life with the knowledge of its unpredictability and the realization that none of this is happening TO us, but FOR us. Nothing is wasted. Not one thing. Life can be both painful and purposeful at the same time. Goodness can come from even the most horrific of experiences, but this isn't to say that the end (i.e., the gift) justifies the means (i.e., the shit). Just because I'm currently experiencing an *end* result that fills me with happiness, doesn't mean *the means* were enjoyable.

Sometimes the light at the "end" gives new purpose to the pain associated with the means it took to get there. It's high time we work to untangle our emotional garden hoses so life can flow freely through, in, and around us. That's where the magic is: doing the work to maintain the free flow of emotions and feelings, resist the inclination to judge and speculate, and—most impactfully—**find the gift**.

Let's take a brief moment to glean from the wisdom of one of my favorite thought leaders, Moira Rose from *Schitt's Creek*:

> You must prepare for life, and whatever it will throw at you. The opportunities will diminish, and the ass will get bigger. Oh, you can bet your bottom dollar it will! Especially yours. You're going to have a huge ass.
>
> **—MOIRA ROSE**[4]

ACKNOWLEDGMENTS

I'd like to express major gratitude to the following people who made this book possible. If I've thanked you in the wrong order, forgot completely to thank you, or not thanked you enough, just know it's because I am a chaotic mess with very little potential of or *interest in* doing everything right.

My three fabulous, fascinating, and sometimes irritating kids, Annabelle, Liv, and Atticus, for their patience and understanding with their mama having to spend so much time over the past few years on this book vs. attending to their every need.

My parents and brother who still call me *Lulu* in public, love me unconditionally, and support me fearlessly despite the challenges I've undoubtedly brought to their lives over the years

My real-life angel Randy aka Mr. Row 11 whose gift changed my life forever. (May he rest in peace and power.)

My three dogs Whiskey, Ellie, and Homie for drooling all over my keyboard as I attempted to write this book.

My literary agent *Debbie-Double-OH-Sh*t* . . . just kidding, I don't have an agent.

My editor, Lindsey Clark, and my editing team for putting up with my initial 262,000 words in a world that prefers a 90,000-word book.

My *Book Doulas* and dear friends who have taken precious time out of their ridiculously busy lives to help me birth this book.

My accountability sergeant, Dena Jansen, for keeping my ass on track through the book launch.

My marketing firm, Zilker Media, for helping me do social media better (sigh) and for bringing this book to the masses.

The entire staff at Greenleaf Book Group for taking a chance on an unknown author with a questionable sense of humor and out-of-the-box writing style.

My mentors Jen Hatmaker and Jon Zieve, and all the therapists who have listened to my madness over the years, who have loved me through my craziness, and who have lifted me up throughout all of life's seasons. (And my psychiatrist . . . thank God for meds.)

A very well-known fast-food restaurant whose name I cannot mention for copyright reasons for providing me with countless taquitos wrapped in orange paper. Where would I be without your priceless provisions?

All the Airbnbs I escaped to over the past few years so I could work on the book in peace. (Side note: please stop charging so much for the cleaning fee . . . I was literally there one night.)

All of the writers, poets, and creatives who have inspired me throughout my life. I stand on your shoulders.

Last but obvi not least, Love Intelligence, Source, Higher Power, God, Universe, insert-name-here: Thank you for creating me to create, for inspiring this book and using it to help heal me, and for showing me the most tender of loves one could ever experience. Oh and also thanks for giving me the gift of perseverance, even though I'm not sure why you thought I needed it. JK. Love you xoxo.

And, finally, to all the readers out there who joined me on this journey, I raise a yummy glass of bourbon and a taco to you. Please, for the love of YOU, never stop looking for gifts and treasures in the unlikeliest of places, always remembering that Life is happening FOR us, not TO us.

Look . . . There's no way I could successfully string together a mere twenty-six letters to accurately express how grateful I am for all of you. This book, my life's legacy, would have NEVER happened without you.

NOTES

INTRODUCTION

1. Richard Saunders [i.e. Benjamin Franklin], *Poor Richard, An Almanack for the Year of Christ 1738* (Philadelphia, PA: B. Franklin, 1738), https://founders.archives.gov/documents/Franklin/01-02-02-0035.

PART 1

1. Dean Holland, dir., "Jerry's Painting," *Parks and Recreation*, Season 3, Episode 11, aired 28 April 2011, https://www.peacocktv.com/stream-tv/parks-and-recreation.

CHAPTER 1: THE GIFT OF FEAR

1. "You Are Your Brain," Cleveland Clinic, https://healthybrains.org/brain-facts/.

2. Don Miguel Ruiz, *The Four Agreements* (San Francisco, CA: Amber-Allen Publishing, 1997), 56.

3. Bruce McCulloch, dir., "RIP Moira Rose," *Schitt's Creek*, Season 4, Episode 5, aired 6 February 2018, https://www.hulu.com/series/schitts-creek-a2e7a946-9652-48a8-884b-3ea7ea4de273/.

CHAPTER 2: THE GIFT OF ADDICTION

1. Ernest Kurtz and Katherine Ketcham, *The Spirituality of Imperfection: Storytelling and the Search for Meaning* (New York: Bantam, 1993).

2. Jean Vanier, *Community and Growth*, 3rd ed. (Mahwah, NJ: Paulist Press, 2018), 74.

3. Jay Roach, dir., *Austin Powers: The Spy Who Shagged Me*, 1999, https://www.netflix.com/watch/21302357/.

4. Terrence Real, *I Don't Want to Talk About It: Overcoming the Secret Legacy of Male Depression* (New York: Scribner, 1998).

CHAPTER 3: THE GIFT OF ANGER

1. Michael Rodio, "The History of the Burpee," *Men's Journal*, 14 June 2018, https://www.mensjournal.com/health-fitness/history-burpee-origin-name-royal-trainer-bodyweight/.

2. Matthew 21:13 (New International Version).

3. Ephesians 4:26 (Revised Standard Version).

4. Ernest Kurtz and Katherine Ketcham, *The Spirituality of Imperfection: Storytelling and the Search for Meaning* (New York: Bantam, 1993), 126.

5. Declan Lowney, dir., "Make Rebecca Great Again," *Ted Lasso*, Season 1, Episode 7, aired 11 September 2020, https://tv.apple.com/us/show/ted-lasso/umc.cmc.vtoh0mn0xn7t3c643xqonfzy/.

CHAPTER 4: THE GIFT OF HUMILIATION

1. Wynonna, if you're reading this book, I'm really sorry I messed up your lyrics. Please forgive me. Thank you. I love you.

CHAPTER 5: THE GIFT OF TRAGEDY

1. Stephanie Petit, "#MeToo: Sexual Harassment and Assault Movement Tweeted Over 500,000 Times as Celebs Share Stories," *People*, 16 October 2017, https://people.com/movies/me-too-alyssa-milano-heads-twitter-campaign-against-sexual-harassment-assault/.

2. "Get to Know Us: History & Inception," Me Too Movement, https://metoomvmt.org/get-to-know-us/history-inception/.

3. "Get to Know Us."

4. John Bradshaw, *Healing the Shame That Binds You* (Deerfield Beach, FL: Health Communications, Inc., 1988), 37.

5. "Post-Traumatic Stress Disorder (PTSD)," Mayo Clinic, https://www.mayoclinic.org/diseases-conditions/post-traumatic-stress-disorder/symptoms-causes/syc-20355967/.

6. Psalm 40:1-3 (Message Translation).

PART 2

1. William Bridges, *Transitions: Making Sense of Life's Changes* (Boston: Da Capo Press, 2004), 10.

CHAPTER 6: THE GIFT OF REJECTION

1. Irving Wallace, *The Square Pegs: Some Americans Who Dared to be Different* (1957),10. As cited in https://en.wikipedia.org/wiki/Square_peg_in_a_round_hole#cite_note-1/.

2. Sydney Smith, *Elementary Sketches of Moral Philosophy, Delivered at the Royal Institution, in the Years 1804, 1805, and 1806* (London: 1850), 111. Quoted in Alan Bell, *Sydney Smith: A Life* (Oxford: Oxford University Press, 1980), 58. As cited in https://en.wikipedia.org/wiki/Square_peg_in_a_round_hole#cite_note-2/.

3. The last thing I need in my life is someone like Simon Cowell trying to sue me. Although, if it meant I could meet him in person, I might just chance it. I love him. And I loved him *before* he stopped being so mean to people. Also, I'm not saying the show was *American Idol*. It wasn't.

4. "The Gift of Rejection," *Black Girl Musings*, 15 April 2020, https://blackgirlmusings.com/2020/04/15/the-gifts-found-in-rejection/.

5. "Rejected," Merriam-Webster Unabridged Dictionary, https://unabridged.merriam-webster.com/collegiate/rejected/.

CHAPTER 7: THE GIFT OF UNANSWERED PRAYERS

1. Romans 8:26-27 (English Standard Version).

2. Wayne Dyer, *Happiness Is the Way: How to Reframe Your Thinking and Work with What You Already Have to Live the Life of Your Dreams* (Carlsbad, CA: Hay House, 2019), xiii.

3. Paul Selig, *The Book of Mastery* (New York: TarcherPerigee, 2016), 108.

4. Brennan Manning, *The Importance of Being Foolish: How to Think Like Jesus* (New York: HarperOne, 2005), 113 and 139.

5. Joe Vitale and Dr. Hew Len, *Zero Limits: The Secret Hawaiian System for Wealth, Health, Peace, and More* (Hoboken, NJ: John Wiley & Sons, 2007), 74.

6. Vitale and Len, *Zero Limits*, 75.

7. Vitale and Len, Zero Limits, 76.

8. Vitale and Len, Zero Limits, 79–80.

9. Anne Lamott, *Help, Thanks, Wow: The Three Essential Prayers* (New York: Riverhead Books, 2012), 19.

CHAPTER 8: THE GIFT OF WAITING

1. Donald Miller, *A Million Miles in a Thousand Years: What I Learned While Editing My Life* (New York: Thomas Nelson, 2009), 36.

2. Mark É. Czeisler et al., "Mental Health, Substance Use, and Suicidal Ideation During the COVID-19 Pandemic—United States, June 24–30, 2020," Morbidity and Mortality Weekly Report 2020; 69:1049–1057, http://dx.doi.org/10.15585/mmwr.mm6932a1. And "Mental Health and Substance Use State Fact Sheets," 20 March 2023, https://www.kff.org/statedata/mental-health-and-substance-use-state-fact-sheets/.

3. If you or someone you know is struggling with emotional dysregulation or BPD, please visit Family Education Webinars at: https://www.borderlinepersonalitydisorder.org/webinars/.

4. Chris Cuomo, "Cuomo on the Couch: Do the Homework," *The Chris Cuomo Project* podcast, 4 May 2023, https://podcasts.apple.com/be/podcast/cuomo-on-the-couch-do-the-homework/id1635418897?i=1000611721451/.

5. Gary Ryan Blair, "Stop Waiting and Start Doing," Medium.com, 8 June 2023, https://medium.com/mind-munchies/stop-waiting-and-start-doing-2b7bf68131f9/.

CHAPTER 9: THE GIFT OF TRAUMA

1. Amy Florian, "Advising Clients Through the Toughest Times of Life," Northwestern Mutual Wealth Management Symposium, 3 August 2020. For more on Amy Florian's message, see: https://www.corgenius.com/.

2. "About EMDR Therapy," Emderia, https://www.emdria.org/about-emdr-therapy/.

3. Megan Devine, *It's OK That You're Not OK: Meeting Grief and Loss in a Culture That Doesn't Understand* (Boulder, CO: Sounds True, 2017), 15.

4. Bessel van der Kolk, *The Body Keeps the Score: Brain, Mind, and Body in the Healing of Trauma* (New York: Penguin Publishing Group, 2014), 97.

5. Danielle Bernock, *Emerging with Wings: A True Story of Lies, Pain, and the LOVE that Heals* (Santa Ana, CA: 4F Media, 2014), 72.

CHAPTER 10: THE GIFT OF LEAVING

1. Karen Kukil, ed., *The Unabridged Journals of Sylvia Plath* (Albany, NY: Anchor, 2000).

2. Henri Nouwen, *The Inner Voice of Love: A Journey through Anguish to Freedom* (New York: Doubleday, 1996), 103.

3. 2 Corinthians 3:17 (New International Version).

4. Matina Horner, "Loneliness: A New Challenge for Psychologists," *American Psychologist*, vol. 36, no. 3, 1981, 218–219.

5. Robyn Schneider, *The Beginning of Everything* (New York: Katherine Tegen Books, 2013), 232.

6. "Elephants Wandered Hundreds of Miles into a Chinese City. Nobody Knows Why," *NPR*, 4 June 2021, https://www.npr.org/2021/06/04/1003268230/elephants-wandered-hundreds-of-miles-into-a-chinese-city-nobody-knows-why/.

7. Ray Bradbury, *Zen in the Art of Writing: Essays on Creativity* (New York: Joshua Odell Editions, 1994), 102.

8. If you or someone you love is experiencing domestic abuse, find help at the National Domestic Violence Hotline, which provides 24/7 support, safety planning, information, and referrals to local resources for people experiencing domestic violence. Call 1-800-799-SAFE (7233) or visit https://www.thehotline.org/.

9. Source unknown.

10. Brianna Wiest, "To Be Successful, You Must Embrace These 5 Fears," *Forbes*, 4 September 2018, https://www.forbes.com/sites/briannawiest/2018/09/04/to-be-successful-you-must-embrace-these-5-fears/.

CHAPTER 11: THE GIFT OF LOSS

1. Lulu Garcia-Navarro, "Vancouver Mourns the Loss of Its Old Apple Tree," *KUOW*, 23 August 2020, https://www.kuow.org/stories/vancouver-mourns-the-loss-of-its-old-apple-tree/.

2. Garcia-Navarro, "Vancouver Mourns."

3. Ernest Kurtz and Katherine Ketcham, *The Spirituality of Imperfection: Storytelling and the Search for Meaning* (New York: Bantam, 1993), 10.

4. Graham Cooke, "Coming Up from the Wilderness," Brilliant Book House, 19 July 2013, https://www.youtube.com/watch?v=2pVyFCoKGBM&ab_channel=BrilliantBookHouse/. While I love this quote, I do not agree with this entire sermon.

PART 3

1. Friedrich Nietzsche, *Human, All Too Human* (1878), Section 236. See also: Bill Murphy Jr., "Want to Have a Great Second Half of 2021? Here Are the Inspiring Words You'll Need," *INC*, 18 July 2021, https://www.inc.com/bill-murphy-jr/want-to-have-a-great-second-half-of-2021-here-are-inspiring-words-youll-need.html/.

CHAPTER 12: THE GIFT OF POWERLESSNESS

1. Mark Van Vugt, "5 Reasons Why It Sucks to Have Power," *Psychology Today*, 26 January 2013, https://www.psychologytoday.com/us/blog/naturally-selected/201301/5-reasons-why-it-sucks-to-have-power/.

2. Source unkown.

3. Henri J. M. Nouwen, *Out of Solitude: Three Meditations on the Christian Life* (Notre Dame, IN: Ave Maria Press, 2004), 24.

4. Wayne Dyer, *Manifest Your Destiny: The Nine Spiritual Principles for Getting Everything You Want* (New York: HarperCollins, 1997).

CHAPTER 13: THE GIFT OF HEARTBREAK

1. Cynthia Occelli, *Resurrecting Venus: A Woman's Guide to Love, Work, Motherhood & Soothing the Sacred Ache* (Carlsbad, CA: Balboa Press, 2013), 61.

2. "Divorce Statistics: Over 115 Studies, Facts and Rates for 2022," Wilkinson & Finkbeiner, 2022, https://www.wf-lawyers.com/divorce-statistics-and-facts/.

3. Amy Chan, "The 11 Best Gifts to Give Yourself When Going Through a Heartbreak," Heart Hackers Club, 9 December 2021, https://hearthackersclub.com/the-11-best-gifts-to-give-yourself-when-going-through-a-heartbreak/.

4. Steve McVey, *Grace Walk* (Eugene, OR: Harvest House Publishers, 1995), 127.

5. Romans 12:2 (New International Version).

6. "Thinking Errors," InnerChange, https://www.innerchange.com/parents-resources/thinking-errors/.

7. Gregory Bateson, *Steps to an Ecology of Mind: Collected Essays in Anthropology, Psychiatry, Evolution, and Epistemology* (Chicago: University of Chicago Press, 1972), 206.

8. Wayne Dyer, *The Power of Intention* (Carlsbad, CA: Hay House, 1995).

9. Bessel van der Kolk, *The Body Keeps the Score: Brain, Mind, and Body in the Healing of Trauma* (New York: Penguin Publishing Group, 2014), 39.

10. "How Does Heartbreak Affect Your Overall Health?" Healthline, 16 March 2016, https://www.healthline.com/health/what-does-heartbreak-do-to-your-health/.

11. "How Does Heartbreak?"

12. Nelson Mandela, "Let Go," in *Long Walk to Freedom* (New York: Back Bay Books, 1995).

13. "Lesbian Couple Celebrates Love with Drive-In Wedding," today.com, https://www.today.com/video/lesbian-couple-celebrates-love-with-drive-in-wedding-86043717763/.

CHAPTER 14: THE GIFT OF EMPTINESS

1. Brianna West, "Why It's Essential To Set Boundaries While Social Distancing," *Forbes*, 30 Apr 2020, https://www.forbes.com/sites/briannawiest/2020/04/30/why-its-essential-to-set-boundaries-while-social-distancing/#45ec135d47f6/.

2. Paul Selig, *The Book of Knowing and Worth: A Channeled Text* (New York: TarcherPerigee, 2013).

CHAPTER 15: THE GIFT OF CONFLICT

1. "Yin and Yang," Wikipedia, https://en.wikipedia.org/wiki/Yin_and_yang/.

2. Jonah Hill, dir., *Stutz*, Netflix, 2022, https://www.netflix.com/title/81387962/.

3. "Albert Camus Quotes," GoodReads, https://www.goodreads.com/author/quotes/957894.Albert_Camus/. This quote is often attributed to Albert Camus, but it seems to be a paraphrase of his words. The exact quote cannot be found in his works. However, the sentiment expressed in the quote is consistent with Camus's philosophy of finding meaning and joy in life despite the difficulties and hardships that one might face.

4. Find my version at: Lindsey Kane, "How Great Thou Art," *Move Me Aside*, 2007, https://music.apple.com/us/album/how-great-thou-art/264428492?i=264429187/.

5. Michael Schur, dir., "Moving Up: Part 1," *Parks & Recreation*, Season 6, Episode 21, aired 24 April 2014, https://www.peacocktv.com/stream-tv/parks-and-recreation/.

6. "Dialectical Behavior Therapy (DBT): What It Is & Purpose," Cleveland Clinic, https://my.clevelandclinic.org/health/treatments/22838-dialectical-behavior-therapy-dbt/. This is a DBT skill called "Dialectical Abstinence," which involves accepting that two seemingly contradictory things can be true at the same time. Once we recognize the existence of opposing perspectives, we'll see the potential for synthesis between them.

CHAPTER 16: THE GIFT OF PAIN

1. Rita DeMaria et al., *Building Intimate Relationships: Bridging Treatment, Education, and Enrichment Through the PAIRS Program* (New York: Routledge, 2003), 57.

2. Daniel Goleman, *Emotional Intelligence: Why It Can Matter More Than IQ* (New York: Bantam Books, 1995), 29.

3. Eckhart Tolle, *The Power of Now: A Guide to Spiritual Enlightenment* (Novato, CA: New World Library, 1997), 32.

4. Brené Brown, *Braving the Wilderness: The Quest for True Belonging and the Courage to Stand Alone* (London: Vermilion, 2017).

5. Brené Brown, *Atlas of the Heart: Mapping Meaningful Connections* (New York: Random House, 2021), 48.

6. Billy Manas, "We're Spiritually Bypassing Our Pain with Empty Positivity (& We Need to Stop)," *Elephant Journal*, 3 February 2021, https://www.elephantjournal.com/2021/02/its-okay-to-be-broken-but-you-cant-sweep-the-pain-under-a-rug-billy-manas/.

7. The Associated Press, "An Elk Had a Tire Around its Neck for 2 Years. It's Just Been Freed," NPR, 12 October 2021, https://www.npr.org/2021/10/12/1045228734/colorado-elk-tire-removed/.

EPILOGUE

1. Elena Ferrante, *In the Margins: On the Pleasures of Reading and Writing* (New York: Europa Editions, 2022), 32.

2. Brené Brown, *The Gifts of Imperfection* (Center City, MN: Hazelden Publishing, 2010), 43.

3. William P. Young, *The Shack* (Newbury Park, CA: Windblown Media, 2008).

BONUS TRACK

1. "Triage Status," DataTech911, https://www.datatech911.com/resources/triage-status/.

2. "Emotion Wheel," http://www.etc.cmu.edu/projects/emotionshop/wp-content/uploads/2015/10/emotion-wheel.jpg/.

3. Mary Tyler Moore, Interview with Barbara Walters, 1976.

4. Jerry Ciccoritti, dir., "Bad Parents," *Schitt's Creek*, Season 1, Episode 4, aired 25 February 2015, https://www.hulu.com/series/schitts-creek-a2e7a946-9652-48a8-884b-3ea7ea4de273/.

ABOUT THE AUTHOR

 **LINDSEY K. LEAVERTON** is a large-aperture, multi-faceted individual with a passion for both finance and laughter. As a devoted (and sometimes flailing) mother of three, including twin girls she adopted from birth and a cherished bonus son, Lindsey holds a special place in her heart for family.

By day, Lindsey serves as the director of wealth management at a boutique financial planning firm in downtown Austin. Her expertise in the field has allowed her to make a positive impact on clients' lives, guiding them toward financial success and freedom.

Beyond her professional pursuits, Lindsey has a strong sense of faith, a vibrant personality, and a refreshing sense of humor. She obsesses over stand-up comedy and secretly wants to pursue a career in stand-up someday. Her love for making people laugh extends beyond the stage and the pages of this book. With seven recorded albums under her belt, Lindsey is a self-taught guitarist and vocalist who brings hope to others through music, storytelling, and songwriting.

Lindsey's compassion for animals shines through her home, where she cares for two rescue dogs and a blind rescue hedgehog. Additionally, she enjoys opening her heart and home to dogs on the euthanasia list, providing them with a second chance at life through fostering.

In her extremely rare "free" time, Lindsey indulges in guilty pleasures such as reality TV, particularly immersing herself in the drama of *The Real Housewives* of all the cities. She has a strong distaste for mayonnaise but finds solace in cheese, pickleball, and the challenge of crossword puzzles.

Unafraid to embrace her whimsical side, Lindsey occasionally dons narwhal onesies to pick up her children from school, much to their embarrassment. She has a profound love for '90s hip-hop, which adds a touch of nostalgia to her life.

Lindsey embodies her own unique blend of neurodivergence, sarcasm, and passion. Her journey, both personally and professionally, is an inspiration to those who strive to make a positive impact on the world while bringing laughter and empathy to those around them.